Nicky Epstein
KNITTING
IN CIRCLES

100 Circular Patterns for Sweaters,
Bags, Hats, Afghans, and More

POTTER
CRAFT
New York

A double dedication
to Jo Brandon,
my lifelong friend,
and Debbie Macomber,
who dubbed me
"the SISTER OF MY HEART"
—it is more than mutual!

Copyright © 2012 by Nicky Epstein

Published in the United States by Potter Craft,
an imprint of the Crown Publishing Group,
a division of Random House, Inc., New York.
www.pottercraft.com
www.crownpublishing.com
POTTER CRAFT and colophon is
a registered trademark of Random House, Inc.

Library of Congress Cataloging-in-Publication Data
Epstein, Nicky.
Knitting in circles: 100 circular patterns for sweaters,
bags, hats, afghans, and more / Nicky Epstein.
p. cm.
Includes bibliographical references and index.
1. Knitting—Patterns I. Title
TT825 .E64215 2012
2011046904

ISBN 978-0-307-58706-0
eISBN 978-0-307-58707-7

Printed in China

Design by Chi Ling Moy and Jess Morphew
Fashion photography by Rose Callahan
Swatch photography by Heather Weston
Technical illustrations by Therese Chynoweth

Cover design by Jess Morphew
Cover photography by Rose Callahan and Heather Weston

10 9 8 7 6 5 4 3 2 1
First Edition

CONTENTS ◯◯◯

INTRODUCTION

Knitting in Circles is the second in a series of books on knitting techniques incorporating geometric shapes. After going "around the block" in my previous book, *Knitting Block by Block*, it seemed only natural that we explore circles. Over the years, I've used a variety of circle shapes in my designs and I thought it was finally time to share their many unique and beautiful uses with knitters of all skill levels.

In this book I'll teach you different ways to shape, create, and embellish knitted circles, using traditional methods as well as some I've come up with on my own.

As you'll see, a few circles—or even just one great big one—can be transformed into fabulous and fashionable knitted sweaters, shawls, afghans, jackets, and more. Every circle in this book can also make an instant pillow (page 210), hat (page 208), or bag (page 210). You'll be astonished at just how many fabulous ways there are to use them!

Although knitted circles have been around for some time, there has never been a book like this. I've created one hundred circles and twenty original designs so you can gain an in-depth understanding of all the fun and creative possibilities a knitted circle can offer. I've also included detailed design diagrams for every project and exclusive mix-and-match circle pages (pages 217–219) so you can choose your own look for each piece.

Knitting circles is very travel-friendly. I like to bring along individual circles to work on, just so I don't have to carry an entire garment. And because they are small, you can practice techniques that might be new to you, like entrelac, Fair Isle, domino, or reversible cables. Get your circle of friends knitting them, too, and you can quickly make wonderful gifts for loved ones, friends, or those in need.

So "circle the wagons," start "thinking in circles," experience the "circle of life," and enjoy knitting "round and round." I loved making this book, and hope it will inspire you and other fellow knitters to think in new, creative ways as you begin *Knitting in Circles*.

Happy Circle Knitting!

NOTES ON TEXTURE AND GAUGE

With all the amazingly beautiful yarns we have access to, you can make the same circle, and get a wide range of incredible looks, simply by changing yarns. Try solid, glitter, self-striping, texture-stranded, thick and thin, beaded, and sequin yarns. The choices are almost endless. Hand-dyed yarn can create beautiful striping and, in effect, often make circles so gorgeous they can take your breath away.

Be adventurous and try some of the unusual yarns in your LYS or in your stash. You will be amazed at how knitting a circle can change and enhance the essence of yarns, even with the simplest of yarns.

These circle swatches show a variety of yarns in different weights, textures, and dyeing methods.

As in all knitting, gauge is important if you want your circles to be approximately the same size. Using a variety of yarn weights and the corresponding needles will change the size of your circle. The same circle pattern knit in lace, DK, worsted, and bulky will give you small to large versions. When you are making a piece, carefully consider adjusting your yarn choice to get the size and drape that you wish.

Note: Almost all the circle samples in this book were made with the same gauge, 4½–5 stitches per 1" (2.5cm) using Cascade 220 Superwash yarn, but because of stitch patterns or different techniques, the finished circles vary up to ¼" to 1½" (6mm–4cm).

(LEFT TO RIGHT) variegated lace weight, metallic, mohair lace weight, hand-dyed baby weight, beaded silk with sequins, wool DK weight, hand-dyed sequins DK weight, silk and wool worsted weight, variegated worsted weight, hand-dyed tweed bulky, wool bulky, wool super bulky

DESIGNING WITH CIRCLES

Designing with circles can open up a whole new world of knitting for you.

In this book, you will find one hundred circle patterns, along with design diagrams for the twenty projects I created using them. You can use the circles I have chosen or design your own look by using any circles that appeal to you. Select the same circles to repeat or get playful with lots of different ones.

Using the mix-and-match circles on pages 217–219, make copies of the circles of your choice, cut them out, and arrange them as desired into the provided design diagrams. Moving and rearranging the circles into different configurations is very satisfying and will help you release your inner designer so you can create your very own one-of-a-kind masterpiece.

The size of your piece will depend on the size of your circles. Choose the yarn you want to use and work a gauge swatch. This will allow you to determine the size of your circle. Most of the circle samples in this book were made with a worsted weight yarn. Here are the gauges I used:

For a 10" circle

18 stitches and 24 rows = 4" (10cm) on size U.S. 8 needles

For a 9" circle

20 stitches and 26 rows = 4" (10cm) on size U.S. 7 needles

As noted on page 6, depending on the circle patterns you choose, your finished circles may vary slightly in size. Here are some ways to adjust circle sizes:

- Change yarn weights. For smaller circles use lighter weight yarns, and for larger circles use bulkier weight yarns with corresponding needle sizes.
- Add or subtract rounds, stitch counts, or rows.
- Change the needle size up or down. To make a cable circle the same size as a stockinette stitch circle, you may need to go up a needle size.
- Block your circle to size. Blocking a circle can add up to 1" (2.5 cm) more.
- Add an edging, like rib or garter stitch (page 48), to increase circumference.

If you have a difficult time making your circles uniformly sized, don't fret. You'll be happy to see that by overlapping the circles, using edgings, or adding the "filler" circles I included for putting large circles together (page 198) it will all work out. Or just see how beautifully the different circle sizes worked in the Circle Sampler Afghan (page 198). The Hemisphere Shrug (page 181) and the Rotunda Cape (page 181) are excellent examples of gauge changes.

See page 215 for methods on joining your circles.

Now get your creative juices flowing and start knitting in circles.

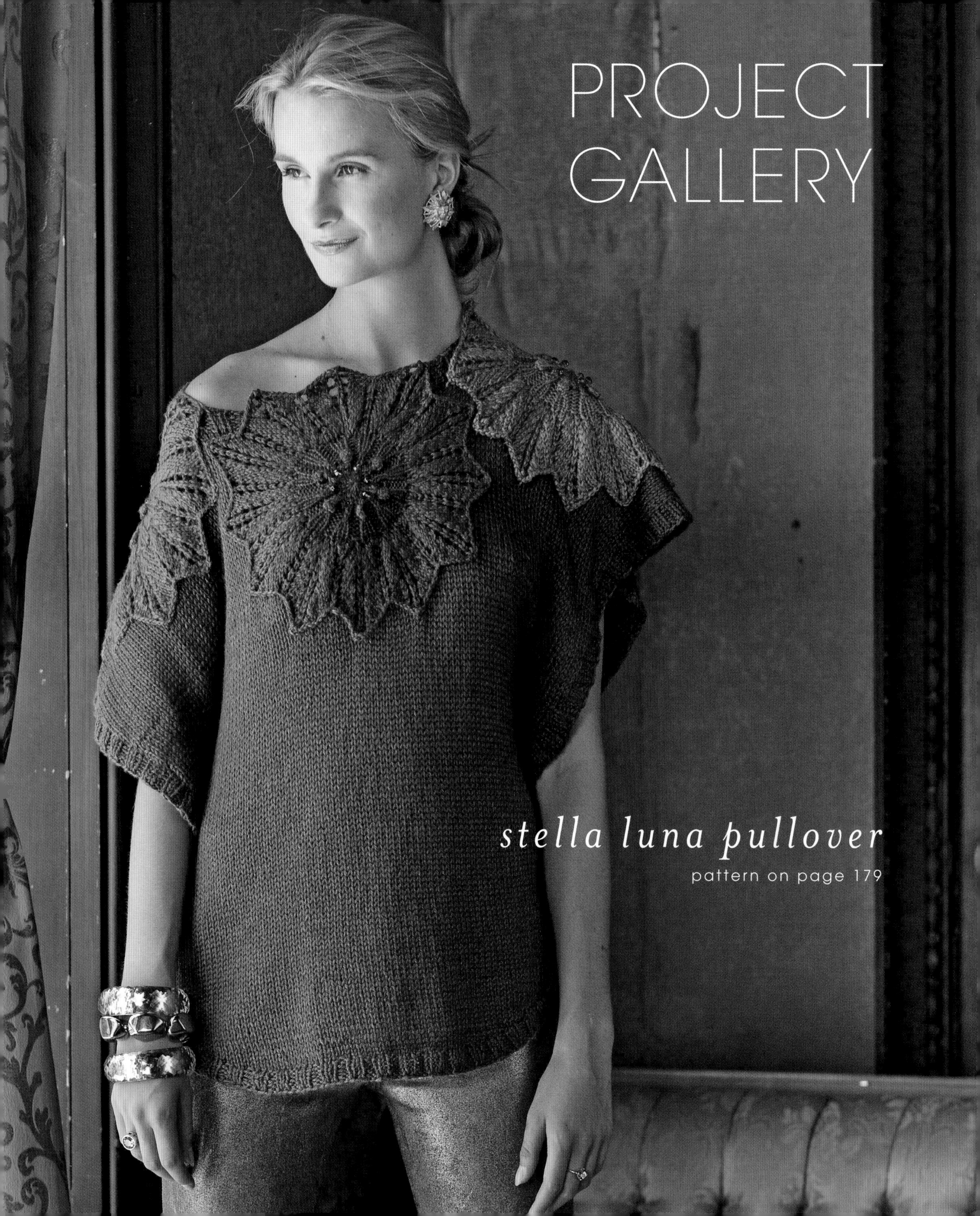

stella luna pullover

pattern on page 179

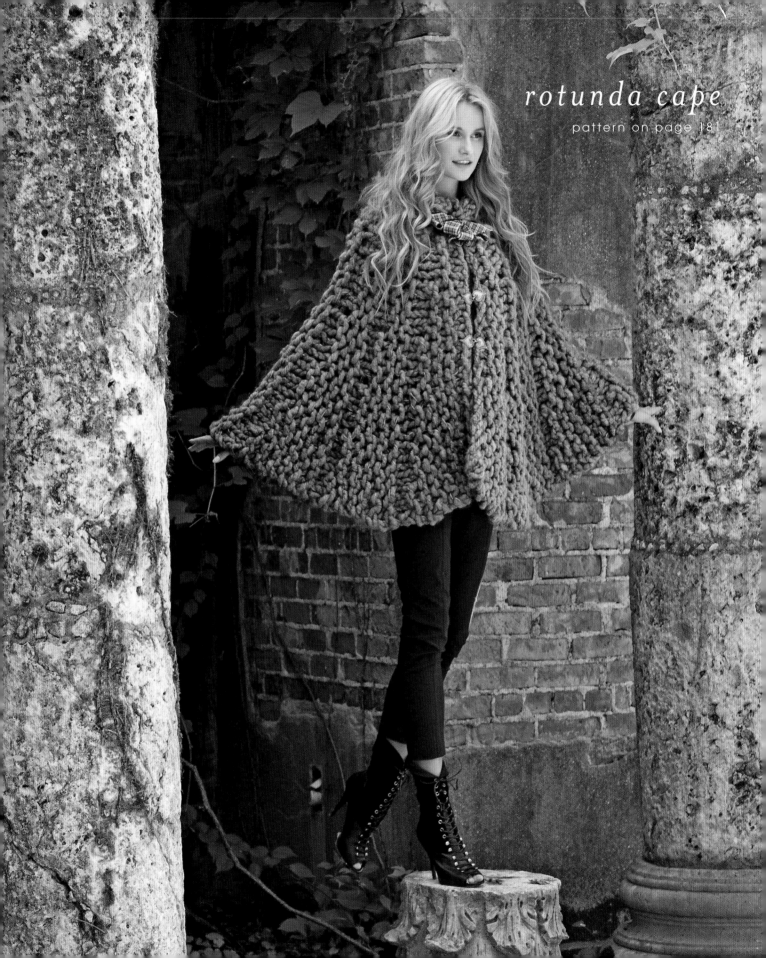

rotunda cape
pattern on page 181

crystal lace jacket
pattern on page 182

spring leaves jacket
pattern on page 186

esther's slouchy hat
pattern on page 189

capella cover-up
pattern on page 190

illuminator fringed vest
pattern on page 191

entrelac capelet
pattern on page 192

daisy mae pullover

pattern on page 194

big blooms capelet
pattern on page 195

starstruck tunic
pattern on page 196

rambling reversible cable scarf

pattern on page 197

circle sampler afghan
pattern on page 198

kaleidoscope afghan
pattern on page 200

hoopla bag
pattern on page 202

celestial shawl
pattern on page 203

eternity dress
pattern on page 204

BASIC CIRCLE SHAPING

In this chapter I've included a wide variety of ways to shape circles. They include spirals, spokes, twists, and turns. By using different knitting increases and decreases, and working with straight, circular, and/or double-pointed needles, circles can be easily shaped in fun and interesting ways. In the instructions, I have indicated the method used for each. The techniques section (page 213) at the back of the book contains information on all these methods as well as joining techniques (page 215) you can use.

These circles will be the basis for the more intricate circles that you will find in later chapters, but they can also be used to create beautiful knitted pieces, such as the Hemisphere Shrug and Rotunda Cape on page 181, and the Autumn Leaf Beret on page 209.

In this chapter and throughout the book, please note the edgings on the circles. Many are interchangeable and can be applied to different circles so you can use them as another design element. They can be worked at the cast-on or bound-off edge, the stitches can be picked up around the circles and then knit, or they can be knit separately and then sewn on after the circle is made.

10–*spiral*
decrease
page 45

10–*spiral*
decrease
(*2 needle with seam*)
page 46

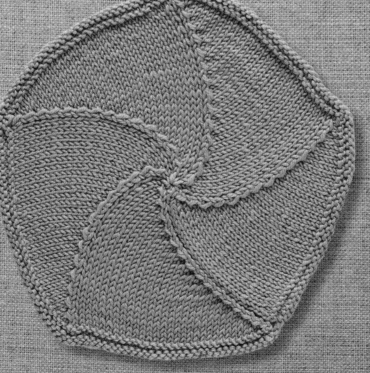

5-spiral decrease
page 46

5-spiral decrease
(with seam)
page 47

petalwork

page 48

burst

page 48

halo
page 49

swirl
page 49

*garter
stitch circle*
page 50

*garter stitch
striped circle*
page 50

corkscrew

page 51

stockinette
stitch circle
page 52

stockinette
stitch
scallops
page 52

*seed stitch
circle*

page 53

*eyelet
points*

page 54

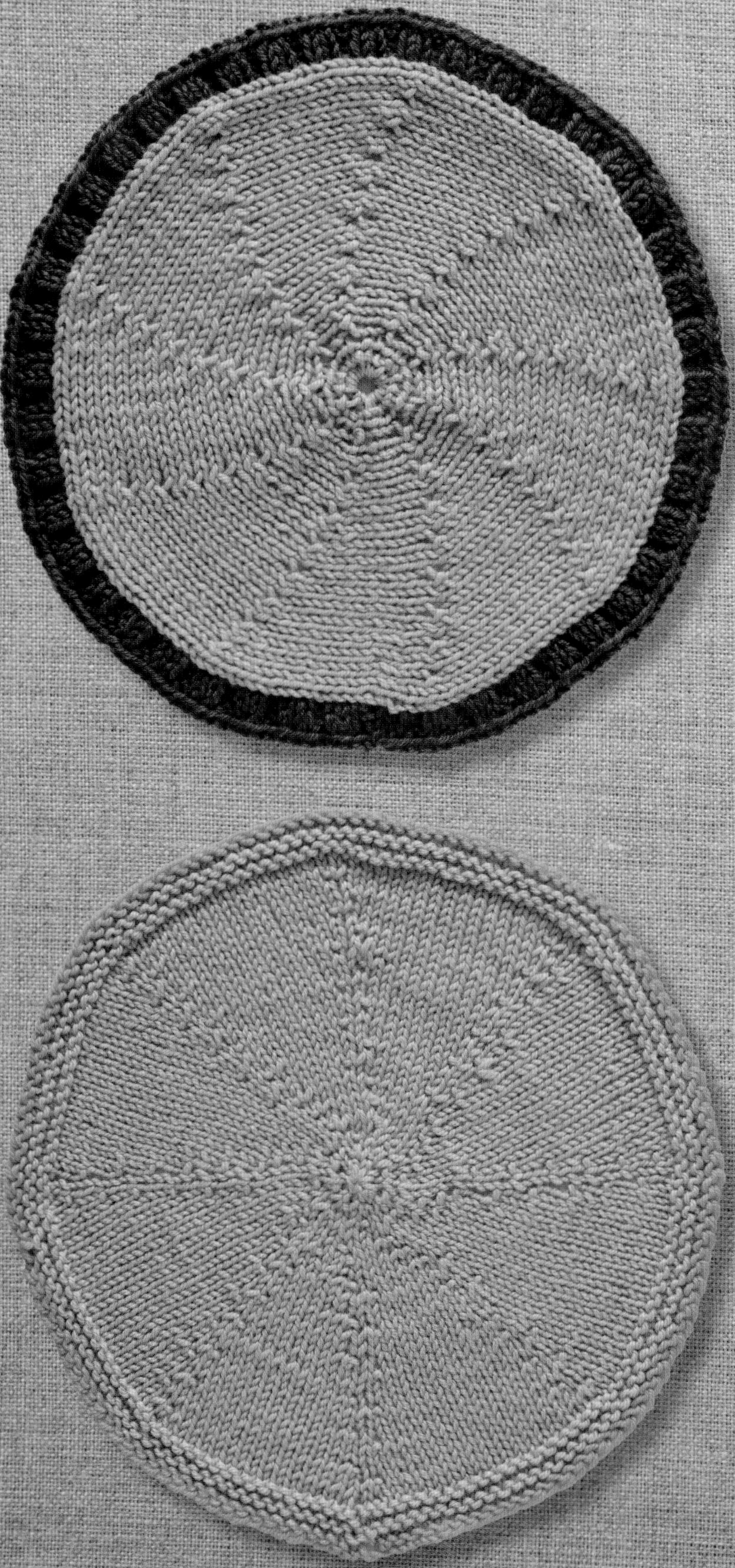

orbit
page 54

pie
page 55

rotate

page 55

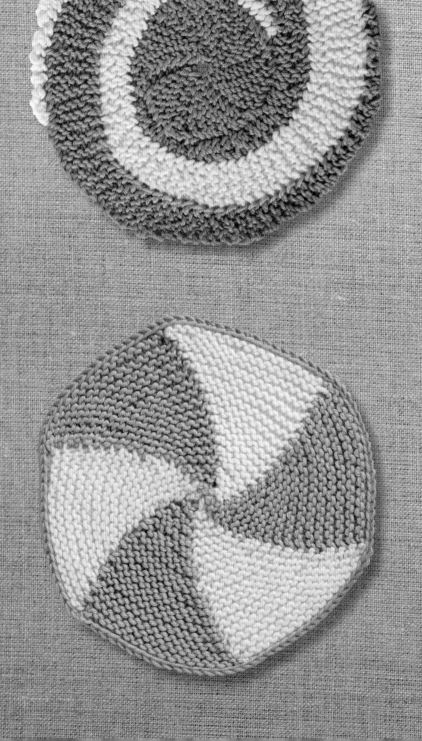

garter spiral
(marble cake)
page 56

pinwheel
page 58

sphere

page 59

SPOKE

Worked from the outer edge to the center
Colors MC and CC

CENTERED DOUBLE DECREASES

S2KP (RS) Sl 2 as if to k2tog, k1, pass the 2 slipped stitches over.
S2PP (WS) [Sl 1 knitwise] twice, slip these 2 stitches back to the left-hand needle, sl 2 to the right-hand needle as if to p2tog tbl, p1, pass the 2 slipped stitches over.

GARTER ST EDGING

With CC, cast on 142 stitches.
Rows 1–5 Knit.
Row 6 With MC, purl.

BODY

Row 1 K1, *k9, S2KP, k8; repeat from * to the last stitch, k1 (128 stitches) (18 stitches each section plus 2 selvedge stitches/128 stitches total).
Row 2 Purl.
Row 3 Knit.
Row 4 P1, *p7, S2PP, p8, pm; repeat from * to the last stitch, p1 (16/114 stitches).
Row 5 Knit.
Row 6 Purl.
Row 7 K1, *k7, S2KP, k6; repeat from * to the last stitch, k1 (14/100 stitches).
Row 8 Purl.
Row 9 Knit.
Row 10 P1, *p5, S2PP, p6; repeat from * to the last stitch, p1 (12/86 stitches).
Row 11 Knit.
Row 12 Purl.
Row 13 K1, *k5, S2KP, k4; repeat from * to the last stitch, k1

(10/72 stitches).
Row 14 Purl.
Row 15 Knit.
Row 16 P1, *p3, S2PP, p4; repeat from * to the last stitch, p1 (8/58 stitches).
Row 17 Knit.
Row 18 Purl.
Row 19 K1, *k3, S2KP, k2; repeat from * to the last stitch, k1 (6/44 stitches).
Row 20 Purl.
Row 21 Knit.
Row 22 P1, *p1, S2PP, p2; repeat from * to the last stitch, p1 (4/30 stitches).
Row 23 Knit.
Row 24 Purl.
Row 25 K1, *k1, S2KP; repeat from * to the last stitch, k1 (2/16 stitches).
Row 26 Purl.
Row 27 Knit.
Row 28 P1, *p2tog; repeat from * to the last stitch, p1 (1/9 stitches).
Break off the yarn, leaving a long tail. Thread the tail through the remaining stitches, pull tight, and secure. Sew seam.

Stitch Key

☐	MC
▨	CC
☐	K on RS, P on WS
⊡	K on WS
⊼	S2KP on RS, S2PP on WS
◿	P2tog on WS
☐	Repeat

Body

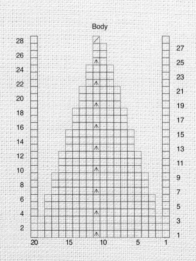

Garter Stitch Edging

RADIATOR

Worked in the round from the center to the outer edge

Colors MC and CC

K1b Knit into the head of the stitch below.

With MC, cast on 7 stitches and divide stitches among 3 dpns; mark the beginning of the round and join.

Rnd 1 *Kfb; repeat from * around (14 stitches).

Rnds 2 and 3 Knit.

Rnd 4 *K1, k1b, pm; repeat from * around (2 stitches each section/28 stitches total).

Rnds 5 and 6 Knit.

Rnd 7 *K2, k1b; repeat from * around (3/42 stitches).

Rnds 8 and 9 Knit.

Rnd 10 *K3, m1; repeat from * around (4/56 stitches).

Rnds 11 and 12 Knit.

Rnd 13 *K4, m1; repeat from * around (5/70 stitches).

Rnds 14 and 15 Knit.

Rnd 16 *K5, m1; repeat from * around (6/84 stitches).

Rnds 17 and 18 Knit.

Rnd 19 *K6, m1; repeat from * around (7/98 stitches).

Rnds 20 and 21 Knit.

Rnd 22 *K7, m1; repeat from * around (8/112 stitches).

Rnds 23 and 24 Knit.

Rnd 25 *K8, m1; repeat from * around (9/126 stitches).

Rnds 26 and 27 Knit.

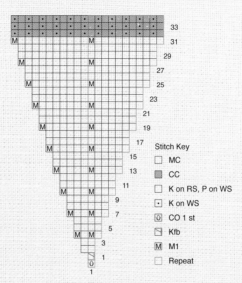

Stitch Key
- ☐ MC
- ▨ CC
- ☐ K on RS, P on WS
- ⊡ K on WS
- ⓪ CO 1 st
- ☒ Kfb
- Ⓜ M1
- ☐ Repeat

Rnd 28 *K9, m1; repeat from * around (10/140 stitches).

Rnds 29 and 30 Knit.

Rnd 31 *K10, m1; repeat from * around (11/154 stitches). Change to CC and work 3 rnds of K1, P1 Rib. Bind off knitwise using a needle one size larger.

For a smaller (larger) circle, increase every 3rd round to desired size, ending after an increase round.

10-SPIRAL DECREASE

Worked in the round from the outer edge to the center

Cast on 160 stitches; mark the beginning of the round and join without twisting.
For Garter st edging, purl 1 rnd, knit 1 rnd, purl 1 rnd.

Rnd 1 *K2tog, k14, pm; repeat from * around (15 stitches each section/150 stitches total).

Rnd 2 and all even-numbered rnds Knit.

Rnd 3 *K2tog, k13; repeat from * around (14/140 stitches).

Rnd 5 *K2tog, k12; repeat from * around (13/130 stitches).

Rnd 7 *K2tog, k11; repeat from * around (12/120 stitches).

Rnd 9 *K2tog, k10; repeat from * around (11/110 stitches).

Rnd 11 *K2tog, k9; repeat from * around (10/100 stitches).

Rnd 13 *K2tog, k8; repeat from * around (9/90 stitches).

Rnd 15 *K2tog, k7; repeat from * around (8/80 stitches).

Rnd 17 *K2tog, k6; repeat from * around (7/70 stitches).

Rnd 19 *K2tog, k5; repeat from * around (6/60 stitches).

Rnd 21 *K2tog, k4; repeat from * around (5/50 stitches).

Rnd 23 *K2tog, k3; repeat from * around (4/40 stitches).

Rnd 25 *K2tog, k2; repeat from * around (3/30 stitches).

Rnd 27 *K2tog, k1; repeat from * around (2/20 stitches).

Rnd 29 *K2tog; repeat from * around (10 stitches).

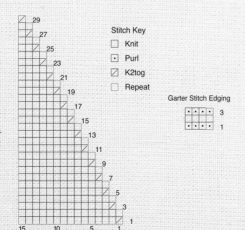

Stitch Key
- ☐ Knit
- ⊡ Purl
- ◩ K2tog
- ☐ Repeat

Garter Stitch Edging

Break off the yarn and thread the tail through the remaining stitches, pull tightly to gather, and secure.

For a smaller (larger) circle, begin with a smaller (larger) multiple of 10 stitches, divide into 10 sections, and decrease every other round at the beginning of each section.

10-SPIRAL DECREASE *(2 needle with seam)*

Worked back and forth from the outer edge to the center

Colors MC and CC

With CC, cast on 162 stitches.

K1, P1 RIBBED EDGING

Rows 1 and 3 (WS) P2, *k1, p1; repeat from * to end.

Row 2 *K1, p1; repeat from * to the last 2 stitches, k2. Change to MC.

Row 1 (RS) K1, pm, *k2tog, k14, pm; repeat from * to the last st, k1 (15 stitches each section plus 2 selvedge stitches/152 stitches total).

Row 2 and all WS rows Purl.

Row 3 K1, *k2tog, knit to the next marker; repeat from * to the last marker, k1 (14/142 stitches).

Row 5 K1, *k2tog, k12; repeat from * to the last stitch, k1 (13/132 stitches).

Row 7 K1, *k2tog, k11; repeat from * to the last stitch, k1 (12/122 stitches).

Row 9 K1, *k2tog, k10; repeat from * to the last stitch, k1 (11/112 stitches).

Row 11 K1, *k2tog, k9; repeat from * to the last stitch, k1 (10/102 stitches).

Row 13 K1, *k2tog, k8; repeat from * to the last stitch, k1 (9/92 stitches).

Row 15 K1, *k2tog, k7; repeat from * to the last stitch, k1 (8/82 stitches)Row 17 K1, *k2tog, k6; repeat from * to end (7/72 stitches).

Row 19 K1, *k2tog, k5; repeat from * to the last stitch, k1 (6/62 stitches).

Row 21 K1, *k2tog, k4; repeat from * to the last stitch, k1 (5/52 stitches).

Row 23 K1, *k2tog, k3; repeat from * to the last stitch, k1 (4/42 stitches).

Row 25 K1, *k2tog, k2; repeat from * to the last stitch, k1 (3/32 stitches).

Row 27 K1, *k2tog, k1; repeat from * to the last stitch, k1 (2/22 stitches).

Row 29 K1, *k2tog; repeat from * to the last stitch, k1 (12 stitches).

Break off the yarn and thread the tail through the remaining stitches, pull together, and secure. Sew side seam.

For a smaller (larger) circle, begin with a smaller (larger) multiple of 10 stitches plus 2 selvedge stitches, divide into 10 sections (with a selvedge stitch at each end), and decrease every RS row at the beginning of each section.

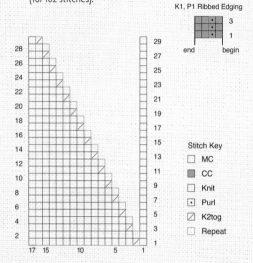

K1, P1 Ribbed Edging

Stitch Key
- ☐ MC
- ▨ CC
- ☐ Knit
- ⊡ Purl
- ▧ K2tog
- ☐ Repeat

5-SPIRAL DECREASE

Worked in the round from the outer edge to the center

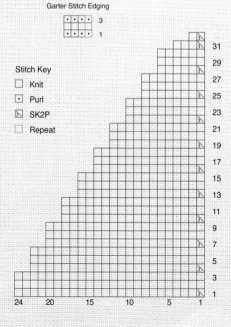

Garter Stitch Edging

Stitch Key
- ☐ Knit
- ⊡ Purl
- ▨ SK2P
- ☐ Repeat

Cast on 130 stitches; mark the beginning of the round and join without twisting.

GARTER ST EDGING

Rnds 1 and 3 Purl.

Rnd 2 Knit.

BODY

Rnd 1 *SK2P, k23, pm; repeat from * around (24 stitches each section/120 stitches total).

Rnds 2 and 3 Knit.

Rnd 4 *SK2P, knit to the next marker; repeat from * around (22/110 stitches).

Rnds 5 and 6 Knit.

Rnd 7 *SK2P, k19; repeat from * around (20/100 stitches).

Rnds 8 and 9 Knit.

Rnd 10 *SK2P, k17; repeat from * around (18/90 stitches).

Rnds 11 and 12 Knit.

Rnd 13 *SK2P, k15; repeat from * around (16/80 stitches).

Rnds 14 and 15 Knit.

Rnd 16 *SK2P, k13; repeat from * around (14/70 stitches).

Rnds 17 and 18 Knit.

Rnd 19 *SK2P, k11; repeat from * around (12/60 stitches).

Rnds 20 and 21 Knit.

Rnd 22 *SK2P, k9; repeat from * around (10/50 stitches).

Rnds 23 and 24 Knit.

Rnd 25 *SK2P, k7; repeat from * around (8/40 stitches).

Rnds 26 and 27 Knit.

Rnd 28 *SK2P, k5; repeat from * around (6/30 stitches).

Rnds 29 and 30 Knit.

Rnd 31 *SK2P, k3; repeat from * around (4/20 stitches).

Rnd 32 *SK2P, k1; repeat from * around (10 stitches).

Break off the yarn and thread the tail through the remaining 10 stitches, pull tightly to gather, and secure.

For a smaller (larger) circle, begin with a smaller (larger) multiple of 10 stitches, divide into 5 sections, and decrease every 3rd round at the beginning of each section.

. . . .

5 – SPIRAL DECREASE (*with seam*)

Worked back and forth from the outer edge to the center

Cast on 162 stitches.

GARTER ST EDGING

Rows 1–3 Knit.

BODY

Row 1 (RS) K1, pm, *SK2P, k29, pm; repeat from * to the last stitch, k1 (30 stitches each section plus 2 selvedge stitches/152 stitches total).

Row 2 and all WS rows Purl.

Row 3 K1, *SK2P, k27; repeat from * to the last stitch, k1 (28/142 stitches).

Row 5 K1, *SK2P, k25; repeat from * to the last stitch, k1 (26/132 stitches).

Row 7 K1, *SK2P, k23; repeat from * to the last stitch, k1 (24/122 stitches).

Row 9 K1, *SK2P, k21; repeat from * to the last stitch, k1 (22/112 stitches).

Row 11 K1, *SK2P, k19; repeat from * to the last stitch, k1 (20/102 stitches).

Row 13 K1, *SK2P, k17; repeat from * to the last stitch, k1 (18/92 stitches).

Row 15 K1, *SK2P, k15; repeat from * to the last stitch, k1 (16/82 stitches).

Row 17 K1, *SK2P, k13; repeat from * to the last stitch, k1 (14/72 stitches).

Row 19 K1, *SK2P, k11; repeat from * to the last stitch, k1 (12/62 stitches).

Row 21 K1, *SK2P, k9; repeat from * to the last stitch, k1 (10/52 stitches).

Row 23 K1, *SK2P, k7; repeat from * to the last stitch, k1 (8/42 stitches).

Row 25 K1, *SK2P, k5; repeat from * to the last stitch, k1 (6/32 stitches).

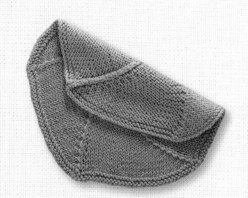

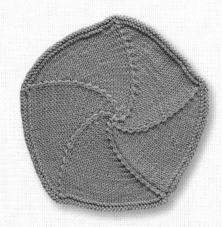

Row 27 K1, *SK2P, k3; repeat from * to the last stitch, k1 (4/22 stitches).

Row 29 K1, *SK2P, k1; repeat from * to the last stitch, k1 (2/12 stitches).

Break off the yarn and thread the tail through the remaining 12 stitches, pull tightly to gather, and secure. Sew seam.

For a smaller (larger) circle, begin with a smaller (larger) multiple of 10 stitches plus 2 selvedge stitches, divide into 5 sections, and decrease every other round at the beginning of each section.

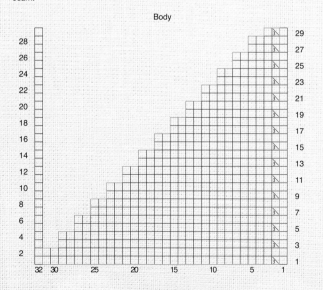

Body

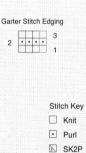

Garter Stitch Edging

Stitch Key

☐ Knit

· Purl

⋋ SK2P

☐ Repeat

PETALWORK

Worked in the round from the center to the outer edge

Cast on 8 stitches (2 stitches each on 4 dpns); mark the beginning of the round and join without twisting.

Rnd 1 *Yo, k1, pm; repeat from * around (2 stitches in each section/16 stitches total).

Rnd 2 and all even-numbered rnds Knit.

Rnd 3 *Yo, k2; repeat from * around (24 stitches).

Rnd 5 *Yo, k3; repeat from * around (32 stitches).

Rnd 7 *Yo, k4; repeat from * around (40 stitches).

Rnd 9 *Yo, k5; repeat from * around (48 stitches).

Rnd 11 *Yo, k6; repeat from * around (56 stitches).

Rnd 13 *Yo, k7; repeat from * around (64 stitches).

Rnd 15 *Yo, k8; repeat from * around (72 stitches).

Rnd 17 *Yo, k9; repeat from * around (80 stitches).

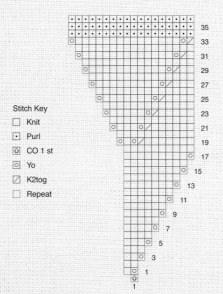

Stitch Key
- ☐ Knit
- · Purl
- ⊙ CO 1 st
- ⊙ Yo
- ⧄ K2tog
- ☐ Repeat

Rnd 19 *K7, k2tog, yo, k1, yo; repeat from * around (11/88 stitches).

Rnd 21 *K6, k2tog, yo, k3, yo; repeat from * around (12/96 stitches).

Rnd 23 *K5, k2tog, yo, k5, yo; repeat from * around (13/104 stitches).

Rnd 25 *K4, k2tog, yo, k7, yo; repeat from * around (14/112 stitches).

Rnd 27 *K3, k2tog, yo, k9, yo; repeat from * around (15/120 stitches).

Rnd 29 *K2, k2tog, yo, k11, yo; repeat from * around (16/128 stitches).

Rnd 31 *K1, k2tog, yo, k13, yo; repeat from * around (17/136 stitches).

Rnd 33 *K2tog, yo, k15, yo; repeat from * around (18/144 stitches).

If not working edging, bind off using a needle one size larger.

REVERSE STOCKINETTE ST EDGING

Rnds 34–36 Purl.

Bind off using a needle one size larger.

BURST

Worked in the round from the center to the outer edge

Cast on 8 stitches (2 stitches each on 4 dpns); mark the beginning of the round and join without twisting.

Rnd 1 *K1 tbl; repeat from * around.

Rnd 2 *Kfb; repeat from * around (16 stitches).

Rnd 3 and all odd-numbered rnds Knit.

Rnd 4 *Kfb, k1, pm; repeat from * around (3 stitches each section/24 stitches total).

Garter St Edging

Stitch Key
- ☐ K on RS, P on WS
- · P on RS, K on WS
- ◩ Kfb
- ☑ K1 tbl
- ⊙ CO 1 st
- ☐ Repeat

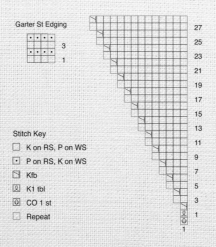

Rnd 6 *K2, kfb; repeat from * around (4/32 stitches).

Rnd 8 *K3, kfb; repeat from * around (5/40 stitches).

Rnd 10 *K4, kfb; repeat from * around (6/48 stitches).

Rnd 12 *K5, kfb; repeat from * around (7/56 stitches).

Rnd 14 *K6, kfb; repeat from * around (8/64 stitches).

Rnd 16 *K7, kfb; repeat from * around (9/72 stitches).

Continue increasing 8 stitches every other rnd, working one more stitch before each increase, to desired size (sample has 15/120 stitches), ending with an increase rnd. If not working edging, bind off using a needle one size larger.

For a smaller (larger) circle, repeat rnds 5–6 and end with an increase round at the desired size, then bind off or work edging.

GARTER ST EDGING

Rnds 1 and 3 Knit.

Rnds 2 and 4 Purl.

Bind off using a needle one size larger.

HALO

Worked in the round from the center to the outer edge

Colors MC and CC

With MC, cast on 8 stitches (2 stitches each on 4 dpns); mark the beginning of the round and join without twisting.

Rnd 1 *K1 tbl; repeat from * around.

Rnd 2 *Kfb, pm; repeat from * around (2 stitches each section/16 stitches total).

Rnds 3–7 Knit.

Rnd 8 *Kfb; repeat from * around (4/32 stitches).

Rnds 9–13 Knit.

Rnd 14 *Kfb; repeat from * around (8/64 stitches).

Rnds 15–19 Knit.

Rnd 20 *K1, kfb; repeat from * around (12/96 stitches).

Rnds 21–25 Knit.

Rnd 26 *K2, kfb; repeat from * around (16/128 stitches).

Rnds 27–31 Knit.

Rnd 32 *K3, kfb; repeat from * around (20/160 stitches). If not working edging, bind off using a needle one size larger.

For a smaller circle, end with an increase round at desired size.

For a larger circle, continue increasing 32 stitches every 6th round as established to desired size, ending with an increase round.

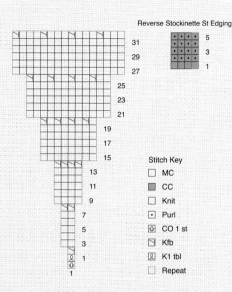

Reverse Stockinette St Edging

Stitch Key

- ☐ MC
- ▨ CC
- ☐ Knit
- · Purl
- ⊙ CO 1 st
- ◥ Kfb
- ⊻ K1 tbl
- ☐ Repeat

REVERSE STOCKINETTE ST EDGING

Change to CC.

Rnd 1 Knit.

Rnds 2–5 Purl.

Bind off knitwise using a needle one size larger.

SWIRL

Worked in the round from the center to the outer edge

Colors MC and CC

With MC, cast on 12 stitches (4 stitches each on 3 dpns); mark the beginning of the round and join without twisting.

Rnd 1 *K1 tbl; repeat from * around.

Rnd 2 *Yo, k2, pm; repeat from * around (3 stitches each section/18 stitches total).

Rnd 3 and all odd-numbered rnds Knit.

Rnd 4 *Yo, k3; repeat from * around (4/24 stitches).

Rnd 6 *Yo, k4; repeat from * around (5/30 stitches).

Rnd 8 *Yo, k5; repeat from * around (6/36 stitches).

Rnd 10 *Yo, k6; repeat from * around (7/42 stitches).

Rnd 12 *Yo, k7; repeat from * around (8/48 stitches).

Rnd 14 *Yo, k8; repeat from * around (9/54 stitches).

Continue increasing every other rnd to desired size, working one more stitch after each yo, ending with an increase rnd (sample has 16/96 stitches).

For a smaller circle, end with an increase round at the desired size.

If not working edging, bind off using a needle one size larger.

K2, P2 Edging

Stitch Key

- ☐ MC
- ▨ CC
- ☐ Knit
- · Purl
- ⊙ Yo
- ◥ Kfb
- ⊻ K1 tbl
- ⊙ CO 1 st
- ■ No stitch
- ☐ Repeat

K2, P2 EDGING (MULTIPLE OF 4 STITCHES)

Rnd 1 Knit.

Change to CC.

Rnd 2 *K1, kfb; repeat from * around (sample has 144 stitches).

Rnds 3–5 *K2, p2; repeat from * around.

Bind off in pattern using a needle one size larger.

GARTER ST CIRCLE

Worked from the bottom up

Cast on 15 stitches.

Inc row Kfb, knit to the last stitch, kfb (17 stitches). Repeat Inc row every row until there are 31 stitches, every other row until there are 39 stitches, every 4th row until there are 41 stitches, then every 6th row until there are 45 stitches.

Work 22 rows even in Garter stitch.

Dec row K2tog, knit to the last 2 stitches, ssk (43 stitches). Repeat Dec row every 6th row until there are 41 stitches; every 4th row until there are 39 stitches, every other row until there are 31 stitches, then every row until there are 15 stitches.

Bind off.

GARTER ST STRIPED CIRCLE

Worked from the bottom up

Colors MC and CC

Stitch Key

☐ K on RS

⊡ K on WS

⊿ K2tog

◺ SSK

◹ Kfb

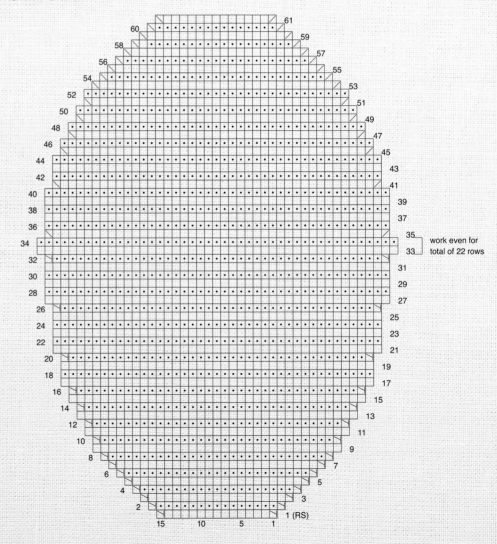

work even for total of 22 rows

With MC, cast on 15 stitches.

Inc row Kfb, knit to the last stitch, kfb (17 stitches).

Repeat Inc row every row until there are 31 stitches, every other row until there are 39 stitches, every 4th row until there are 41 stitches, then every 6th row until there are 45 stitches and AT THE SAME TIME, change colors every 4 rows.

Work 22 rows even in Garter stitch.

Dec row K2tog, knit to the last 2 stitches, ssk (43 stitches).

Repeat Dec row every 6th row until there are 41 stitches, every 4th row until there are 39 stitches, every other row until there are 31 stitches, then every row until there are 15 stitches.

Bind off.

LOOP ST EDGING

With MC, cast on 135 stitches.

Row 1 (WS) K1, *insert the right-hand needle into the next stitch knitwise; wind yarn over the right-hand needle and the first and second fingers of your left hand 3 times, then over the right-hand needle point once more; draw all 4 loops through the stitch and slip them onto the left-hand needle; insert the right-hand needle through the back of these 4 loops and the original stitch and knit them together tbl, k1; repeat from * to the last stitch, k1.

Bind off.

CORKSCREW

EDGING

With CC, loosely cast on 141 stitches.

Row 1 Knit into the front, back, and front again of each stitch across (423 stitches).

Bind off purlwise. Use fingers to twist and squeeze to shape corkscrew.

Row 1 With CC, *after corkscrew is shaped, use needle to pick up a stitch on each twist, with 2nd needle and yarn, knit 1 stitch from one of the corkscrew twists, cast on 2 stitches; repeat from * until there are 120 or more stitches.

Rows 2 and 3 Knit.

Bind off.

Pin the edging evenly around the edge of the circle and sew in place.

Note This edging may need to be adjusted to fit circle if using a different weight yarn. Make a swatch.

Corkscrew Edging

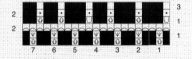

Stitch Key

☐ K on RS, P on WS

· P on RS, K on WS

⍉ K1 tbl

Ⓥ CO 1 st

Ⓥ Knit (front, back, front) in 1 st

⌣ Bind off 1 st

■ No stitch

☐ Repeat

STOCKINETTE ST CIRCLE

Work 13 rows even in Stockinette stitch, ending with a WS row.

Continuing in Stockinette stitch, work a Dec row on the next row and every 4th row until there are 41 stitches, every other row until there are 35 stitches, then every row until there are 15 stitches.

Bind off.

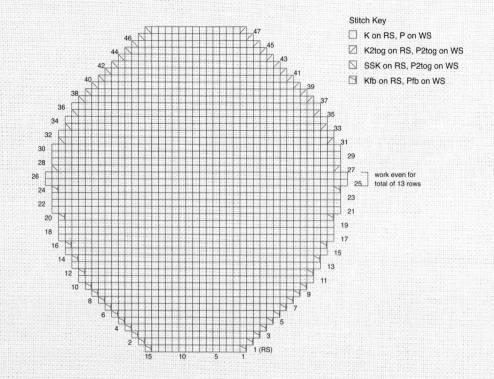

Stitch Key
- ☐ K on RS, P on WS
- ◩ K2tog on RS, P2tog on WS
- ◪ SSK on RS, P2tog on WS
- ◩ Kfb on RS, Pfb on WS

work even for total of 13 rows

Worked from the bottom up

Inc row 1 (RS) Kfb, knit to the last stitch, kfb.
Inc row 2 (WS) Pfb, purl to the last stitch, pfb.
Dec row 1 (RS) Ssk, knit to the last 2 stitches, k2tog.
Dec row 2 (WS) P2tog, purl to the last 2 stitches, ssp.

Cast on 15 stitches.

Continuing in Stockinette stitch, work an Inc row every row until there are 35 stitches, every other row until there are 41 stitches, then every 4th row until there are 45 stitches.

STOCKINETTE ST SCALLOPS

EDGING (FINAL MULTIPLE OF 13 STITCHES)

Each point is worked separately and then joined on the same row. Break the yarn after all but the last point, leaving stitches on the needle.

Cast on 6 stitches.
Row 1 K6.
Rows 2–8 Kfb, knit to end (13 stitches after row 8).

Break the yarn, leaving stitches on the needle.

On the same needle, cast on 6 stitches and work rows 1–8 to make another point. Continue making desired number of points. When the last point is complete, turn and knit across all points on the needle to join.

Bind off and sew to the edge of the circle or continue with circle.

Stitch Key
- ☐ K on RS
- ⊡ K on WS
- ⊚ CO 1 st
- ◩ Kfb on RS
- ◪ Kfb on WS
- ☐ Repeat

Horizontal Garter St Scallops

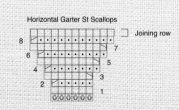

Joining row

SEED ST CIRCLE

Worked from the bottom up

Cast on 11 stitches.

Row 1 (RS) Kfb, *k1, p1; repeat from * to the last 2 stitches, k1, kfb (13 stitches).

Row 2 Kfb, *p1, k1; repeat from * to the last 2 stitches, p1, kfb (15 stitches).

Inc row Kfb, work in Seed st to the last stitch, kfb (17 stitches).

Continuing in Seed st as established, work Inc row every row until there are 31 stitches, every other row until there are 35 stitches, every 4th row once, then every 6th row until there are 45 stitches.

Work 11 rows even in Seed st.

Dec row K2tog, work in Seed st to the last 2 stitches, ssk (43 stitches).

Work Dec row every 6th row until there are 37 stitches, every 4th row once, every other row until there are 31 stitches, then every row until there are 11 stitches.

Bind off.

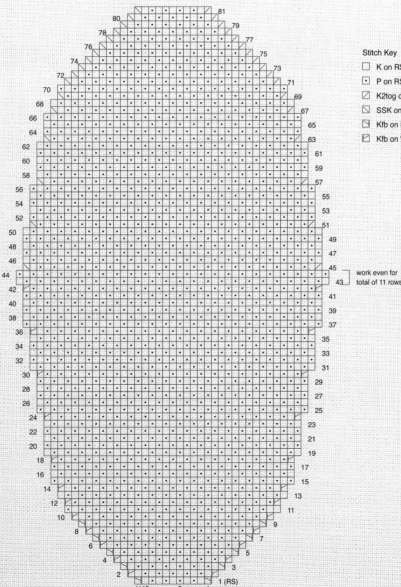

Stitch Key

- ☐ K on RS, P on WS
- ☐ P on RS, K on WS
- ◩ K2tog on RS, P2tog on WS
- ◲ SSK on RS, P2tog tbl on WS
- ◩ Kfb on RS
- ◩ Kfb on WS

work even for
total of 11 rows

EYELET POINTS

EDGING

Cast on 5 stitches.

Row 1 Sl 1, k1, [yo] twice, k2tog, k1 (6 stitches).

Stitch Key

- ☐ K on RS
- • K on WS
- ⊙ CO 1 st
- ⊡ Yo
- ⧄ K2tog
- ⊻ Slip 1 st
- ⌢ Bind off 1 st
- ☐ Repeat

Row 2 Sl 1, k1, [k1, p1] in double yo, k2.

Row 3 Sl 1, k3, [yo] twice, k2 (8 stitches).

Row 4 Sl 1, k1, [k1, p1] in double yo, k4.

Row 5 Sl 1, k1, [yo] twice, k2tog, k4 (9 stitches).

Row 6 Sl 1, k4, [k1, p1] in double yo, k2.

Row 7 Sl 1, k8.

Row 8 Bind off 4 stitches, k4 (5 stitches).

Repeat rows 1–8 to desired length. Bind off.

Sew bound-off edge to cast-on edge. Sew edging to edge of circle.

ORBIT

Worked in short rows

Colors MC and CC

With MC and using a provisional cast-on (see page 214), cast on 20 stitches.

Row 1 and all odd-numbered rows Knit.

Row 2 P18. Turn, leaving the last 2 stitches unworked.

Row 4 P16. Turn, leaving the last 4 stitches unworked.

Row 6 P14. Turn, leaving the last 6 stitches unworked.

Row 8 P12. Turn, leaving the last 8 stitches unworked.

Row 10 P10. Turn, leaving the last 10 stitches unworked.

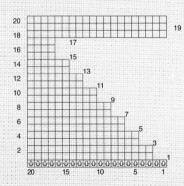

K2, P2 Edging

Stitch Key

- ☐ MC
- ■ CC
- ☐ K on RS, P on WS
- • P on RS, K on WS
- ⊙ CO 1 st
- ☐ Repeat

Row 12 P8. Turn, leaving the last 12 stitches unworked.

Row 14 P6. Turn, leaving the last 14 stitches unworked.

Row 16 P4. Turn, leaving the last 16 stitches unworked.

Row 18 Purl.

Row 20 Purl.

Repeat rows 1–20 eight more times (9 sections).

Graft beginning to end.

For a smaller (larger) circle, cast on fewer (more) stitches with a multiple of 2. Work the first short row to the last 2 stitches and work the last short row ending with p4.

Optional To close the center, thread the yarn through the end stitches at the center, pull tightly to gather, and secure.

K2, P2 EDGING (MULTIPLE OF 4 STITCHES)

With CC, pick up and knit 180 stitches evenly around edge of circle, pm.

Rnds 1–3 *K2, p2; repeat from * around.

Bind off in pattern using a needle one size larger.

PIE

Worked in the round from the center to the outer edge

Cast on 8 stitches (2 stitches each on 4 dpns); mark the beginning of the round and join without twisting.

Rnd 1 *K1 tbl; repeat from * around.

Rnd 2 *Kfb; repeat from * around (16 stitches).

Rnd 3 and all odd-numbered rnds Knit.

Rnd 4 *Kfb, k1, pm; repeat from * around (3 stitches each section/24 stitches total).

Rnd 6 *K2, kfb; repeat from * around (4/32 stitches).

Rnd 8 *Kfb, k3; repeat from * around (5/40 stitches).

Rnd 10 *K4, kfb; repeat from * around (6/48 stitches).

Rnd 12 *Kfb, k5; repeat from * around (7/56 stitches).

Rnd 14 *K6, kfb; repeat from * around (8/64 stitches).

Rnd 16 *Kfb, k7; repeat from * around (9/72 stitches).

Continue increasing 8 stitches every other rnd as established, working one more stitch before or after each increase, until circle is desired size, ending with an Inc rnd (sample has 18/144 stitches). End with an Inc rnd.

For a smaller (larger) circle, repeat rnds 5–8 and end with an Inc round at the desired size, then bind off or work edging.

If not working edging, bind off using a needle one size larger.

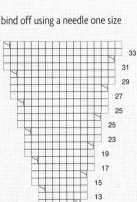

Garter St Edging

3

1

Stitch Key
- ☐ Knit
- ⊡ Purl
- ◩ Kfb
- ⍉ K1 tbl
- ⍟ CO 1 st
- ☐ Repeat

GARTER ST EDGING

Rnds 1 and 3 Knit.

Rnds 2 and 4 Purl.

Bind off purlwise using a needle one size larger.

ROTATE

Worked in short rows

Cast on 21 stitches.

Row 1 (RS) K3, turn, leaving 18 stitches unworked.

Row 2 and all WS rows through Row 12 Knit.

Row 3 K6, turn, leaving 15 stitches unworked.

Row 5 K9, turn, leaving 12 stitches unworked.

Row 7 K12, turn, leaving 9 stitches unworked.

Row 9 K15, turn, leaving 6 stitches unworked.

Row 11 K18, turn, leaving 3 stitches unworked.

Row 13 Knit.

Row 14 Purl.

Repeat rows 1–14 eighteen more times (19 sections).

Bind off, leaving a long tail. Sew cast-on edge to bound-off edge. Thread the tail through the stitches at the center, pull tight to gather, and secure.

For a smaller (larger) circle, cast on a smaller (larger) multiple of 3 stitches.

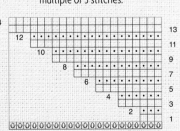

Stitch Key
- ☐ K on RS
- ⊡ K on WS
- ⍟ CO 1 st
- ☐ Repeat

GARTER SPIRAL *(Marble Cake)*

Colors MC and CC

Note This circle looks a bit long and tricky but isn't; for an easier version, see page 173.

CENTER

With MC, cast on 8 stitches, leaving a long tail.

Row 1 and all WS rows Knit.

Row 2 K6, k2tog.

Row 4 K5, k2tog.

Row 6 K4, k2tog.

Row 8 K3, k2tog.

Row 10 K2, k2tog.

Row 12 K1, k2tog.

Row 14 K2tog.

Row 16 K1, pick up and knit 7 stitches (1 in each ridge along edge of piece) (8 stitches).

Repeat rows 1–16 five more times (6 sections). Bind off; do not cut yarn. With cast-on tail, close the center and sew the bound-off edge to the cast-on edge.

Note Use removable stitch markers.

CENTER EDGE

With RS facing, join MC. Using a circular needle, *pick up and knit 4 stitches in the next 4 Garter st ridges along the edge of the piece, 1 stitch between the 4th and 5th ridges, then 4 stitches in the next 4 ridges, pm; repeat from * 5 more times (9 stitches each section/54 stitches total).

*SECTION 1

Use double-pointed or straight needles.

Row 1 With MC, k1 from circular needle.

Row 2 K1.

Rows 3, 5, 7, 9, 11, 13, 15, and 17 K1, k1 from circular needle.

Rows 4, 6, 8, 10, 12, 14, and 16 Ssk.

Pm.

SECTION 2

Row 1 Kfb, k1 from circular needle.

Row 2 Ssk, k1 (2 stitches).

Rows 3, 5, 7, and 9 K2, k1 from circular needle.

Rows 4, 6, 8, and 10 Ssk, k1.

Row 11 K1, W&T.

Row 12 K1.

Rows 13–20 Repeat rows 3–10 (lifting wraps and working together with wrapped stitches).

Pm.

SECTION 3

Row 1 K1, kfb, k1 from circular needle.

Row 2 Ssk, k2 (3 stitches).

Rows 3, 5, and 7 K3, k1 from circular needle.

Rows 4, 6, and 8 Ssk, k2.

Row 9 K1, W&T.

Row 10 K1.

Rows 11–14 Repeat rows 3–6 (lifting wraps and working together with wrapped stitches).

Rows 15 and 16 Repeat rows 9 and 10.

Rows 17–22 Repeat rows 3–8 (lifting wraps and working together with wrapped stitches).

Pm.

Move Section 1 marker one ridge to the left. Repeat for Section 2 marker (10 ridges in each section). Do not break yarn.*

Transfer the 3 working MC stitches to a holder.

Join CC and repeat from * to * over the remaining 27 stitches, then transfer the 3 working CC stitches to a holder.

SECTION 4

Transfer the 3 MC stitches from the holder back to the needle.

**Row 1 With MC, k2, m1, k1, pick up and knit 1 stitch in the next ridge on the circle.

Row 2 Ssk, k3 (4 stitches).

Row 3 K4, pick up and knit 1 stitch in the next ridge.

Row 4 Ssk, k3.

Row 5 K2, W&T.

Row 6 K2.

Rows 7 and 9 K4 (lifting wraps and working together with wrapped stitches), pick up and knit 1 stitch in the next ridge.

Rows 8 and 10 Ssk, k3.

Rows 11–28 Repeat rows 5–10 (lifting wraps and working together with wrapped stitches).

Move marker to outer edge.

SECTION 5

Row 1 K2, m1, k2, pick up and knit 1 stitch in the next ridge.

Row 2 Ssk, k4 (5 stitches).

Row 3 K5, pick up and knit 1 stitch in the next ridge.

Row 4 Ssk, k4.

Row 5 K2, W&T.

Row 6 K2.

Rows 7 and 9 K5 (lifting wraps and working together with wrapped stitches), pick up and knit 1 stitch in the next ridge.

Rows 8 and 10 Ssk, k4.

Row 11–28 Repeat rows 5–10.

Move marker to outer edge.

SECTION 6

Row 1 K2, m1, k3, pick up and knit 1 stitch in the next ridge.

Row 2 Ssk, k5 (6 stitches).

Row 3 K6, pick up and knit 1 stitch in the next ridge.

Row 4 Ssk, k5.

Row 5 K3, W&T.

Row 6 K3.

Rows 7 and 9 K6 (lifting wraps and working together with wrapped stitches), pick up and knit 1 stitch in the next ridge.

Rows 8 and 10 Ssk, k5.

Rows 11–28 Repeat rows 5–10 (lifting wraps and working together with wrapped stitches). Move marker to outer edge.

Transfer the 6 working MC stitches to a holder. DO NOT BREAK YARN.**

Transfer the 3 CC stitches from the holder back to the needle and repeat from ** to ** using CC.

SECTION 7

Transfer the 6 MC stitches from the holder back onto the needle.

***Rows 1, 3, and 5** With MC, k6, pick up and knit 1 stitch in the next ridge.

Rows 2, 4, and 6 Ssk, k5.

Row 7 K3, W&T.

Row 8 K3.

Rows 9–16 Repeat rows 1–8 (lifting wraps and working together with wrapped stitches).

Row 17 K2, k2tog, k2, pick up and knit 1 stitch in the next ridge.

Row 18 Ssk, k4.

Rows 19, 21, and 23 K5, pick up and knit 1 stitch in the next ridge.

Rows 20, 22, and 24 Ssk, k4.

Rows 25 and 26 Repeat rows 7 and 8.

Rows 27–34 Repeat rows 19–26 (lifting wraps and working together with wrapped stitches).

Row 35 K2, k2tog, k1, pick up and knit 1 stitch in the next ridge.

Row 36 Ssk, k3 (4 stitches). Move marker to outer edge.

SECTION 8

Rows 1, 3, and 5 K4, pick up and knit 1 stitch in the next ridge.

Rows 2, 4, and 6 Ssk, k3.

Row 7 K2, W&T.

Row 8 K2.

Rows 9–16 Repeat rows 1–8 (lifting wraps and working together with wrapped stitches).

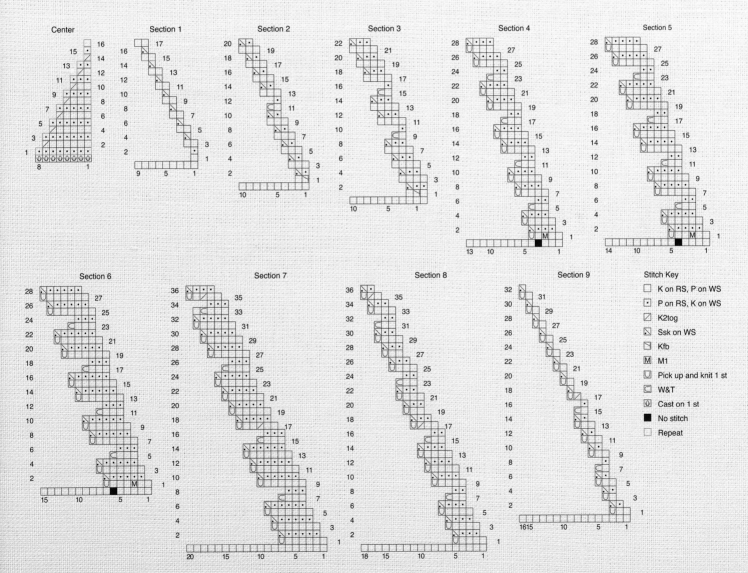

Stitch Key

- ☐ K on RS, P on WS
- ⊡ P on RS, K on WS
- ◿ K2tog
- ◺ Ssk on WS
- ◹ Kfb
- Ⓜ M1
- ∪ Pick up and knit 1 st
- ⊍ W&T
- ⓤ Cast on 1 st
- ■ No stitch
- ☐ Repeat

Row 17 K2, k2tog, pick up and knit 1 stitch in the next ridge.

Row 18 Ssk, k2 (3 stitches).

Rows 19 and 21 K3, pick up and knit 1 stitch in the next ridge.

Rows 20 and 22 Ssk, k2.

Rows 23 and 24 Repeat rows 7 and 8.

Rows 25–30 Repeat rows 19–24 (lifting wraps and working together with wrapped stitches).

Rows 31 and 34 Repeat rows 19–22.

Row 35 K1, k2tog, pick up and knit 1 stitch in the next ridge.

Row 36 Ssk, k1.

Move marker to outer edge.

SECTION 9

Rows 1, 3, and 5 K2, pick up and knit 1 stitch in the next ridge.

Rows 2, 4, and 6 Ssk, k1.

Row 7 K1, W&T.

Row 8 K1.

Rows 9–16 Repeat rows 1–8 (lifting wraps and working together with wrapped stitches).

Row 17 K2tog, pick up and knit 1 stitch in the next ridge.

Row 18 Ssk.

Rows 19, 21, 23, 25, 27, 29, and 31 K1, pick up and knit 1 stitch in the next ridge.

Rows 20, 22, 24, 26, 28, 30, and 32 Ssk.

Fasten off.***

Transfer the 3 CC stitches from the holder back to the needle and repeat from *** to *** using CC.

PINWHEEL

Worked back and forth in wedges from the center to the outer edge

Colors A and B

SECTION 1

With A, cast on 1 stitch.

Row 1 (RS) Kfb (2 stitches).

Row 2 Knit.

Row 3 Knit to the last stitch, kfb.

Row 4 Knit.

Repeat rows 3 and 4 until there are 18 stitches, ending with a WS row.

Break the yarn and place the stitches on hold.

Note Stitches can be placed on a circular needle as you continue making the sections.

SECTION 2

With RS facing and B, pick up and knit 1 stitch in the right-hand side of the cast-on stitch of Section 1.

Row 1 (WS) Knit.

Row 2 K1, pick up and knit 1 from the first Garter st ridge on the side of Section 1.

Row 3 Knit.

Row 4 Knit to the end, pick up and knit 1 from the next Garter st ridge on the side of Section 1.

Repeat rows 3 and 4 until there are 18 stitches, ending with a WS row.

Break the yarn and place the stitches on hold together with Section 1.

SECTIONS 3-8

Work the same as for Section 2 onto the previous Section, alternating colors A and B.

Sew the side of Section 8 to the side of Section 1. Place all 144 stitches onto a circular needle. Pm and join. With either A or B, knit 1 rnd. Bind off knitwise with a needle one size larger.

Note For a multicolored pinwheel, change the yarn color at each section pickup.

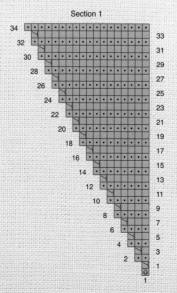

Section 1

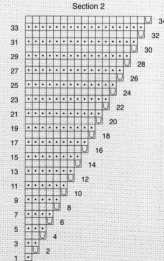

Section 2

Stitch Key

- ▨ A
- ☐ A or B
- ☐ K on RS
- ⊡ K on WS
- Ⓤ Cast on 1 st
- ⊠ Kfb
- ⊔ Pick up and knit 1 st

SPHERE

Worked in the round from the center to the outer edge
Sewn on beaded fringe (optional)

Cast on 8 stitches (2 stitches each on 4 dpns); mark the beginning of the round and join without twisting.

Rnd 1 *K1 tbl; repeat from * around.

Rnd 2 *Kfb; repeat from * around (16 stitches).

Rnd 3 and all odd-numbered rnds Knit.

Rnd 4 *K1, kfb; repeat from * around (24 stitches).

Rnd 6 K1, kfb, *k2, kfb; repeat from * to the last stitch, k1 (32 stitches).

Rnd 8 *K3, kfb; repeat from * around (40 stitches).

Rnd 10 K1, kfb; *k4, kfb; repeat from * to the last 3 stitches, k3 (48 stitches).

Rnd 12 *Kfb, k5; repeat from * around (56 stitches).

Rnd 14 K4, kfb, *k6, kfb; repeat from * to the last 2 stitches, k2 (64 stitches).

Rnd 16 K1, kfb, *k7, kfb; repeat from * to the last 6 stitches, k6 (72 stitches).

Rnd 18 *Kfb, k8; repeat from * around (80 stitches).

Rnd 20 K5, kfb, *k9, kfb; repeat from * to the last 4 stitches, k4 (88 stitches).

Rnd 22 K1, kfb, *k10, kfb; repeat from * to the last 9 stitches, k9 (96 stitches).

Rnd 24 *Kfb, k11; repeat from * around (104 stitches).

Rnd 26 K6, kfb, *k12, kfb; repeat from * to the last 6 stitches, k6 (112 stitches).

Rnd 28 K1, kfb, *k13, kfb; repeat from * to the last 12 stitches, k12 (120 stitches).

Rnd 30 *Kfb, k14; repeat from * around (128 stitches).

Rnd 32 K7, kfb, *k15, kfb; repeat from * to the last 8 stitches, k8 (136 stitches).

If not working edging, bind off using a needle one size larger.

GARTER ST EDGING
Rnds 1 and 3 Knit.
Rnds 2 and 4 Purl.
Bind off knitwise using a needle one size larger.

Garter Stitch Edging

Stitch Key
- ☐ Knit
- ⊡ Purl
- ◹ Kfb
- ⬚ K1 tbl
- ⬚ CO 1 st
- ☐ Repeat

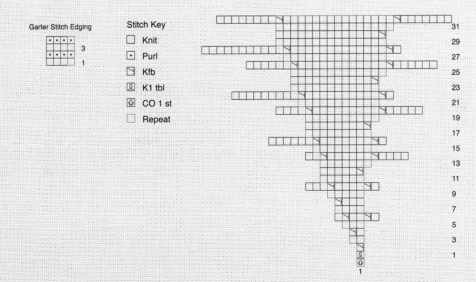

TEXTURE & TECHNIQUES

Much like knitted blocks, knitted circles can be used to learn and practice different knitting techniques on a small scale. This chapter includes circles made using entrelac, cables, reversible cables, bobbles, leaves, brioche, domino, short-row knitting techniques, and more.

The circles in this chapter are wonderful for designing. They make unique statements, which will give your garments gorgeous interest and appeal. The reversible patterns are especially versatile. Good examples of projects that use the circles featured here are Rambling Reversible Cable Scarf on page 197, Brunhilda's Whirl on page 190, and Spring Leaves Jacket on page 186.

Use these circles to experiment with techniques you may not be familiar with, and give your pieces added flair. Enjoy!

cathedral window

page 74

bobble swirl

page 75

honeycomb circle
page 76

corona
(running cable circle)
page 77

meridian
(cable circle)
page 78

seed stitch
spoke
page 78

periphery
page 79

*daisy mae
circle*
page 80

domino disk
page 81

*ribbed
round*
page 81

ringed leaves
page 82

brunhilda's whirl
page 83

entrelac
encircle
page 84

cirque
page 85

stellar
page 86

bobble burst
page 87

bulbiform brioche

page 87

bold reversible cable

page 88

capella
(textures)
page 89

tree circle
page 90

CATHEDRAL WINDOW

Worked in the round from the outer edge to the center
Colors MC and CC
1/1 RPC Sl 1 stitch onto the cn and hold in back, k1, p1 from the cn.
1/1 LPC Sl 1 stitch onto the cn and hold in front, p1, k1 from the cn.

GARTER ST EDGING

With CC and circular needle, loosely cast on 143 stitches; pm and join without twisting. Change to dpns when stitches no longer fit comfortably on circular needle.

Rnds 1 and 3 Purl.

Rnds 2 and 4 Knit.

Rnd 5 Change to MC. *K4, k2tog, k5, pm; repeat from * around (10 stitches each section/130 stitches total).

BODY

Rnd 1 *P3, 1/1 RPC, 1/1 LPC, p3; repeat from * around.

Rnd 2 *P3, sl 1, p2, sl 1, p3; repeat from * around.

Rnd 3 *P2, 1/1 RPC, p2, 1/1 LPC, p2; repeat from * around.

Rnd 4 *P2, sl 1, p4, sl 1, p2; repeat from * around.

Rnd 5 *P1, 1/1 RPC, p4, 1/1 LPC, p1; repeat from * around.

Rnd 6 *P1, sl 1, p6, sl 1, p1; repeat from * around.

Rnd 7 *1/1 RPC, p6, 1/1 LPC; repeat from * around.

Rnds 8 and 10 *Sl 1, p8, sl 1; repeat from * around.

Rnd 9 *K1, p8, k1; repeat from * around.

Rnd 11 *1/1 LPC, p6, 1/1 RPC; repeat from * around.

Rnd 12 *P1, sl 1, p6, sl 1, p1; repeat from * around.

Rnd 13 *P1, 1/1 LPC, p4, 1/1 RPC, p1; repeat from * around.

Rnd 14 *P2, sl 1, p4, sl 1, p2; repeat from * around.

Rnd 15 *P2, 1/1 LPC, p2, 1/1 RPC, p2; repeat from * around.

Rnd 16 *P3, sl 1, p2, sl 1, p3; repeat from * around.

Rnd 17 *P3, ssk, k2tog, p3; repeat from * around (8/104 stitches).

Rnd 18 *P3, k2, p3; repeat from * around.

Rnd 19 *P3, sl 2, p3; repeat from * around.

Rnd 20 *P2, 1/1 RPC, 1/1 LPC, p2; repeat from * around.

Rnd 21 *[P2, sl 1] twice, p2; repeat from * around.

Rnd 22 *P1, 1/1 RPC, p2, 1/1 LPC, p1; repeat from * around.

Rnds 23 and 25 *Sl 1, p4, sl 1, p1; repeat from * around.

Rnd 24 *P1, k1, p4, k1, p1; repeat from * around.

Rnd 26 *P1, 1/1 LPC, p2, 1/1 RPC, p1; repeat from * around.

Rnd 27 *[P2, sl 1] twice, p2; repeat from * around.

Rnd 28 *P2, 1/1 LPC, 1/1 RPC, p2; repeat from * around.

Rnd 29 *P3, sl 2, p3; repeat from * around.

Rnd 30 *P2, k2tog, ssk, p2; repeat from * around (6/78 stitches).

Rnd 31 *P2, sl 2, p2; repeat from * around.

Rnd 32 *P1, k2tog, ssk, p1; repeat from * around (4/52 stitches).

Rnd 33 *P1, sl 2, p1; repeat from * around.

Rnd 34 *P1, k1, k2tog; repeat from * around (3/39 stitches).

Rnd 35 *P1, sl 2; repeat from * around.

Rnd 36 *P1, k2tog; repeat from * around (2/26 stitches).

Rnd 37 *P1, sl 1; repeat from * around.

Rnd 38 *K2tog; repeat from * around (13 stitches).

Break the yarn. Thread the tail through the remaining 13 stitches, pull tight, and secure.

I-CORD EDGING

With CC, cast 5 stitches onto a double-pointed needle. *Do not turn, slide stitches onto the other end of the needle. K5; repeat from * until cord is long enough to match the circumference of the circle. Sew ends together and sew to the inside edge of the Garter stitch edging.

Using Lazy Daisy stitch and CC, embroider 5-petaled flowers at the outer edge of each section and in the center.

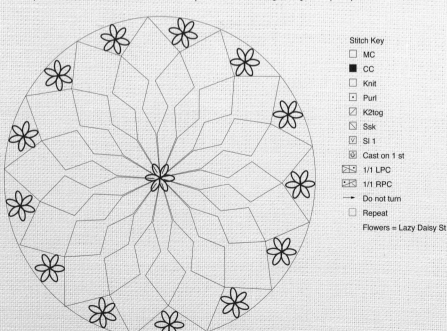

Stitch Key
- □ MC
- ■ CC
- □ Knit
- · Purl
- ⧄ K2tog
- ⧅ Ssk
- ⧈ Sl 1
- Ⓤ Cast on 1 st
- ⧖ 1/1 LPC
- ⧗ 1/1 RPC
- → Do not turn
- □ Repeat
- Flowers = Lazy Daisy St

Body

I-Cord Edging

BOBBLE SWIRL

Worked in the round from the center to the outer edge
Colors MC and CC

MB (make bobble) [P1, k1] twice in the same stitch,
turn; k4, turn; p4, turn; k4, turn; pass the 2nd, 3rd, and
4th stitches, one at a time, over the first stitch. Slip the
bobble stitch onto the right-hand needle.

With MC, cast on 4 stitches.
Setup row 1 (RS) *Kfb; repeat from * around (8 stitches).
Divide stitches evenly over 4 dpns (2 stitches on each);
mark the beginning of the rnd and join without twisting.
Rnd 1 *Kfb; repeat from * around (16 stitches).
Rnd 2 *K2, m1; repeat from * around (24 stitches).
Rnd 3 *K3, p3, pm; repeat from * around (6 stitches each
section/24 stitches total).
Rnd 4 *K3, m1, p3, m1; repeat from * around (8/32
stitches).
Rnd 5 *K4, p4; repeat from * around.
Rnd 6 *K4, m1, p4, m1; repeat from * around (10/40
stitches).
Rnd 7 *K5, p2, MB, p2; repeat from * around.
Rnd 8 *K5, m1, p5, m1; repeat from * around (12/48
stitches).
Rnd 9 *K6, p6; repeat from * around.
Rnd 10 *K6, m1, p6, m1; repeat from * around (14/56
stitches).
Rnd 11 *K7, p7; repeat from * around.
Rnd 12 *K7, m1, p7, m1; repeat from * around (16/64
stitches).

Rnd 13 *K8, p8; repeat from * around.
Rnd 14 *K8, m1, p8, m1; repeat from * around (18/72
stitches).
Rnd 15 *K9, p2, MB, p3, MB, p2; repeat from * around.
Rnd 16 *K9, m1, p9, m1; repeat from * around (20/80
stitches).
Rnd 17 *K10, p10; repeat from * around.
Rnd 18 *K10, m1, p10, m1; repeat from * around (22/88
stitches).
Rnd 19 *K11, p11; repeat from * around.
Rnd 20 *K11, m1, p11, m1; repeat from * around (24/96
stitches).
Rnd 21 *K12, p12; repeat from * around.
Rnd 22 *K12, m1, p12, m1; repeat from * around (26/104
stitches).
Rnd 23 *K13, p2, [MB, p3] twice, MB, p2; repeat from *
around.
Rnd 24 *K13, m1, p13, m1; repeat from * around (28/112
stitches).
Rnd 25 *K14, p14; repeat from * around.
Rnd 26 *K14, m1, p14, m1; repeat from * around (30/120
stitches).
Rnd 27 *K15, p15; repeat from * around.
Rnd 28 *K15, m1, p15, m1; repeat from * around (32/128
stitches).
Rnd 29 *K16, p16; repeat from * around.
Rnd 30 *K16, m1, p16, m1; repeat from * around (34/136
stitches).
Rnd 31 *K17, p2, [MB, p3] 3 times, MB, p2; repeat from *
around.

Rnd 32 *K17, m1, p17, m1; repeat from * around (36/144
stitches).
Bind off using a needle one size larger.

CROCHET EDGING

With the right side facing and using CC, pull up a loop
with the crochet hook.
Rnd 1 Chain 1, single crochet evenly around in a multiple
of 3 stitches. Join to the first single crochet with a slip
stitch.
Rnd 2 Chain 1, single crochet in each stitch around. Join to
the first single crochet with a slip stitch.
Rnd 3 Chain 1, single crochet in the first 3 stitches, *chain
4, slip stitch in the single crochet just made, single crochet in the next 3 stitches; repeat from * around.
Fasten off.

Bobble

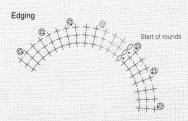

Edging

Start of rounds

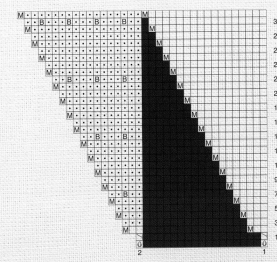

Stitch Key

Knit Stitches

☐ Knit
· Purl
M M1
B Make bobble
⟋ Kfb
⌄ Cast on 1 st
V [P1, k1] twice in 1 st
▭ Stitch over
■ No stitch
☐ Repeat

Crochet Stitches

0 Chain
+ Single crochet
· Slip stitch
⊛ Chain 4, slip stitch in single crochet just made

HONEYCOMB CIRCLE

Worked in the round from the outer edge to the center
Colors MC and CC
Optional 24 pearl beads (½"/13mm)

2/2 RC Slip 2 stitches to cn and hold in back, k2, k2 from cn.
2/2 LC Slip 2 stitches to cn and hold in front, k2, k2 from cn.

With MC, cast on 152 stitches (38 stitches each on 4 dpns); mark the beginning of the round and join without twisting.

Rnd 1 *P2, k8, p2, k7, pm; repeat from * around (19 stitches each section/152 stitches total).
Rnd 2 *P2, 2/2RC, 2/2LC, p2, k7; repeat from * around.
Rnds 3 and 4 *P2, k8, p2, k7; repeat from * around.
Rnd 5 * P2, k8, p2, k3, k2tog, k2; repeat from * around (18/144 stitches).
Rnd 6 *P2, 2/2LC, 2/2RC, p2, k6; repeat from * around.
Rnds 7–9 * P2, k8, p2, k6; repeat from * around.
Rnd 10 *P2, 2/2RC, 2/2LC, p2, k6; repeat from * around.
Rnd 11 *P2, k8, p2, k2, k2tog, k2; repeat from * around (17/136 stitches).
Rnds 12 and 13 *P2, k8, p2, k5; repeat from * around.
Rnd 14 *P2, 2/2LC, 2/2RC, p2, k5; repeat from * around.
Rnds 15 and 16 *P2, k8, p2, k5; repeat from * around.
Rnd 17 *P2, k8, p2, k1, k2tog, k2; repeat from * around (16/128 stitches).
Rnd 18 *P2, 2/2RC, 2/2LC, p2, k4; repeat from * around.
Rnds 19 and 20 *P2, k8, p2, k4; repeat from * around.
Rnd 21 *P2, k8, p2, k1, k2tog, k1; repeat from * around (15/120 stitches).
Rnd 22 *P2, 2/2LC, 2/2RC, p2, k3; repeat from * around.
Rnds 23 and 24 *P2, k8, p2, k3; repeat from * around.
Rnd 25 *P2, k8, p2, k1, k2tog; repeat from * around (14/112 stitches).
Rnd 26 *P2, 2/2RC, 2/2LC, p2, k2; repeat from * around.

Rnds 27 and 28 * P2, k8, p2, k2; repeat from * around.
Rnd 29 *P2, k8, p2, k2tog; repeat from * around (13/104 stitches).
Rnd 30 *P2, 2/2 LC, 2/2 RC, p2, k1; repeat from * around.
Rnd 31 *P2, k8, p1, p2tog; repeat from * around (12/96 stitches).
Rnd 32 *P2, k8, p2; repeat from * around.
Rnd 33 *P2tog, [k2tog] 4 times, p2tog; repeat from * around (6/48 stitches).
Rnd 34 *K2tog; repeat from * around (3/24 stitches).
Rnd 35 *K3tog; repeat from * around (8 stitches).
Break off the yarn, leaving a 6" (15cm) tail. Thread the tail through the remaining 8 stitches, draw up firmly, and secure.

GARTER ST EDGING
With RS facing and CC, pick up and knit 152 stitches evenly around edge of circle. Pm.
Rnds 1 and 3 Purl.
Rnd 2 Knit.
Bind off using a needle one size larger.

Optional Sew a bead to the center of each honeycomb opening.

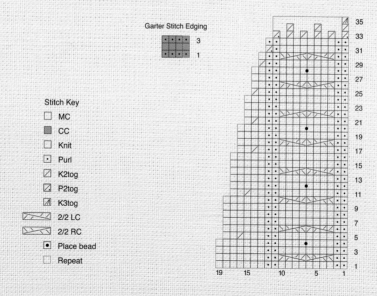

Garter Stitch Edging

Stitch Key
- ☐ MC
- ▨ CC
- ☐ Knit
- ⊡ Purl
- ⧄ K2tog
- ⧄ P2tog
- ⧄ K3tog
- ⧅ 2/2 LC
- ⧅ 2/2 RC
- ⊙ Place bead
- ☐ Repeat

CORONA (*running cable circle*)

Worked in the round from the center to the outer edge
Colors MC and CC

M1P (make 1 purlwise) Insert the left-hand needle from front to back under the horizontal strand between the last stitch and the next stitch, purl through the back loop of this strand.

M2 (make 2) Insert the left-hand needle from front to back under the horizontal strand between the last stitch and the next stitch, knit in the front and back loop of this strand.

2/2 LC inc Slip 2 stitches to the cn and hold in front, k2, M2, k2 from the cn.

3/3 LC inc Slip 3 stitches to the cn and hold in front, k3, M2, k3 from the cn.

4/4 LC inc Slip 4 stitches to the cn and hold in front, k4, M2, k4 from the cn.

With MC, cast on 8 stitches (2 stitches each on 4 dpns); mark the beginning of the round and join without twisting.
Rnd 1 *Kfb, pm; repeat from * around (2 stitches each section/16 stitches total).
Rnd 2 *Kfb; repeat from * around (4/32 stitches).
Rnd 3 Knit.
Rnd 4 *K4, m1P; repeat from * around (5/40 stitches).
Rnd 5 *K4, p1; repeat from * around.
Rnd 6 *2/2 LC inc, m1P, p1; repeat from * around (8/64 stitches).

Rnd 7 *K6, p2; repeat from * around.
Rnd 8 *K6, p1, m1P, p1; repeat from * around (9/72 stitches).
Rnd 9 *K6, p3; repeat from * around.
Rnd 10 *K6, p1, m1P, p2; repeat from * around (10/80 stitches).
Rnd 11 *K6, p4; repeat from * around.
Rnd 12 *K6, p1, m1P, p3; repeat from * around (11/88 stitches).
Rnd 13 *K6, p5; repeat from * around.
Rnd 14 *3/3 LC inc, p5; repeat from * around (13/104 stitches).
Rnd 15 *K8, p5; repeat from * around.
Rnd 16 *K8, p1, m1P, p4; repeat from * around (14/112 stitches).
Rnds 17–21 *K8, p6; repeat from * around.
Rnd 22 *K8, p1, m1P, p5; repeat from * around (15/120 stitches).
Rnd 23 *K8, p7; repeat from * around.
Rnd 24 *4/4 LC inc, p7; repeat from * around (17/136 stitches).
Rnds 25–27 *K10, p7; repeat from * around.
Rnd 28 *K10, p1, m1P, p6; repeat from * around (18/144 stitches).
Rnds 29 and 30 *K10, p8; repeat from * around.
If not working edging, bind off using a needle one size larger.

2-COLOR GARTER ST EDGING
Change to CC.
Rnd 1 Knit.
Rnd 2 Purl.
Change to MC.
Rnds 3 and 4 Repeat rnds 1 and 2.
Change to CC.
Rnds 5 and 6 Repeat rnds 1 and 2.
Bind off using a needle one size larger.

Garter Stitch Edging

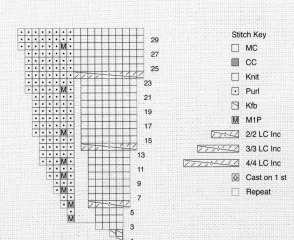

Stitch Key
- ☐ MC
- ▨ CC
- ☐ Knit
- · Purl
- ◹ Kfb
- M M1P
- ◿ 2/2 LC Inc
- ◿ 3/3 LC Inc
- ◿ 4/4 LC Inc
- ◌ Cast on 1 st
- ☐ Repeat

MERIDIAN (*cable circle*)

Worked in the round from the center to the outer edge

Colors MC and CC

2/2 RC Slip 2 stitches to cn and hold in back, k2, k2 from cn.

M1P (make 1 purlwise) Insert the left-hand needle from front to back under the horizontal strand between the last stitch and the next stitch, purl through the back loop of this strand.

Cast on 8 stitches (2 stitches each on 4 dpns). Mark the beginning of the round and join without twisting.

Rnd 1 *Kfb; repeat from * around (16 stitches).

Rnd 2 *Kfb, pm; repeat from * around (2 stitches each section/32 stitches total).

Rnd 3 *Kfb; repeat from * around (4/64 stitches).

Rnd 4 Knit.

Rnd 5 *K4, m1P; repeat from * around (5/80 stitches).

Rnd 6 *2/2 RC, p1; repeat from * around.

Rnds 7 and 8 *K4, p1; repeat from * around.

Rnd 9 *K4, p1, m1P; repeat from * around (6/96 stitches).

Rnds 10 and 11 *K4, p2; repeat from * around.

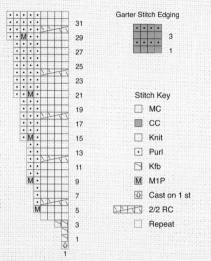

Garter Stitch Edging

Stitch Key
- ☐ MC
- ▨ CC
- ☐ Knit
- · Purl
- ◹ Kfb
- M M1P
- Ⓤ Cast on 1 st
- ◸◹ 2/2 RC
- ☐ Repeat

Rnd 12 *2/2 RC, p2; repeat from * around.

Rnds 13 and 14 *K4, p2; repeat from * around.

Rnd 15 *K4, p1, m1P, p1; repeat from * around (7/112 stitches).

Rnds 16 and 17 *K4, p3; repeat from * around.

Rnd 18 *2/2 RC, p3; repeat from * around.

Rnds 19 and 20 *K4, p3; repeat from * around.

Rnd 21 *K4, p1, m1P, p2; repeat from * around (8/128 stitches).

Rnds 22 and 23 *K4, p4; repeat from * around.

Rnd 24 *2/2 RC, p4; repeat from * around.

Rnds 25–28 *K4, p4; repeat from * around.

Rnd 29 *K4, p2, m1P, p2; repeat from * around (9/144 stitches).

Rnd 30 *2/2 RC, p5; repeat from * around.

Rnds 31 and 32 *K4, p5; repeat from * around.

If you're not working the edging, bind off knitwise with a needle one size larger.

GARTER ST EDGING

Change to CC.

Rnds 1 and 3 Knit.

Rnds 2 and 4 Purl.

Bind off knitwise using a needle one size larger.

Optional Sew a decorative button at the center of the circle.

···

SEED STITCH SPOKE

Worked in the round from the center to the outer edge

Cast on 7 stitches. Divide on 3 dpns as 2-2-3; mark beginning of the round and join without twisting.

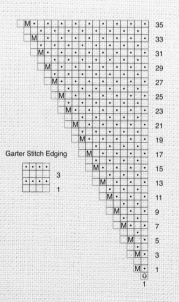

Garter Stitch Edging

Stitch Key
- ☐ Knit
- · Purl
- M M1
- Ⓤ Cast on 1 st
- ☐ Repeat

Rnd 1 *P1, m1, pm; repeat from * around (2 stitches each section/14 stitches total).

Rnd 2 Knit.

Rnd 3 *P1, m1, k1; repeat from * around (3/21 stitches).

Rnd 4 *Work in Seed st to 1 stitch before marker, k1; repeat from * around.

Rnd 5 *Work in Seed st to 1 stitch before marker, M1, k1; repeat from * around (4/28) stitches.

Rnds 6–35 Repeat rnds 4 and 5 (19/133 stitches after rnd 35).

If not working edging, bind off in pattern using a needle one size larger.

GARTER ST EDGING

Rnds 1 and 3 Knit.

Rnds 2 and 4 Purl.

Bind off using a needle one size larger.

PERIPHERY

Worked in the round from the center to the outer edge

1/1 RC Slip 1 stitch onto the cn and hold in back, k1, k1 from cn.

1/1 LC Slip 1 stitch onto the cn and hold in front, k1, k1 from cn.

1/1 RPC Slip 1 stitch onto the cn and hold in back, k1, p1 from cn.

1/1 LPC Slip 1 stitch onto the cn and hold in front, p1, k1 from cn.

Dec 4 Slip 3 stitches onto the right-hand needle, *pass the 2nd stitch over the first stitch, slip the first stitch onto the left-hand needle, pass the 2nd stitch over the first stitch*, slip the first stitch onto the right-hand needle; repeat from * to * once, k1.

Cast on 8 stitches (2 stitches each on 4 dpns). Mark the beginning of the round and join without twisting.

Rnd 1 *Kfb, pm; repeat from * around (2 stitches in each section/16 stitches total).

Rnd 2 *Kfb; repeat from * around (4/32 stitches).

Rnd 3 *P1, k2, p1; repeat from * around.

Rnd 4 *P1, m1P, k2, m1P, p1; repeat from * around (6/48 stitches).

Rnd 5 *P2, 1/1 RC, p2; repeat from * around.

Rnd 6 *P1, m1P, p1, k2, p1, m1P, p1; repeat from * around (8/64 stitches).

Rnd 7 *P3, 1/1 RC, p3; repeat from * around.

Rnd 8 *P1, m1P, p2, k2, p2, m1P, p1; repeat from * around (10/80 stitches).

Rnd 9 *P4, 1/1 RC, p4; repeat from * around.

Rnd 10 *P2, m1P, p2, k2, p2, m1P, p2; repeat from * around (12/96 stitches).

Rnds 11 and 13 *P5, 1/1 RC, p5; repeat from * around.

Rnd 12 *P5, k2, p5; repeat from * around.

Rnd 14 *P2, m1P, p3, k2, p3, m1P, p2; repeat from * around (14/112 stitches).

Rnds 15 and 17 *P6, 1/1 RC, p6; repeat from * around.

Rnd 16 *P6, k2, P6; repeat from * around.

Rnd 18 *P3, m1P, p3, k2, p3, m1P, p3; repeat from * around (16/128 stitches).

Rnd 19 *([K1, yo] twice, k1) in the same stitch, p6, 1/1 RC, p7; repeat from * around (20/160 stitches).

Rnd 20 *K5, p6, k2, p7; repeat from around.

Rnd 21 *Kfb, k3, kfb, p5, 1/1 RC, 1/1 LC, p6; repeat from * around (22/176 stitches).

Rnd 22 *K7, p3, m1P, p2, k4, p6; repeat from * around (23/184 stitches).

Rnd 23 *Kfb, k5, kfb, p5, 1/1 RPC, k2 tbl, 1/1 LPC, p5; repeat from * around (25/200 stitches).

Rnd 24 *K9, p5, k1, p1, k2 tbl, p1, k1, p5; repeat from * around.

Rnd 25 *K9, p4, 1/1 RPC, p1, k2 tbl, p1, 1/1 LPC, p4; repeat from * around.

Rnd 26 *K9, p4, k1, p2, k2 tbl, p2, k1, p4; repeat from * around,

Rnd 27 *Ssk, k5, k2tog, p3, 1/1 RPC, p2, k2 tbl, p2, 1/1 LPC, p3; repeat from * around (23/184 stitches).

Rnd 28 *K7, p3, k1, p3, k2 tbl, p3, k1, p3; repeat from * around.

Rnd 29 *Ssk, k3, k2tog, p7, k2 tbl, p7; repeat from * around (21/168 stitches).

Rnd 30 *Dec 4, p7, k2 tbl, p7; repeat from * around (17/136 stitches).

Rnd 31 *P13, m1P, p4; repeat from * around (18/144 stitches).

Rnd 32 Purl.

Bind off purlwise using a needle one size larger.

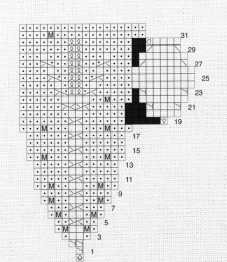

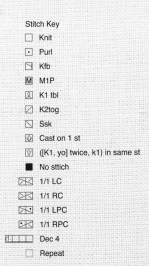

Stitch Key

☐	Knit
·	Purl
Ꙅ	Kfb
M	M1P
Ꝺ	K1 tbl
╱	K2tog
╲	Ssk
Ꙩ	Cast on 1 st
Ꝟ	([K1, yo] twice, k1) in same st
■	No sttich
⋈	1/1 LC
⋈	1/1 RC
⋈	1/1 LPC
⋈	1/1 RPC
⬚	Dec 4
☐	Repeat

DAISY MAE CIRCLE

Worked in the round from the center to the outer edge
Colors MC and CC

MB (make bobble) K in (front, back, front, back, front) in next stitch, turn; [p5, turn; k5, turn] twice, slip the 2nd, 3rd, 4th, and 5th stitches over the first stitch.

S2KP Slip 2 stitches as if to k2tog, k1, pass the 2 slipped stitches over.

S2PP [Slip 1 stitch knitwise] twice, slip these 2 stitches back onto the left-hand needle in their twisted position, slip these 2 stitches as if to p2tog tbl, p1, pass the 2 slipped stitches over.

With MC, cast on 6 stitches (2 stitches each on 3 dpns); mark the beginning of the round and join.

Rnds 1, 3, 5, and 7 Knit.

Rnd 2 *K1, m1, pm; repeat from * around (2 stitches in each section/12 stitches total).

Rnd 4 *K1, m1; repeat from * around (4/24 stitches).

Rnd 6 *K1, m1, k2, m1, k1; repeat from * around (6/36 stitches).

Rnd 8 *K3, m1P, k3; repeat from * around (7/42 stitches).

Rnd 9 *K3, p1, k3; repeat from * around.

Rnd 10 *K3, m1P, p1, m1P, k3; repeat from * around (9/54 stitches).

Rnd 11 *K3, p3, k3; repeat from * around.

Rnd 12 *Yo, k3, m1P, p1, MB, p1, m1P, k3; repeat from * around (12/72 stitches).

Rnd 13 *P1, k3, p5, k3; repeat from * around.

Rnd 14 *P1, yo, k3, m1P, p5, m1P, k3, yo; repeat from * around (16/96 stitches).

Rnd 15 *P2, k3, p7, k3, p1; repeat from * around.

Rnd 16 *P2, yo, k3, p7, k3, yo, p1; repeat from * around (18/108 stitches).

Rnd 17 *P3, k3, p7, k3, p2; repeat from * around.

Rnd 18 *P3, yo, k3, p3, MB, p3, k3, yo, p2; repeat from * around (20/120 stitches).

Rnd 19 *P4, k3, p7, k3, p3; repeat from * around.

Rnd 20 *P4, yo, k3, p7, k3, yo, p3; repeat from * around (22/132 stitches).

Rnd 21 *P5, k3, p7, k3, p4; repeat from * around.

Rnd 22 *P5, yo, k3, p7, k3, yo, p4; repeat from * around (24/144 stitches).

Rnd 23 *P6, k3, p7, k3, p5; repeat from * around.

Rnd 24 *P6, yo, k3, p7, k3, yo, p5; repeat from * around (26/156 stitches).

Rnd 25 *P7, k3, p7, k3, p6; repeat from * around.

Rnd 26 *P7, yo, k3, p2tog, p1, MB, p1, p2tog tbl, k3, yo, p6; repeat from * around.

Rnd 27 *P8, k3, p5, k3, p7; repeat from * around.

Rnd 28 *P8, yo, k3, p2tog, p1, p2tog tbl, k3, yo, p7; repeat from * around.

Rnd 29 *P9, k3, p3, k3, p8; repeat from * around.

Rnd 30 *P9, yo, k3, S2PP, k3, yo, p8; repeat from * around.

Rnd 31 *P10, k3, p1, k3, p9; repeat from * around.

Rnd 32 *P10, yo, k2, S2KP, k2, yo, p9; repeat from * around.

Rnd 33 *P11, k5, p10; repeat from * around.

Rnd 34 *P11, yo, k1, S2KP, k1, yo, p10; repeat from * around.

Rnd 35 *P12, k3, p11; repeat from * around.

Rnd 36 *P12, yo, S2KP, yo, p11; repeat from * around.

If not working edging, bind off purlwise with a needle one size larger.

GARTER ST EDGING
Change to CC.
Rnds 1 and 3 Knit.
Rnds 2 and 4 Purl.
Bind off knitwise with a needle one size larger.

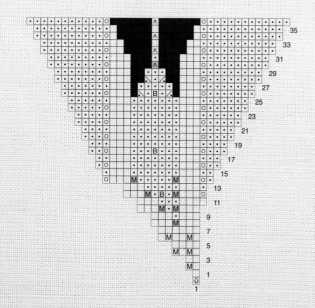

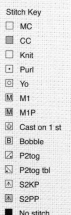

Garter Stitch Edging

Stitch Key

☐	MC
▨	CC
☐	Knit
·	Purl
⦿	Yo
Ⰼ	M1
Ⰼ	M1P
ⓤ	Cast on 1 st
B	Bobble
⟋	P2tog
⟍	P2tog tbl
⋏	S2KP
⋏	S2PP
■	No stitch
☐	Repeat

DOMINO DISK

Worked in quadrants

Colors MC and CC

S2PP [Slip 1 stitch knitwise] twice, slip these 2 stitches back onto the left-hand needle in their twisted positions, slip these 2 stitches to the right-hand needle as if to p2tog tbl, p1, pass the 2 slipped stitches over.

SECTION A (LOWER LEFT)

With MC, cast on 39 stitches using knitted cast-on. Mark the center stitch.

Row 1 (WS) With MC, knit.

Row 2 With CC, ssk, knit to 1 stitch before the center stitch, S2KP, knit to the last 2 stitches, k2tog.

Row 3 With CC, knit to the center stitch, p1, knit to end. Change to MC.

Repeat rows 2 and 3, alternating 2 rows MC with 2 rows CC until 7 stitches remain.

Next row Ssk, S2KP, k2tog (3 stitches).

Last row S2PP (1 stitch).

Fasten off.

SECTION B (LOWER RIGHT)

With RS facing and MC, pick up and k19 stitches along straight edge (from curved edge to corner) and 1 stitch in corner of Section A, turn work and cast on 19 stitches (39 stitches). Beginning with row 1, work the same as for Section A.

SECTION C (UPPER RIGHT)

Work the same as for Section B, picking up stitches along straight edge of Section B.

SECTION D (UPPER LEFT)

With RS facing and MC, pick up and knit 19 stitches along straight edge of Section C, 1 stitch at the inner corner, and 19 stitches along straight edge of Section A. Beginning with row 1, work the same as for Section A.

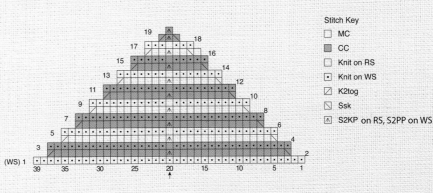

Stitch Key
- ☐ MC
- ▨ CC
- ☐ Knit on RS
- ⊡ Knit on WS
- ◿ K2tog
- ◹ Ssk
- ⬆ S2KP on RS, S2PP on WS

RIBBED ROUND

Worked in the round from the outer edge to the center

Cast on 150 stitches; mark the beginning of the round and join without twisting.

Rnds 1–4 *P2, k3; repeat from * around.

Rnd 5 *[P2, k3] 4 times, p2, k1, k2tog, pm; repeat from * around (24 stitches each section, 144 stitches total).

Rnd 6 *Work in P2, K3 Rib as established to 2 stitches before the next marker, k2tog; repeat from * around. Repeat rnd 6 until 6 stitches remain.

Break the yarn. Thread the tail through the remaining 6 stitches, pull tight, and secure.

Stitch Key
- ☐ Knit
- ⊡ Purl
- ▨ K2tog
- ☐ Repeat

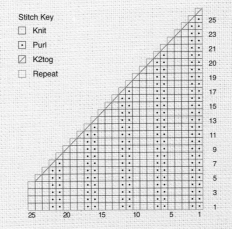

RINGED LEAVES

Worked in the round from the center to the outer edge
Colors MC and CC

With MC, cast on 10 stitches. Divide over 4 dpns as
3-2-3-2; mark the beginning of the round and join without
twisting.

Rnd 1 *K1 tbl; repeat from * around.
Rnd 2 *K1 tbl, m1P, pm; repeat from * around (2 stitches
each section, 20 stitches total).
Rnd 3 *K1 tbl, p1; repeat from * around.
Rnd 4 *M1P, k1 tbl, p1; repeat from * around (3/30
stitches).
Rnd 5 *P1, k1 tbl, p1; repeat from * around.

Rnd 6 *P1, m1P, k1 tbl, m1P, p1; repeat from * around (5/50
stitches).
Rnds 7–9 *P2, k1 tbl, p2; repeat from * around.
Rnd 10 *P1, m1P, p1, k1 tbl, p1, m1P, p1; repeat from * around
(7/70 stitches).
Rnds 11 and 12 *P3, k1 tbl, p3; repeat from * around .
Rnd 13 *P3, yo, k1, yo, p3; repeat from * around (9/90
stitches).
Rnd 14 *P2, m1P, p1, k3, p1, m1P, p2; repeat from * around
(11/110 stitches).
Rnd 15 *P4, k1, yo, k1, yo, k1, p4; repeat from * around
(13/130 stitches).
Rnd 16 *P4, k5, p4; repeat from * around.
Rnd 17 *P4, k2, yo, k1, yo, k2, p4; repeat from * around
(15/150 stitches).
Rnd 18 *P2, m1P, p2, k7, p2, m1P, p2; repeat from * around
(17/170 stitches).
Rnd 19 *P5, k3, yo, k1, yo, k3, p5; repeat from * around
(19/190 stitches).
Rnd 20 *P5, k9, p5; repeat from * around.
Rnd 21 *P5, k4, yo, k1, yo, k4, p5; repeat from * around
(21/210 stitches).
Rnd 22 *P5, k11, p5; repeat from * around.
Rnd 23 *P5, ssk, k7, k2tog, p5; repeat from * around (19/190
stitches).
Rnd 24 *P2, m1P, p3, k9, p3, m1P, p2; repeat from * around
(21/210 stitches).

Rnd 25 *P6, ssk, k5, k2tog, p6; repeat from * around
(19/190 stitches).
Rnd 26 *P6, k7, p6; repeat from * around.
Rnd 27 *P6, ssk, k3, k2tog, p6; repeat from * around (17/170
stitches).
Rnd 28 *P6, k5, p6; repeat from * around.
Rnd 29 *P6, ssk, k1, k2tog, p6; repeat from * around
(15/150 stitches).
Rnd 30 *P6, k3, p6; repeat from * around.
Rnd 31 *P6, SK2P, p6; repeat from * around (13/130
stitches).
Rnd 32 *[P6, m1P] twice, p1; repeat from * around (15/150
stitches).
Rnd 33 Purl.

If not working edging, bind off purlwise with a needle one
size larger.

GARTER ST EDGING

Change to CC.
Rnds 1 and 3 Knit.
Rnds 2 and 4 Purl.
Bind off knitwise with a needle one size larger.

Optional Sew a decorative button at the center of the
circle.

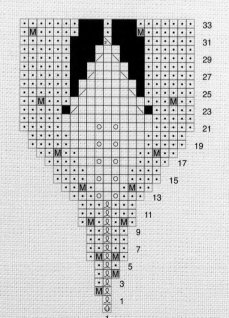

Stitch Key
- ☐ MC
- ▨ CC
- ☐ Knit
- · Purl
- ○ Yo
- ◎ K1 tbl
- Ⓜ M1P
- ◍ Cast on 1 st
- ╱ K2tog
- ╲ SSK
- ◺ SK2P
- ■ No stitch
- ☐ Repeat

Garter Stitch Edging

BRUNHILDA'S WHIRL

Worked in the round from the outer edge to the center

2/2 RC Slip 2 stitches to cn and hold in back, k2, k2 from cn.

Cast on 168 stitches; mark the beginning of the round and join without twisting.

Rnd 1 *K1, yo, k20, pm; repeat from * around (22 stitches each section/176 stitches total).

Rnd 2 *K3, p3, [k1, p3] 4 times; repeat from * around.

Rnd 3 *[K1, yo] twice, [k1, p3] 5 times; repeat from * around (24/192 stitches).

Rnd 4 *K5, p3, [k1, p3] 4 times; repeat from * around.

Rnd 5 *[K1, yo] 4 times, [ssk, p2] 5 times; repeat from * around (23/184 stitches).

Rnd 6 *K9, p2, [k1, p2] 4 times; repeat from * around.

Rnd 7 *[K1, yo] 3 times, S2KP, [yo, k1] twice, yo, [ssk, p1] 5 times; repeat from * around (22/176 stitches).

Rnd 8 *K13, p1, [k1, p1] 4 times; repeat from * around.

Rnd 9 *K12, ssk 5 times; repeat from * around (17/136 stitches).

Rnd 10 *K13, k4 and slip these 4 stitches to cn and wrap yarn counterclockwise around these stitches 3 times, slip stitches to the right-hand needle; repeat from * around.

Rnd 11 *P1, k4, S2KP, k4, p1, k4; repeat from * around (15/120 stitches).

Rnds 12 and 14 *P1, k9, p1, k4; repeat from * around.

Rnd 13 *P1, k9, p1, 2/2 RC; repeat from * around.

Rnd 15 *P1, k3, S2KP, k3, p1, k4; repeat from * around (13/104 stitches).

Rnds 16 and 18 *P1, k7, p1, k4; repeat from * around.

Rnd 17 *P1, k7, p1, 2/2 RC; repeat from * around.

Rnd 19 *P1, k2, S2KP, k2, p1, k4; repeat from * around (11/88 stitches).

Rnds 20 and 22 *P1, k5, p1, k4; repeat from * around.

Rnd 21 *P1, k5, p1, 2/2 RC; repeat from * around.

Rnd 23 *P1, k1, S2KP, k1, p1, k4; repeat from * around (9/72 stitches).

Rnd 24 *P1, k3, p1, k4; repeat from * around.

Rnd 25 *P1, S2KP, p1, 2/2 RC; repeat from * around (7/56 stitches).

Rnd 26 *P1, k1, p1, k4; repeat from * around.

Rnd 27 *S2KP, k4; repeat from * around (5/40 stitches).

Rnd 28 K39. Pm for new end of rnd.

Rnd 29 *S2KP, k2; repeat from * around (24 stitches).

Rnd 30 K23. Pm for new end of rnd.

Rnd 31 *S2KP; repeat from * around (8 stitches).

Break the yarn and thread the tail through the remaining 8 stitches. Pull tight to gather and secure.

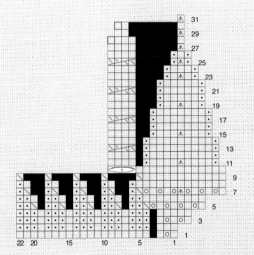

Stitch Key

- ☐ Knit
- ⊡ Purl
- ⊙ Yo
- ◩ SSK
- ◮ S2KP
- ◻ 2/2 RC
- ⬭ K4 and slip these 4 sts to cn and wrap yarn counterclockwise around these sts 3 times
- ■ No stitch
- ☐ Knit in each rep until last rep, then end last rep before this st; it is worked with the dec at the beg of the next rnd
- ☐ Repeat

ENTRELAC ENCIRCLE

Worked in the round from the outer edge to the center
Colors A, B, C, and D

With circular needle and A, loosely cast on 112 stitches. Mark the beginning of the round and join without twisting. (Change to dpns when there are too few stitches to go around the circular needle.)

BASE TRIANGLES

*K2, turn; p2, turn; k3, turn; p3, turn; k4, turn; p4, turn; k5, turn; p5, turn; k6, turn; p6, turn; k7, turn; p7, turn; k8; repeat from * 13 more times (14 triangles). Break the yarn.

FIRST-ROUND RECTANGLES (RIGHT-LEANING)

**With WS facing and B, working from tip to base of last triangle, pick up and purl 6 stitches, *turn; k6, turn; p5, p2tog; repeat from * until all stitches from the triangle have been worked. Repeat from ** for each triangle. Break the yarn.

SECOND-ROUND RECTANGLES (LEFT-LEANING)

Tip To avoid holes, you can pick up the last stitch in the stitch that is in the row below the stitch on the left-hand needle. Another way to say this: Pick up the second to the last stitch in the lowest spot on the rectangle side and last one actually under one stitch on left-hand needle— part of the next rectangle.

**With RS facing and C, working from the tip to the base of the last rectangle on the left side, pick up and knit 6 stitches, *turn; p6, turn; k5, ssk; repeat from * until all stitches from rectangle have been worked. Repeat from ** for each rectangle. Break the yarn.

THIRD-ROUND RECTANGLES

**With WS facing and D, working from tip to base of the last rectangle, pick up and purl 4 stitches, *turn; k4, turn; p3, p2tog; repeat from * until all stitches from the rectangle have been worked.
Repeat from ** for each rectangle. Break the yarn.

FOURTH-ROUND RECTANGLES

**With RS facing and A, working from tip to base of the last rectangle on the left side, pick up and knit 4 stitches, *turn; p4, turn; k3, ssk; repeat from * until all stitches from the rectangle have been worked. Repeat from ** for each rectangle. Break the yarn.

FIFTH-ROUND RECTANGLES

Tip Pick up stitches closer to the corner of the rectangles, skipping the upper parts to prevent holes from forming.
**With WS facing and B, working from tip to base of the last rectangle, pick up and purl 4 stitches, *turn; k4, turn; p3, p2tog; repeat from * until all stitches from the

rectangle have been worked.
Repeat from ** for each rectangle. Break the yarn.

SIXTH-ROUND RECTANGLES

**With RS facing and C, pick up and knit 3 stitches as follows: 2 from the left side of B rectangle, one in the stitch below the last stitch on the left-hand needle, turn. *P3, turn; k2, ssk, turn; repeat from * until all stitches from the rectangle have been worked.
Repeat from ** for each rectangle. Break the yarn.

SEVENTH-ROUND RECTANGLES

**With WS facing and D, pick up and purl 2 stitches, *turn; k3, turn; p1, p2tog; repeat from * until all stitches from the rectangle have been worked.
Repeat from ** for each rectangle (28 stitches).

CENTER

Rnd 1 *P2tog; repeat from * around (14 stitches).
Rnd 2 Repeat rnd 1 (7 stitches).
Break the yarn. Thread the tail through the remaining 7 stitches, pull tight, and secure.

I-CORD EDGING

With D, cast on 5 stitches. *Do not turn, slide stitches onto other end of the needle. K5, repeat from* until cord matches circumference of the circle. Sew ends together and sew edging to the circle.

BASE TRIANGLES

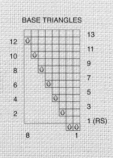

FIRST ROUND RECTANGLES

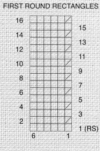

SECOND ROUND RECTANGLES

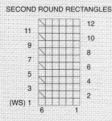

THIRD ROUND RECTANGLES

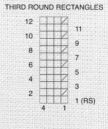

FOURTH ROUND RECTANGLES

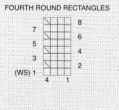

FIFTH ROUND RECTANGLES

SIXTH ROUND RECTANGLES

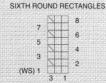

SEVENTH ROUND RECTANGLES

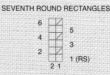

CENTER

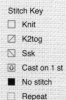

Stitch Key
☐ Knit
☑ K2tog
◲ Ssk
Ⓞ Cast on 1 st
■ No stitch
☐ Repeat

CIRQUE

Worked in the round from the outer edge to the center

2/1/2 RPC Sl 3 stitches onto the cn and hold in back, k2, sl the purl stitch back onto the left-hand needle from the cn and purl this stitch, k2 from cn.

2/3 LC Sl 2 stitches onto the cn and hold in front, k3, k2 from cn.

1/2 RC Sl 2 stitches onto the cn and hold in back, k1, k2 from cn.

1/2 LC Sl 1 stitch onto the cn and hold in front, k2, k1 from cn.

2/2 LC Sl 2 stitches onto the cn and hold in front, k2, k2 from cn.

Cast on 152 stitches; mark the beginning of the round and join without twisting.

Rnd 1 *P14, k4, p1, pm; repeat from * around (19 stitches each section/152 stitches total).

Rnd 2 *P4, 2/3 LC, p5, 2/2 LC, p1; repeat from* around.

Rnd 3 *P4, k5, p5, k4, p1; repeat from * around.

Rnd 4 *P4, k2, p1, k2, p5, k4, p1; repeat from * around.

Rnd 5 *P4, [k1, p1] twice, k1, p5, k4, p1, repeat from * around.

Rnd 6 *P2, 1/2 RC, k1, p1, k1, 1/2 LC, p3, 2/2 LC, p1; repeat from * around.

Rnd 7 *P2, [k1, p1] 4 times, k1, p3, k4, p1; repeat from * around.

Rnd 8 *1/2 RC, [k1, p1] 3 times, k1, 1/2 LC, p1, k4, p1; repeat from * around.

Rnd 9 *K3, [p1, k1] 3 times, p1, k3, p1, k2, ssk, p1; repeat from * around (18/144 stitches).

Rnd 10 *K3, [k1, p1] 3 times, k1, k3, p1, k1, ssk, p1; repeat from * around (17/136 stitches).

Rnd 11 *K3, [p1, k1] 3 times, p1, k3, p1, k2, p1; repeat from * around.

Rnd 12 *K3, [k1, p1] 3 times, k1, k3, p1, ssk, p1; repeat from * around (16/128 stitches).

Rnd 13 *K3, [p1, k1] 3 times, p1, k3, p1, k1, p1; repeat from * around.

Rnd 14 *K3, [k1, p1] 3 times, k1, k3, p2tog tbl, p1; repeat from * around (15/120 stitches).

Rnd 15 *K3, [p1, k1] 3 times, p1, k3, p2; repeat from * around.

Rnd 16 *K3, [k1, p1] 3 times, k1, k3, p2tog tbl; repeat from * around (14/112 stitches).

Note In rnd 17 each section will move 3 sts to the left. Remove marker (RM) and replace as indicated.

Rnd 17 RM, sl 3, *pm, [p1, k1] 3 times, p1, k3, p1, RM, k3; repeat from * around.

Rnd 18 *[K1, p1] 3 times, k1, k2tog, k1, p1, k1, ssk; repeat from * around (12/96 stitches).

Rnd 19 *[P1, k1] 3 times, p1, 2/1/2 RPC; repeat from * around.

Rnd 20 *[K1, p1] 3 times, k1, k2, p1, k2; repeat from * around.

Rnd 21 *[P1, k1] 3 times, p1, k2, p1, k2; repeat from * around.

Rnd 22 *P2tog, k1, p1, k1, p2tog, k2, p1, k2; repeat from * around (10/80 stitches).

Rnd 23 *[K1, p1] twice, k1, k2, p1, k2; repeat from * around.

Rnd 24 *K2tog, p1, ssk, k2, p1, k2; repeat from * around (8/64 stitches).

Rnd 25 *P1, k1, p1, 2/1/2 RPC; repeat from * around.

Rnd 26 *P3tog, k2, p1, k2; repeat from * around (6/48 stitches).

Rnd 27 *K3, p1, k2; repeat from * around.

Rnd 28 *K2tog, k1, p1, k2; repeat from * around (5/40 stitches).

Rnd 29 *K1, ssk, k2; repeat from * around (4/32 stitches).

Rnd 30 *K2, ssk; repeat from * around (3/24 stitches).

Rnd 31 *Ssk, k1; repeat from * around (2/16 stitches).

Rnd 32 *Ssk; repeat from * around (8 stitches).

Break the yarn. Thread the tail through the remaining 8 stitches, pull tight, and secure.

BOBBLES (MAKE 9)

Cast on 1 stitch. Knit in front, back, front, back, and front of stitch (5 stitches). [Turn, k5; turn, p5] twice. Pass the 2nd, 3rd, 4th, and 5th stitches over the first stitch. Fasten off.

Sew bobbles to the circle, as pictured.

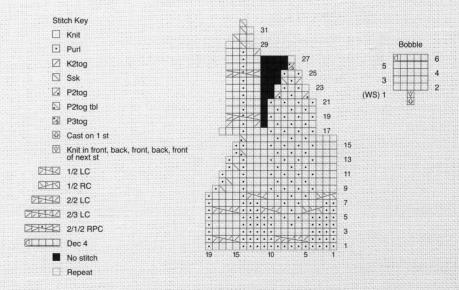

Stitch Key

- ☐ Knit
- ⊡ Purl
- ╱ K2tog
- ╲ Ssk
- ◢ P2tog
- ◣ P2tog tbl
- ▨ P3tog
- ⓪ Cast on 1 st
- ⓥ Knit in front, back, front, back, front of next st
- 1/2 LC
- 1/2 RC
- 2/2 LC
- 2/3 LC
- 2/1/2 RPC
- Dec 4
- ■ No stitch
- ☐ Repeat

STELLAR

Worked flat in sections and sewn together

4/3 RC Sl 3 stitches onto the cn and hold in back, k4, k3 from cn.

1/1 LPC Sl 1 stitch onto the cn and hold in front, p1, k1 from cn.

1/1 RPC Sl 1 stitch onto the cn and hold in back, k1, p1 from cn.

1/1 LC Sl 1 stitch onto the cn and hold in front, k1, k1 from cn.

1/1 RC Sl 1 stitch onto the cn and hold in back, k1, k1 from cn.

W3 Sl 3 stitches onto the cn and wrap yarn clockwise 3 times around these 3 stitches (ending with yarn in back), k3 from cn.

SECTION (MAKE 5)

Cast on 3 stitches.

Row 1 (RS) Knit.

Row 2 K1, p1, k1.

Row 3 K1, [m1, k1] twice (5 stitches).

Row 4 K1, p3, k1.

Row 5 K1, m1, k3, m1, k1 (7 stitches).

Row 6 K1, p5, k1.

Row 7 K1, m1, k5, m1, k1 (9 stitches).

Row 8 K1, p7, k1.

Row 9 K1, m1, 4/3 RC, m1, k1 (11 stitches).

Row 10 K2, p7, k2.

Row 11 K1, m1, p1, k7, p1, m1, k1 (13 stitches).

Row 12 K3, p7, k3.

Row 13 K1, m1, p2, k7, p2, m1, k1 (15 stitches).

Row 14 K4, p7, k4.

Row 15 K1, m1, p3, k7, p3, m1, k1 (17 stitches).

Row 16 K1, p1, k4, p5, k4, p1, k1.

Row 17 K1, m1, 1/1 LPC, p4, k3, p4, 1/1 RPC, m1, k1 (19 stitches).

Row 18 K3, p1, k4, p3, k4, p1, k3.

Row 19 K1, m1, p2, 1/1 LPC, p4, k1, p4, 1/1 RPC, p2, m1, k1 (21 stitches).

Row 20 K1, p1, k3, p1, k4, p1, k4, p1, k3, p1, k1.

Row 21 K1, m1, 1/1 LPC, p2, 1/1 LPC, p3, k1, p3, 1/1 RPC, p2, 1/1 RPC, m1, k1 (23 stitches).

Row 22 [K3, p1] twice, k7, [p1, k3] twice.

Row 23 K1, m1, p2, 1/1 LC, p2, 1/1 LPC, p5, 1/1 RPC, p2, 1/1 RC, p2, m1, k1 (25 stitches).

Row 24 K4, p2, k3, p1, k5, p1, k3, p2, k4.

Row 25 K1, m1, p2, 1/1 RPC, 1/1 LPC, p2, 1/1 LPC, p3, 1/1 RPC, p2, 1/1 RPC, 1/1 LPC, p2, m1, k1 (27 stitches).

Row 26 K4, p1, k2, p1, [k3, p1] 3 times, k2, p1, k4.

Row 27 K1, m1, p2, 1/1 RPC, p2, 1/1 LC, p2, 1/1 LPC, p1, 1/1 RPC, p2, 1/1 RC, p2, 1/1 LPC, p2, m1, k1 (29 stitches).

Row 28 K4, p1, k3, p2, k3, p3, k3, p2, k3, p1, k4.

Row 29 K1, m1, [p2, 1/1 RPC] twice, 1/1 LPC, p2, W3, p2, 1/1 RPC, [1/1 LPC, p2] twice, m1, k1 (31 stitches).

Row 30 K4, p1, k3, p1, k2, p1, k7, p1, k2, p1, k3, p1, k4,

Row 31 K1, m1, p2, [1/1 RPC, p2] twice, 1/1 LC, p5, 1/1 RC, [p2, 1/1 LPC] twice, p2, m1, k1 (33 stitches).

Row 32 K4, [p1, k3] twice, p2, k5, p2, [k3, p1] twice, k4.

Row 33 K1, m1, [p2, 1/1 RPC] 3 times, 1/1 LPC, p3, 1/1 RPC, [1/1 LPC, p2] 3 times, m1, k1 (35 stitches).

Row 34 K4, p1, [k3, p1] twice, k2, p1, k3, p1, k2, [p1, k3] twice, p1, k4.

Row 35 K1, m1, [p2, 1/1 RPC] 3 times, p2, 1/1 LC, p1, 1/1 RC, p2, [1/1LPC, p2] 3 times, m1, k1 (37 stitches).

Row 36 K4, [p1, k3] 3 times, p5, [k3, p1] 3 times, k4.

Row 37 K1, m1, [p2, 1/1 RPC] 4 times, W3, [1/1 LPC, p2] 4 times, m1, k1 (39 stitches).

Row 38 K4, [p1, k3] 3 times, p1, k5, p1, [k3, p1] 3 times, k4. Bind off using a needle one size larger. Sew sections together to form a circle.

Optional Sew twenty 8mm beads to the circle, as pictured.

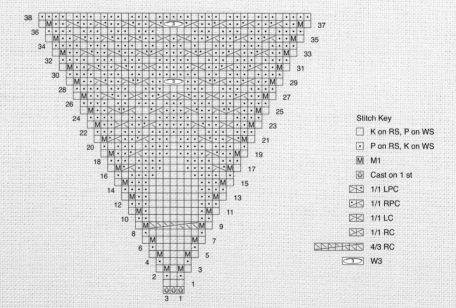

Stitch Key

☐ K on RS, P on WS

• P on RS, K on WS

Ⓜ M1

Ⓞ Cast on 1 st

⧄ 1/1 LPC

⧅ 1/1 RPC

⧄ 1/1 LC

⧅ 1/1 RC

⧄⧄⧄ 4/3 RC

⬭ W3

BOBBLE BURST

Worked in the round from the center to the outer edge

MBinc (make bobble increase) K into the front, back, front, back, and front of the next stitch (5 stitches), turn; p4, turn; k4, turn; p4 (do not turn), pass the 2nd, 3rd, and 4th stitches over the first stitch, turn; place stitch on right-hand needle.

Cast on 8 stitches (2 stitches each on 4 dpns). Mark the beginning of the round and join without twisting.

Rnd 1 *K1 tbl; repeat from * around.

Rnd 2 *Kfb, pm; repeat from * around (2 stitches each section/16 stitches total).

Rnds 3–5 Knit.

Rnd 6 *Kfb, MBinc; repeat from * around (4/32 stitches).

Rnds 7–11 Knit.

Rnd 12 *Kfb, MBinc; repeat from * around (8/64 stitches).

Rnds 13–19 Knit.

Rnd 20 *K1, kfb, k1, MBinc; repeat from * around (12/96 stitches).

Rnds 21–25 Knit.

Rnd 26 *K2, kfb, k2, MBinc; repeat from * around (16/128 stitches).

Rnds 27–31 Knit.

If not working edging, bind off using a needle one size larger.

GARTER ST EDGING

Rnds 1 and 3 Purl.

Rnd 2 Knit.

Bind off knitwise using a needle one size larger.

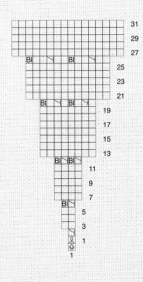

Bobble

| 4 | | | | | D |
| 2 | | | | | |

5
3
1 (RS)

Garter Stitch Edging

| · | · | · | · | · | 3 |
| · | · | · | · | · | 1 |

Stitch key

☐ Knit
· Purl
Bl MBinc
◣ Kfb
⊻ Cast on 1 st
⊽ Knit into front, back, front, back, then front of next st
▭▭▭▭D Pass 2nd, 3rd, and 4th sts over first st
☐ Repeat

BULBIFORM BRIOCHE

Worked in the round from the outer edge to the center
Colors A and B

With circular needle and A, cast on 156 stitches. Mark the beginning of the round and join without twisting. Change to dpns when there are too few stitches to fit around the circular needle.

Note The end of the round changes every round, as noted in rnd 2.

Rnd 1 *K1 A, k1 B; repeat from * around.

Rnd 2 *K1 A, k1 B; repeat from * to the last stitch. Pm for new end of rnd.

Rnd 3 *S2KP with A, [k1 A, k1 B] 8 times, k1 A, pm, ssk with B, [k1 B, k1 A] 18 times, k1 B, k2tog with B, pm, [k1 A, k1 B] 8 times, k1 A, pm; repeat from * once more (148 stitches).

Rnd 4 *S2KP with A, work in color pattern as established to next marker, ssk with B, work in color pattern to 2 stitches before next marker, k2tog with B, work in color pattern to 1 stitch before next marker; repeat from * once more (8 stitches decreased).

Repeat rnd 4 until 12 stitches remain.

Break the yarn. Thread the tail through the remaining 12 stitches, pull tight, and secure.

See chart on page 88.

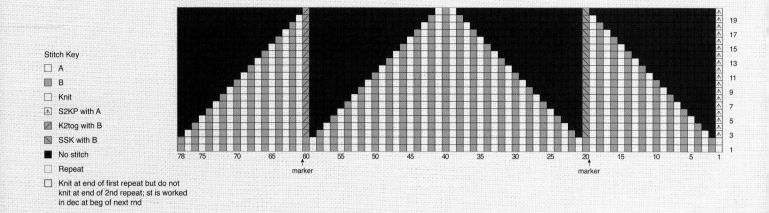

Stitch Key

☐ A
▨ B
☐ Knit
⬆ S2KP with A
⧄ K2tog with B
⧅ SSK with B
■ No stitch
☐ Repeat
☐ Knit at end of first repeat but do not knit at end of 2nd repeat; st is worked in dec at beg of next rnd

BOLD REVERSIBLE CABLE

Worked back and forth from the outer edge to the center

12/12 LC Sl 12 stitches onto the cn and hold in front, [k2, p2] 3 times, then [k2, p2] 3 times from the cn.

Cast on 158 stitches.

Row 1 (RS) K1, pm, *k4, [p2, k2] 5 times, p2, pm; repeat from * to the last stitch, k1 (26 stitches each section plus 2 selvedge stitches/158 stitches total).

Row 2 P1, *p4, [k2, p2] 5 times, k2; repeat from * to the last stitch, p1.

Rows 3–12 Repeat rows 1 and 2.

Row 13 K1, *k2, 12/12 LC; repeat from * to the last stitch, k1.

Rows 14, 16, and 18 Repeat row 2.

Rows 15 and 17 Repeat row 1.

Row 19 K1, *ssk, [k2, p2tog] 6 times; repeat from * to the last stitch, k1 (19/116 stitches).

Row 20 P1, *p1, [p2tog, k1] 6 times; repeat from * to the last stitch, p1 (13/80 stitches).

Rows 21 and 22 Knit.

Row 23 K1, *k2tog; repeat from * to the last stitch, k1 (41 stitches).

Row 24 P1, *p3tog; repeat from * to the last stitch, p1 (15 stitches).

Row 25 Knit.

Break the yarn, leaving a long tail. Thread the tail through the remaining 15 stitches, pull tight, and secure. Sew seam.

Stitch Key

☐ K on RS, P on WS
⊡ P on RS, K on WS
⧄ K2tog on RS, P2tog on WS
⧅ Ssk
⧄ P2tog on RS
⧄ 12/12 LC
⬈ P3tog on WS
■ No stitch
☐ Repeat

* Decrease across all stitches as follows:
Row 23: K1, *k2tog; repeat from * to the last stitch, k1 (41 sts)
Row 24: K1, *k3tog; repeat from * to the last stitch, k1 (15 sts)
Row 25: Knit.

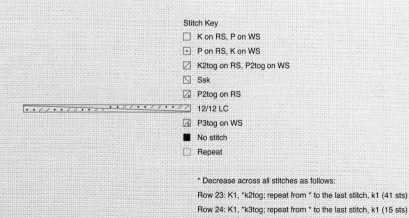

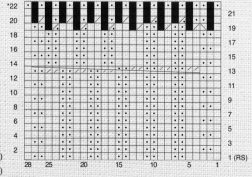

CAPELLA (textures)

Worked in the round from the center to the outer edge

MB (make bobble) ([K1, p1] twice, k1) in the same stitch, turn; k5, turn; k5tog.

1/1 RC Sl 1 stitch onto the cn and hold in back, k1, k1 from cn.

Cast on 8 stitches (2 stitches each on 4 dpns); mark the beginning of the round and join without twisting.

Rnd 1 *P1, pm; repeat from * around (1 stitch in each section/8 stitches total).

Rnd 2 *K1, m1; repeat from * around (2/16 stitches).

Rnds 3, 5, 7, 9, and 11 Purl.

Rnd 4 *K2, m1; repeat from * around (3/24 stitches).

Rnd 6 *K3, m1; repeat from * around (4/32 stitches).

Rnd 8 *K4, m1; repeat from * around (5/40 stitches).

Rnd 10 *K5, m1; repeat from * around (6/48 stitches).

Rnd 12 *K6, m1; repeat from * around (7/56 stitches).

Rnds 13 and 15 Knit.

Rnd 14 *K7, m1; repeat from * around (8/64 stitches).

Note The repeat in rnds 16–21 is worked over 2 sections (4 times each rnd). The stitch count is still given for each of the 8 sections.

Rnd 16 *[K2, p2] twice, m1, sm, [p2, k2] twice, m1P; repeat from * around (9/72 stitches).

Rnd 17 *[K2, p2] twice, k1, sm, [p2, k2] twice, p1; repeat from * around.

Rnd 18 *[K2, p2] twice, k1, m1, sm, [p2, k2] twice, p1, m1P; repeat from * around (10/80 stitches).

Rnds 19–21 *K2, p2; repeat from * around.

Rnd 22 *K10, m1; repeat from * around (11/88 stitches).

Rnds 23, 25, 27, 31, 33, and 35 Knit.

Rnd 24 *K11, m1; repeat from * around (12/96 stitches).

Rnd 26 *P12, m1P; repeat from * around (13/104 stitches).

Rnd 28 *K13, m1; repeat from * around (14/112 stitches).

Rnd 29 *K2, [MB, k4] twice, MB, k1; repeat from * around.

Rnd 30 *K14, m1; repeat from * around (15/120 stitches).

Rnd 32 *P15, m1P; repeat from * around (16/128 stitches).

Rnd 34 *K16, m1; repeat from * around (17/136 stitches).

Rnd 36 *K17, m1; repeat from * around (18/144 stitches).

Rnds 37, 39, and 41 *K2, p1; repeat from * around.

Rnds 38, 40, and 42 *1/1 RC, p1; repeat from * around.

Rnd 43 *[K2, p1] 6 times, m1; repeat from * around (19/152 stitches).

Bind off knitwise using a needle one size larger.

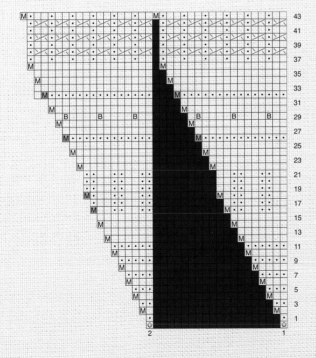

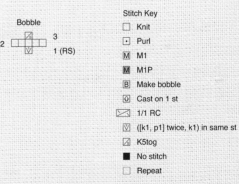

Bobble

2 — 1 (RS)

3

Stitch Key

☐ Knit
· Purl
M M1
M M1P
B Make bobble
Ⓞ Cast on 1 st
⤬ 1/1 RC
Ⅴ ([k1, p1] twice, k1) in same st
⧄ K5tog
■ No stitch
☐ Repeat

TREE CIRCLE

Worked from the bottom up

1/1 LPC (RS) Sl 1 stitch onto the cn and hold in front, p1, k1 tbl from the cn.

(WS) Sl 1 stitch onto the cn and hold in front, p1 tbl, k1 from the cn.

1/1 RPC (RS) Sl 1 stitch onto the cn and hold in back, k1 tbl, p1 from the cn.

(WS) Sl 1 stitch onto the cn and hold in back, k1, p1 tbl from the cn.

1/1 LT Sl 1 stitch onto the cn and hold in front, k1 tbl, k1 tbl from the cn.

1/1 RT Sl 1 stitch onto the cn and hold in front, k1 tbl, k1 tbl from the cn.

2/2 LPC (RS) Sl 2 stitches onto the cn and hold in front, p2, k2 tbl from the cn.

(WS) Sl 2 stitches onto the cn and hold in front, p2 tbl, k2 from the cn.

2/2 RPC (RS) Sl 2 stitches onto the cn and hold in back, k2 tbl, p2 from the cn.

(WS) Sl 2 stitches onto the cn and hold in back, k2, p2 tbl from the cn.

Cast on 13 stitches.

Row 1 (WS) K6, p1 tbl, k6.

Row 2 P1, m1P, p5, k1 tbl, p5, m1P, p1 (15 stitches).

Row 3 K1, m1, k6, p1 tbl, k6, m1, k1 (17 stitches).

Row 4 P1, m1P, p7, k1 tbl, p6, k1 tbl, m1P, p1 (19 stitches).

Row 5 K1, m1, k1, p3 tbl, k4, p1 tbl, k4, p4 tbl, m1, k1 (21 stitches).

Row 6 P1, m1P, p1, [1/1 LPC] twice, p3, k2 tbl, p3, 1/1 RPC, p4, m1P, p1 (23 stitches).

Row 7 K1, m1, k6, p2 tbl, k2, p2 tbl, k1, p3 tbl, k5, m1, k1 (25 stitches).

Row 8 P1, m1P, p7, 1/1 LPC, p1, k2 tbl, p1, 1/1 RPC, p8, m1P, p1 (27 stitches).

Row 9 K1, m1, k10, p6 tbl, k9, m1, k1 (29 stitches).

Row 10 P1, m1P, p10, k6 tbl, p11, m1P, p1 (31 stitches).

Row 11 K1, m1, k12, p6 tbl, k11, m1, k1 (33 stitches).

Row 12 P1, m1P, p12, k6 tbl, p13, m1P, p1 (35 stitches).

Row 13 K15, p6 tbl, k14.

Row 14 P1, m1P, p13, k6 tbl, p14, m1P, p1 (37 stitches).

Row 15 K16, p6 tbl, k15.

Row 16 P1, m1P, p14, k6 tbl, p15, m1P, p1 (39 stitches).

Row 17 K17, p6 tbl, k16.

Row 18 P1, m1P, p15, k1 tbl, 1/1 RPC, 1/1 LPC, k1 tbl, p16, m1P, p1 (41 stitches).

Rows 19 and 21 K18, p2 tbl, p2, p2 tbl, k17.

Row 20 P17, k2 tbl, k2, k2 tbl, p18.

Row 22 P1, m1P, p16, k2 tbl, k2, k2 tbl, p17, m1P, p1 (43 stitches).

Row 23 K19, p2 tbl, p2, p2 tbl, k18.

Row 24 P18, k1 tbl, 1/1 LT, 1/1 RT, k1 tbl, p19.

Row 25 K19, p6 tbl, k18.

Row 26 P1, m1P, p17, k6 tbl, p18, m1P, p1 (45 stitches).

Row 27 K19, p8 tbl, k18.

Row 28 P18, k8 tbl, p10, k1 tbl, p8.

Row 29 K8, 1/1 RPC, k8, p10 tbl, k12, p1 tbl, k4.

Row 30 P4, 1/1 LPC, p11, k10 tbl, p7, 1/1 RPC, p9.

Row 31 K10, p6 tbl, 2/2 LPC, p6 tbl, 2/2 RPC, p10 tbl, k5.

Row 32 P1, k3 tbl, 1/1 RPC, p9, k2 tbl, p2, k6 tbl, p2, k3 tbl, p4, 1/1 LPC, k1 tbl, p8.

Row 33 K6, p1 tbl, 1/1 LPC, k4, 2/2 LPC, k2, p8 tbl, k2, 2/2 RPC, k12.

Row 34 P12, k2 tbl, p4, k8 tbl, p4, k2 tbl, p7, k2 tbl, p4.

Row 35 K11, 2/2 LPC, k3, p10 tbl, k3, p1 tbl, 2/2 RPC, k5, p1 tbl, k3.

Row 36 P4, k1 tbl, p4, k2 tbl, p6, k10 tbl, p5, 2/2 LPC, p4, k2 tbl, p3.

Row 37 K3, p2 tbl, k4, p2 tbl, k5, 2/2 LPC, p6 tbl, 2/2 RPC, k4, 2/2 RPC, p3 tbl, k4.

Row 38 P6, k2 tbl, p7, k2 tbl, p2, k6 tbl, p2, k2 tbl, p5, k2 tbl, p2, 2/2 LPC, p3.

Row 39 Ssk, k3, 2/2 RPC, p2 tbl, k3, 2/2 LPC, k2, p6 tbl, k2, 2/2 RPC, k5, p2 tbl, k4, k2tog (43 stitches).

Row 40 [P5, k2 tbl] twice, p4, k6 tbl, p4, k2 tbl, p3, k2 tbl, p8.

Row 41 K4, p3 tbl, 1/1 LPC, p1 tbl, k3, p2 tbl, k4, p6 tbl, k4, 2/2 RPC, k3, p1 tbl, 1/1 RPC, p3 tbl, k1.

Row 42 P4, k1 tbl, p1, k1 tbl, p3, k2 tbl, p6, k6 tbl, p4, k2 tbl, p3, k1 tbl, p1, k1 tbl, p7.

Row 43 Ssk, [k4, 1/1 LPC] twice, p1 tbl, k2, 2/2 LPC, p2 tbl, 2/2 RPC, k4, p2 tbl, k5, 1/1 RPC, k1, k2tog (41 stitches).

Row 44 P2, k1 tbl, p6, k2 tbl, p4, [k2 tbl, p2] 3 times, k1 tbl, p1, [k1 tbl, p5] twice.

Row 45 [K4, 1/1 LPC] twice, k2, 2/2 LPC, k2, p2 tbl, k2, 2/2 RPC, k2, p1 tbl, 1/1 RPC, k5, 1/1 RPC, k1.

Row 46 P1, k1 tbl, p6, k1 tbl, p1, k1 tbl, p2, [k2 tbl, p4] twice, k2 tbl, p3, k1 tbl, p5, k1 tbl, p4.

Row 47 Ssk, k7, 1/1 LPC, k3, [p2 tbl, k4] 3 times, 1/1 RPC, k5, k2tog (39 stitches).

Row 48 P6, k1 tbl, p5, [k2 tbl, p4] 3 times, k1 tbl, p8.

Row 49 Ssk, k5, 1/1 LPC, k3, 1/1 LPC, p1 tbl, k4, p2 tbl, k4, p1 tbl, 1/1 RPC, k4, 1/1 RPC, k3, k2tog (37 stitches).

Row 50 P4, k1 tbl, p5, k1 tbl, p1, k1 tbl, p4, k2 tbl, p4, k1 tbl, p1, k1 tbl, p4, k1 tbl p6.

Row 51 Ssk, k8, 1/1 LPC, k5, 1/1 LPC, 1/1 RPC, k5, 1/1 RPC, k7, k2tog (35 stitches).

Row 52 P8, k1 tbl, p6, k1 tbl, p2, k1 tbl, p6, k1 tbl, p9.

Row 53 Ssk, k6, 1/1 LPC, k5, 1/1 LPC, k2, 1/1 RPC, k5, 1/1 RPC, k5, k2tog (33 stitches).

Row 54 P2tog, p4, k1 tbl, p6, k1 tbl, p4, k1 tbl, p6, k1 tbl, p5, p2tog tbl (31 stitches).

Row 55 Ssk, k10, 1/1 LPC, k4, 1/1 RPC, k9, k2tog (29 stitches).

Row 56 P2tog, p8, k1 tbl, p6, k1 tbl, p9, p2tog tbl (27 stitches).

Row 57 Ssk, k8, p1 tbl, k6, p1 tbl, k7, k2tog (25 stitches).

Row 58 P2tog, p6, k1 tbl, p6, k1 tbl, p7, p2tog tbl (23 stitches).

Rows 59 and 61 Ssk, knit to the last 2 stitches, k2tog (17 stitches after row 61).

Rows 60 and 62 P2tog, p to the last 2 stitches p2tog tbl (15 stitches after row 62).

Row 63 Repeat row 59 (13 stitches).

Bind off.

GARTER ST EDGING

With the RS facing, pick up and knit 148 stitches evenly around the edge of the circle. Pm and join.

Rnds 1 and 3 Purl.

Rnd 2 Knit.

Bind off using a needle one size larger.

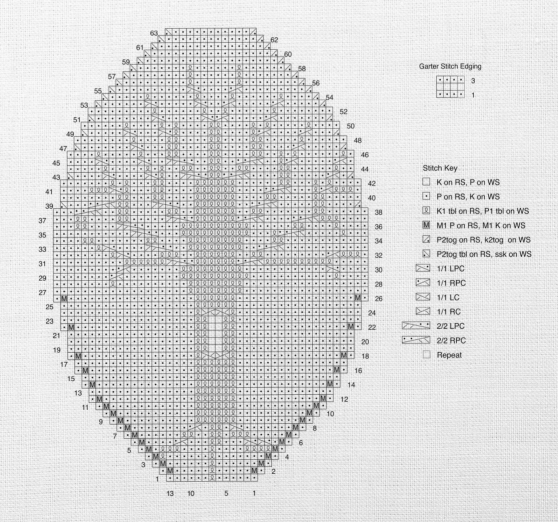

Garter Stitch Edging

Stitch Key

☐ K on RS, P on WS
• P on RS, K on WS
Ω K1 tbl on RS, P1 tbl on WS
M M1 P on RS, M1 K on WS
◩ P2tog on RS, k2tog on WS
◪ P2tog tbl on RS, ssk on WS
1/1 LPC
1/1 RPC
1/1 LC
1/1 RC
2/2 LPC
2/2 RPC
☐ Repeat

ROUND 3

LACE & POINTS

As sisters to crochet circles, there are many beautiful knitted vintage lace circles that are just as delicate. While designing the circles for this chapter, I found myself inspired by one of my favorite vintage pieces. I've included a few vintage circles for you to work with such as the star medallions, elegant leaf lace, picot lace ringlets, and lacy swirl. There are also patterns for what I call "points," circles that have striking points or scalloped edges. Short rows and yarn overs are key techniques in this chapter.

Examples of projects that use these are Stella Luna Pullover on page 179, Eternity Dress on page 204, and Illuminator Fringed Vest on page 191.

elegant leaf lace
page 105

8-point star lace medallion

page 106

sunburst
page 106

6-point
star lace
medallion
page 107

sawtooth lace
page 107

3-color point pinwheel
page 108

petal circle
page 108

cycle point II
page 109

picot-lace
ringlet
page 110

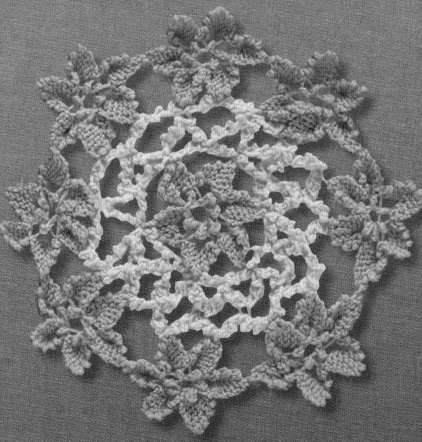

posies
page 110

aureole

page 111

celestial
bloom
page 112

fanfare
page 112

wheel web
page 113

star bright
page 114

*morning
bloom*
page 115

lacy swirl
page 116

stella luna
page 117

illuminator
page 117

ELEGANT LEAF LACE

Worked in the round from the center to the outer edge

Cast on 8 stitches (2 stitches each on 4 dpns); mark the beginning of the round and join without twisting.

Rnds 1 and 2 Knit.

Rnd 3 *Yo, k1 tbl, pm; repeat from * around (2 stitches each section/16 stitches total).

Rnd 4 and all even-numbered rnds Knit.

Rnd 5 *Yo, k1, yo, k1 tbl; repeat from* around (4/32 stitches).

Rnd 7 *Yo, k3, yo, k1 tbl; repeat from * around (6/48 stitches).

Rnd 9 *Yo, k2tog, yo, k1, yo, ssk, yo, k1 tbl; repeat from * around (8/64 stitches).

Rnd 11 *Yo, k2tog, yo, k3, yo, ssk, yo, k1 tbl; repeat from * around (10/80 stitches).

Rnd 13 *[Yo, k2tog] twice, yo, k1, yo, [ssk, yo] twice, k1 tbl; repeat from * around (12/96 stitches).

Rnd 15 *[Yo, k2tog] twice, yo, k3, yo, [ssk, yo] twice, k1 tbl; repeat from * around (14/112 stitches).

Rnd 17 *[Yo, k2tog] 3 times, yo, k1, yo, [ssk, yo] 3 times, k1 tbl; repeat from * around (16/128 stitches).

Rnd 19 *[K2tog, yo] 3 times, k3, [yo, ssk] 3 times, yo, k1 tbl, yo; repeat from * around (18/144 stitches).

Rnd 21 *[Ssk, yo] 3 times, S2KP, [yo, k2tog] 3 times, k1, yo, k1 tbl, yo, k1; repeat from * around.

Rnd 23 *[Ssk, yo] twice, ssk, k1, [k2tog, yo] twice, k2tog, k2, yo, k1 tbl, yo, k2; repeat from * around.

Rnd 25 *[Ssk, yo] twice, S2KP, [yo, k2tog] twice, k3, yo, k1 tbl, yo, k3; repeat from * around.

Rnd 27 *Ssk, yo, ssk, k1, k2tog, yo, k2tog, k4, yo, k1 tbl, yo, k4; repeat from * around.

Rnd 29 *Ssk, yo, S2KP, yo, k2tog, ssk, k2, yo, k1, yo, k1 tbl, yo, k1, yo, k2, k2tog; repeat from * around.

Rnd 31 *Ssk, k1, k2tog, ssk, [k2, yo] twice, k1 tbl, [yo, k2] twice, k2tog; repeat from * around.

Rnd 33 *S2KP, yo, ssk, k2, yo, k3, yo, k1 tbl, yo, k3, yo, k2, k2tog, yo; repeat from * around (20/160 stitches).

Rnd 35 *[K1 tbl, yo] twice, ssk, k2, yo, ssk, k5, k2tog, yo, k2, k2tog, yo, k1 tbl, yo; repeat from * around (22/176 stitches).

Rnd 37 *[Yo, k1 tbl, yo, k1] twice, ssk, k2, yo, ssk, k3, k2tog, yo, k2, k2tog, k1, yo, k1 tbl, yo, k1; repeat from * around (26/208 stitches).

Rnd 39 *Yo, S2KP, yo, k2, yo, k1 tbl, yo, k2, ssk, k2, yo, ssk, k1, k2tog, yo, k2, k2tog, k2, yo, k1 tbl, yo, k2; repeat from * around (28/224 stitches).

Rnd 41 *Yo, S2KP, yo, k3, yo, k1 tbl, yo, k3, ssk, k2, yo, S2KP, yo, k2, k2tog, k3, yo, k1 tbl, yo, k3; repeat from * around (30/240 stitches).

Rnd 43 *Yo, S2KP, yo, k4, yo, k1 tbl, yo, k4, ssk, k5, k2tog, k4, yo, k1 tbl, yo, k4; repeat from * around (32/256 stitches).

Rnd 45 *Yo, S2KP, yo, ssk, k2, yo, k1, yo, k1 tbl, yo, k1, yo, k2, k2tog, ssk, k3, k2tog, ssk, k2, yo, k1, yo, k1 tbl, yo, k1, yo, k2, k2tog; repeat from * around (34/272 stitches).

Rnd 47 *Yo, S2KP, yo, ssk, [k2, yo,] twice, k1 tbl, [yo, k2] twice, k2tog, ssk, k1, k2tog, ssk, [k2, yo] twice, k1 tbl, [yo, k2] twice, k2tog; repeat from * around (36/288 stitches).

Rnd 49 *S2KP, yo, ssk, k2, yo, k3, yo, k1 tbl, yo, k3, yo, k2, k2tog, yo, S2KP, yo, ssk, k2, yo, k3, yo, k1 tbl, yo, k3, yo, k2, k2tog, yo; repeat from * around (40/320 stitches).

Rnd 50 Knit.

Bind off using a needle one size larger.

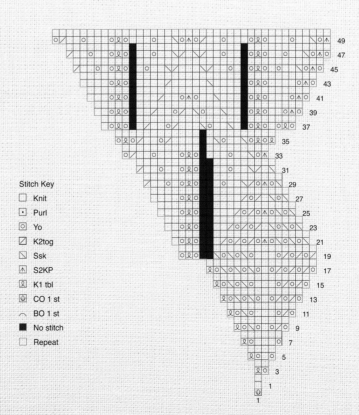

Stitch Key

☐	Knit
·	Purl
○	Yo
⟋	K2tog
⟍	Ssk
⋀	S2KP
℺	K1 tbl
⊍	CO 1 st
⌢	BO 1 st
■	No stitch
☐	Repeat

8-POINT STAR LACE MEDALLION

Worked in the round from the center to the outer edge

Cast on 8 stitches (2 stitches each on 4 dpns); mark the beginning of the round and join without twisting.

Rnd 1 *K1 tbl; repeat from * around.

Rnd 2 *Yo, k1, pm; repeat from * around (2 stitches each section/16 stitches total).

Rnd 3 and all odd-numbered rnds Knit.

Rnd 4 *Yo, k2; repeat from * around (3/24 stitches).

Rnd 6 *Yo, k3; repeat from * around (4/32 stitches).

Rnd 8 *Yo, k4; repeat from * around (5/40 stitches).

Rnd 10 *Yo, k5; repeat from * around (6/48 stitches).

Rnd 12 *Yo, k6; repeat from * around (7/56 stitches).

Rnd 14 *Yo, k7; repeat from * around (8/64 stitches).

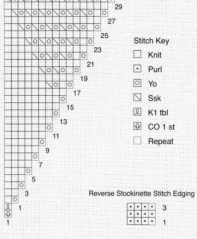

Stitch Key

- ☐ Knit
- · Purl
- ⊙ Yo
- ⊡ Ssk
- ⊠ K1 tbl
- ⊍ CO 1 st
- ☐ Repeat

Reverse Stockinette Stitch Edging

Rnd 16 *Yo, k8; repeat from * around (9/72 stitches).

Rnd 18 *Yo, k1, yo, ssk, k6; repeat from * around (10/80 stitches).

Rnd 20 *Yo, k1, [yo, ssk] twice, k5; repeat from * around (11/88 stitches).

Rnd 22 *Yo, k1, [yo, ssk] 3 times, k4; repeat from * around (12/96 stitches).

Rnd 24 *Yo, k1, [yo, ssk] 4 times, k3; repeat from * around (13/104 stitches).

Rnd 26 *Yo, k1, [yo, ssk] 5 times, k2; repeat from * around (14/112 stitches).

Rnd 28 *Yo, k1, [yo, ssk] 6 times, k1; repeat from * around (15/120 stitches).

Rnd 30 *Yo, k1, [yo, ssk] 7 times; repeat from * around (16/128 stitches).

If not working edging, bind off using a needle one size larger.

REVERSE STOCKINETTE ST EDGING

Rnds 1, 2, and 3 Purl.

Bind off using a needle one size larger.

SUNBURST

Worked with short rows

Cast on 22 stitches.

Row 1 K7, turn (15 stitches unworked).

Row 2 K7, turn.

Row 3 Bind off 1 stitch, k8, turn (12 stitches unworked).

Row 4 K9, turn.

Row 5 Bind off 1 stitch, k10, turn (9 stitches unworked).

Row 6 K11, turn.

Row 7 Bind off 1 stitch, k12, turn (6 stitches unworked).

Row 8 K13, turn.

Row 9 Bind off 1 stitch, knit next 14 stitches, turn (3 stitches unworked).

Row 10 K15, turn.

Row 11 Bind off 1 stitch, k16, turn.

Row 12 K17, cast on 5 stitches (22 stitches).

Repeat rows 1–12 seventeen more times, then rows 1–11 once.

Bind off all stitches, leaving a long tail. Sew the cast-on edge to the bound-off edge, then pick up each ridge in the center of the motif, draw tight, and secure.

Stitch Key

- ☐ Knit on RS
- · Knit on WS
- ⊍ CO 1 st
- ⊠ BO 1 st
- ☐ Repeat

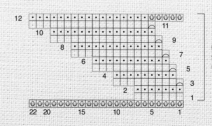

Repeat Rows 1-12 seventeen times, then repeat Rows 1-11 once

6-POINT STAR LACE MEDALLION

Worked in the round from the center to the outer edge

Cast on 6 stitches (2 stitches each on 3 dpns); mark the beginning of the round and join without twisting.

Rnd 1 *Yo, k1, pm; repeat from * around (2 stitches each section/12 stitches total).

Rnds 2, 4, 6, 8, 10, 12, and 14 Knit.

Rnd 3 *Yo, k2; repeat from * around (3/18 stitches).

Rnd 5 *Yo, k3; repeat from * around (4/24 stitches).

Rnd 7 *Yo, k4; repeat from * around (5/30 stitches).

Rnd 9 *Yo, k5; repeat from * around (6/36 stitches).

Rnd 11 *Yo, k6; repeat from * around (7/42 stitches).

Rnd 13 *Yo, k7; repeat from * around (8/48 stitches).

Rnd 15 *Yo, k8; repeat from * around (9/54 stitches).

Rnd 16 *K1, yo, ssk, k6; repeat from * around.

Rnd 17 *Yo, k9; repeat from * around (10/60 stitches).

Rnd 18 *K1, yo, k2tog, yo, ssk, k5; repeat from * around.

Rnd 19 *Yo, k10; repeat from * around (11/66 stitches).

Rnd 20 *K1, [yo, k2tog] twice, yo, ssk, k4; repeat from * around.

Rnd 21 *Yo, k11; repeat from * around (12/72 stitches).

Rnd 22 *K1, [yo, k2tog] 3 times, yo, ssk, k3; repeat from * around.

Rnd 23 *Yo, k12; repeat from * around (13/78 stitches).

Rnd 24 *K1, [yo, k2tog] 4 times, yo, ssk, k2; repeat from * around.

Rnd 25 *Yo, k13; repeat from * around (14/84 stitches).

Rnd 26 *K1, [yo, k2tog] 5 times, yo, ssk, k1; repeat from * around.

Rnd 27 *Yo, k14; repeat from * around (15/90 stitches).

Rnd 28 *K1, [yo, k2tog] 6 times, yo, ssk; repeat from * around.

Rnd 29 *Yo, k15; repeat from * around (16/96 stitches).

Rnds 30 and 31 Purl.

Rnd 32 *Yo, p2tog; repeat from * around.

Rnd 33 *(P1, k1) into yo of previous rnd, p1; repeat from * around (24/144 stitches).

Rnd 34 Purl.

Bind off using a needle one size larger.

Optional Weave ribbon through the eyelets in round 32.

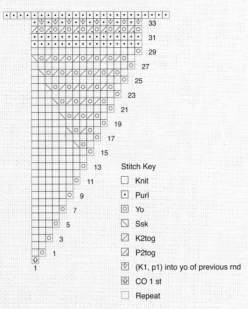

33
31
29
27
25
23
21
19
17
15
13
11
9
7
5
3
1

1

Stitch Key

☐	Knit
⊡	Purl
⊙	Yo
◺	Ssk
⁄	K2tog
⁄	P2tog
▽	(K1, p1) into yo of previous rnd
⊍	CO 1 st
☐	Repeat

SAWTOOTH LACE

Worked in short rows

Provisionally cast on (page 214) 18 stitches.

Row 1 (RS) K12, [yo, k2tog] twice, yo, k2 (19 stitches).

Row 2 K9, p7, W&T, leaving 3 stitches unworked.

Row 3 K10, [yo, k2tog] twice, yo, k2 (20 stitches).

Row 4 K10, p7, k3.

Row 5 K14, [yo, k2tog] twice, yo, k2 (21 stitches).

Row 6 K11, p7, W&T, leaving 3 stitches unworked.

Row 7 P7, k5, [yo, k2tog] twice, yo, k2 (22 stitches).

Row 8 K22.

Row 9 K3, p7, k6, [yo, k2tog] twice, yo, k2 (23 stitches).

Row 10 K20, W&T, leaving 3 stitches unworked.

Row 11 P7, k13.

Row 12 Bind off 5 stitches, knit to the end (18 stitches).

Repeat rows 1–12 fifteen more times (16 points).

Carefully remove provisional cast-on and graft beginning to end. Thread the end tail through the end stitches at the center, pull tight, and secure.

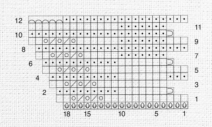

12
10
8
6
4
2

11
9
7
5
3
1

18   15   10   5   1

Stitch Key

☐	Knit on RS, Purl on WS
⊡	Purl on RS, Knit on WS
⊙	Yo
⁄	K2tog
◠	W&T on WS
⊍	CO 1 st
⌢	BO 1 st
☐	Repeat

Optional Sew a decorative button at the center of the circle.

3-COLOR POINT PINWHEEL

Worked in short rows

Colors A, B, and C

With A, cast on 22 stitches.

Row 1 (WS) K5, yo, k15, W&T (23 total stitches; 2 stitches unworked).

Row 2 and all RS rows Knit.

Row 3 K5, yo, k12, k2tog, W&T (4 stitches unworked).

Row 5 K5, yo, k12, W&T (24 total stitches, 6 stitches unworked).

Row 7 K5, yo, k9, k2tog, W&T (8 stitches unworked).

Row 9 K5, yo, k9, W&T (25 total stitches, 10 stitches unworked).

Row 11 K5, yo, k6, k2tog, W&T (12 stitches unworked).

Row 13 K5, yo, k6, W&T (26 total stitches, 14 stitches unworked).

Row 15 K5, yo, k3, k2tog, W&T (16 stitches unworked).

Row 17 K5, yo, k3, W&T (27 total stitches, 18 stitches unworked).

Row 19 K5, yo, k1, k2tog, W&T (19 stitches unworked).

Row 21 Bind off 5 stitches, knit to the last st, slip 1. Break off the yarn and join to the next color.

Row 22 Knit.

Repeat rows 1–22 eleven more times, alternating colors by changing to B, C, or A after row 21.

Sew the last row to the cast-on edge, thread the tail through the end stitches at the center, pull tight to gather, and secure.

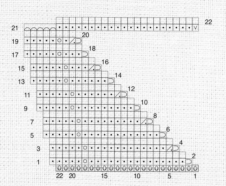

Stitch Key

☐	Knit on RS
·	Knit on WS
⊙	Yo
◢	K2tog on WS
◻	W&T on WS
⌒	Bind off 1 st
V	Slip 1 st
⊚	CO 1 st
☐	Repeat

PETAL CIRCLE

Worked in the round from the center to the outer edge

Cast on 12 stitches (3 stitches each on 4 dpns); mark the beginning of the round and join without twisting.

Rnd 1 *K1 tbl; repeat from * around.

Rnd 2 *Yo, k1, pm; repeat from * around (2 stitches each section/24 stitches total).

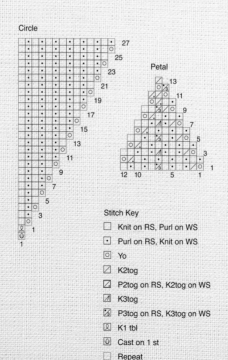

Circle

Petal

Stitch Key

☐	Knit on RS, Purl on WS
·	Purl on RS, Knit on WS
⊙	Yo
◹	K2tog
◿	P2tog on RS, K2tog on WS
◸	K3tog
◺	P3tog on RS, K3tog on WS
ⵜ	K1 tbl
⊚	Cast on 1 st
☐	Repeat

Rnds 3, 7, 11, 15, 19, and 23 *P1, k1; repeat from * around.

Rnd 4 *Yo, p1, k1; repeat from * around (3/36 stitches).

Rnd 5 *K1, p1, k1; repeat from * around.

Rnd 6 *Yo, k1, p1, k1; repeat from * around (4/48 stitches).

Rnd 8 *Yo, [p1, k1] twice; repeat from * around (5/60 stitches).

Rnd 9 *K1, [p1, k1] twice; repeat from * around.

Rnd 10 *Yo, k1, [p1, k1] twice; repeat from * around (6/72 stitches).

Rnd 12 *Yo, [p1, k1] 3 times; repeat from * around (7/84 stitches).

Rnd 13 *K1, [p1, k1] 3 times; repeat from * around.

Rnd 14 *Yo, k1, [p1, k1] 3 times; repeat from * around (8/96 stitches)

Rnd 16 *Yo, [p1, k1] 4 times; repeat from * around (9/108 stitches).

Rnd 17 *K1, [p1, k1] 4 times; repeat from * around.

Rnd 18 *Yo, k1, [p1, k1] 4 times; repeat from * around (10/120 stitches).

Rnd 20 *Yo, [p1, k1] 5 times; repeat from * around (11/132 stitches).

Rnd 21 *K1, [p1, k1] 5 times; repeat from * around.

Rnd 22 *Yo, k1, [p1, k1] 5 times; repeat from * around (12/144 stitches).

Rnd 24 *Yo, [p1, k1] 6 times; repeat from * around (13/156 stitches).

Rnd 25 *K1, [p1, k1] 6 times; repeat from * around.

Rnd 26 *Yo, k1, [p1, k1] 6 times; repeat from * around (14/168 stitches).

Rnd 27 *P1, k1; repeat from * around. Do not break yarn.

PETAL

Note Each petal is worked back and forth over 14 stitches using 2 double-pointed needles. Leave unworked stitches on the needle until you are ready to work them.

Row 1 (RS) Yo, k2tog, [p1, k1] twice, p3tog, [k1, p1] twice, k1 (12 stitches). Turn.

Rows 2, 4, 6, 8, and 10 Yo, k2tog, *p1, k1; repeat from * to end. Turn.

Row 3 Yo, k2tog, p1, k1, p1, k3tog, [p1, k1] twice (10 stitches).

Row 5 Yo, k2tog, p1, k1, p3tog, k1, p1, k1 (8 stitches).

Row 7 Yo, k2tog, p1, k3tog, p1, k1 (6 stitches).

Row 9 Yo, k2tog, p3tog, k1 (4 stitches).

Row 11 Yo, k2tog, p2tog (3 stitches).

Row 12 Yo, k3tog (2 stitches).

Row 13 K2tog.

Fasten off.

Rejoin yarn to the next stitch and work rows 1–13 of the petal over the next 14 stitches. Repeat until 12 petals have been completed.

Thread the cast-on tail through the cast-on stitches at the center, pull tight, and secure.

CYCLE POINT II

Worked in short rows

Cast on 26 stitches loosely.

Row 1 Yo, k25. Turn, leaving 1 stitch unworked.

Row 2 Sl 1, knit to end.

Row 3 Yo, knit to slipped stitch. Turn, leaving 1 more stitch unworked.

Row 4 Sl 1, knit to end.

Rows 5 and 6 Repeat rows 3 and 4.

Row 7 Bind off 3 stitches, (k2tog, [yo] twice, k2tog) 4 times, k5. Turn, leaving 4 stitches unworked.

Row 8 Sl 1, p5, [(p1, k1) in double yo, p2] 4 times.

Rows 9–14 Repeat rows 3 and 4.

Row 15 Bind off 3 stitches, (k2tog, [yo] twice, k2tog) 3 times, k5. Turn, leaving 8 stitches unworked.

Row 16 Sl 1, p5, [(p1,k1) in double yo, p2] 3 times.

Rows 17–22 Repeat rows 3 and 4.

Row 23 Bind off 3 stitches, (k2tog, [yo] twice, k2tog) twice, k5. Turn, leaving 12 stitches unworked.

Row 24 Sl 1, p5, [(p1, k1) in double yo, p2] twice.

Rows 25–30 Repeat rows 3 and 4.

Row 31 Bind off 3 stitches, k2tog, [yo] twice, k2tog, k5. Turn, leaving 16 stitches unworked.

Row 32 Sl 1, p5, (p1, k1) in double yo, p2.

Rows 33–38 Repeat rows 3 and 4.

Row 39 Bind off 3 stitches, k5. Turn, leaving 20 stitches unworked.

Row 40 Sl 1, knit to end.

Rows 41–46 Repeat rows 3 and 4.

Row 47 Bind off 3 stitches, k26.

Row 48 Sl 1, p25.

Repeat rows 1–48 five more times.

Bind off loosely. Sew bound-off edge to cast-on edge.

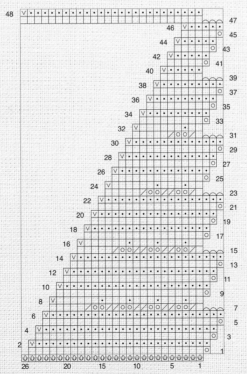

Stitch Key

☐ Knit on RS, Purl on WS

· Purl on RS, Knit on WS

◯ Yo

◿ K2tog

⌒ Bind off 1 st

Ⅴ Slip 1 st

⊡ CO 1 st

☐ Repeat

PICOT-LACE RINGLET

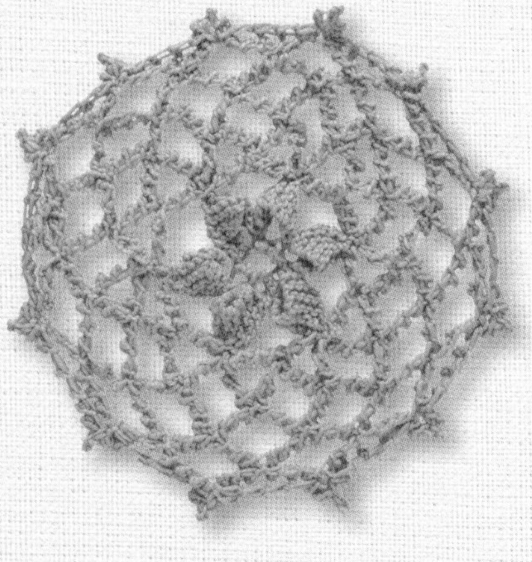

Worked in the round from the center to the outer edge

CENTER

Place a slip knot on the left-hand needle.

[Cast on 3 stitches, bind off 3 stitches] 6 times.

Join by picking up and knitting 1 in the beginning slip knot and passing the first stitch over the picked-up stitch. Place the remaining stitch on the left-hand needle.

PETALS

Cast on 1 stitch (2 stitches).

Row 1 K1, kfb (3 stitches).

Rows 2 and 4 Knit.

Row 3 K2, kfb (4 stitches).

Row 5 K3, kfb (5 stitches).

Rows 6, 7, 8, and 9 Knit.

Row 10, 12, and 14 Bind off 1 stitch, knit to end.

Rows 11, 13, and 15 Knit.

Bind off 1 stitch (1 stitch remains). Pick up and knit 1 between the next 2 picots, then bind off 1 stitch. Place the remaining stitch on the left-hand needle. Repeat rows 1–15 to complete 6 petals, end by joining the last petal at the base of the first petal. Fasten off.

BODY

Picot Cast on 2 stitches, bind off 2 stitches.

Join yarn by picking up and knitting 1 at the center tip of any petal.

Rnd 1 *Make 6 picots, join to the center tip of the next petal by (pick up and knit 1, bind off 1 stitch); repeat from * around.

Rnd 2 *Make 6 picots, join between the 3rd and 4th picots before the next petal of the previous round, make 6 picots, join to the center tip of the next petal; repeat from * around. Fasten off.

Rnds 3, 4, and 5 Rejoin yarn between the 3rd and 4th picots of any picot strand. *Make 6 picots, join between the 3rd and 4th picots of the next picot strand; repeat from * around. Fasten off.

Rnd 6 Rejoin yarn between the 3rd and 4th picots of any picot strand. *Make 3 picots, join to the base of this strand, make 4 picots, join between the 3rd and 4th picots of the next strand; repeat from * around. Fasten off.

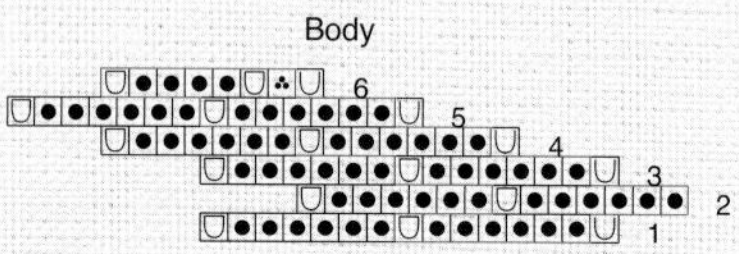

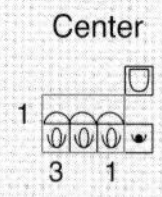

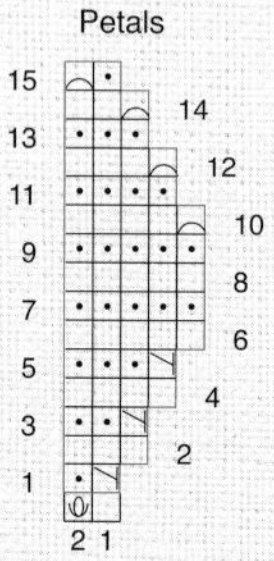

Stitch Key

- Knit on RS
- Knit on WS
- Kfb
- Cast on 1 st
- Slip knot
- Bind off 1 st
- Pick up and knit 1 st
- Pick up and knit 1 st, bind off 1 st;
- Picot
- 3 Picots
- Repeat

POSIES

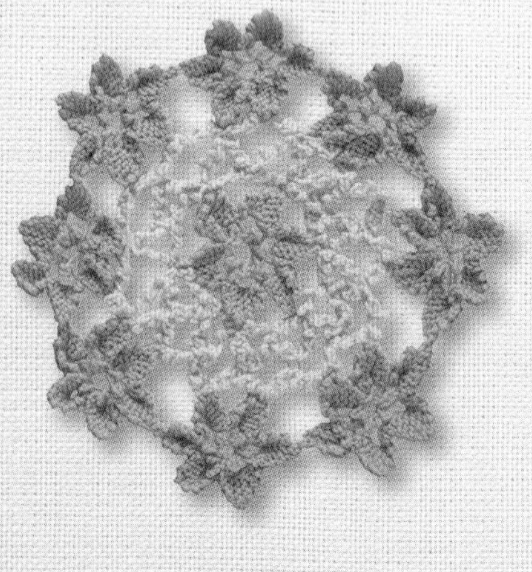

Worked in the round from the center to the outer edge

Colors MC and CC

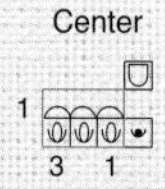

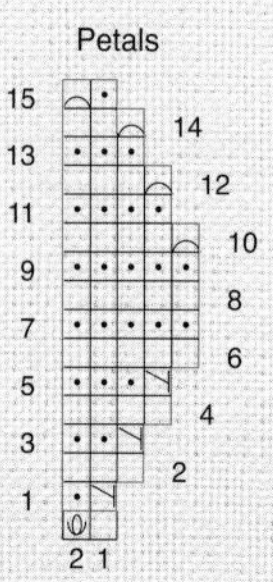

Stitch Key

- MC
- CC
- Knit on RS
- Knit on WS
- Kfb
- Cast on 1 st
- Slip knot
- Bind off 1 st
- Pick up and knit 1 st
- Pick up and knit 1 st, bind off 1 st;
- Picot
- Repeat

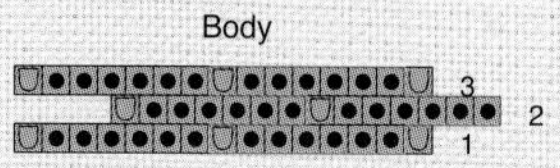

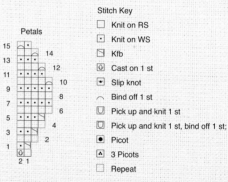

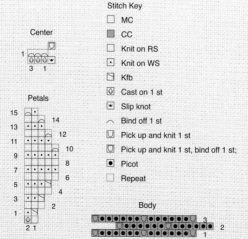

CENTER

With MC, place a slip knot on the left-hand needle.

[Cast on 3 stitches, bind off 3 stitches] 6 times.

Join by picking up and knitting 1 stitch in the beginning slip knot and passing the first stitch over the picked-up stitch. Place the remaining stitch on left-hand needle.

PETALS

Cast on 1 stitch (2 stitches).

Row 1 K1, kfb (3 stitches).

Rows 2 and 4 Knit.

Row 3 K2, kfb (4 stitches).

Row 5 K3, kfb (5 stitches).

Rows 6, 7, 8, and 9 Knit.

Rows 10, 12, and 14 Bind off 1 stitch, knit to end.
Rows 11, 13, and 15 Knit.
Bind off 1 stitch (1 stitch remains). Pick up and knit 1 between the next 2 picots, then bind off 1 stitch. Place the remaining stitch on the left-hand needle. Repeat rows 1–15 to complete 6 petals, end by joining last petal at the base of the first petal. Fasten off.

BODY
Picot Cast on 2 stitches, bind off 2 stitches.

Join CC by picking up and knitting 1 stitch at the center tip of any petal.
Rnd 1 *Make 6 picots, join to the center tip of the next petal by (pick up and knit 1, bind off 1 stitch); repeat from * around.
Rnd 2 *Make 6 picots, join between the 3rd and 4th picots before the next petal of the previous rnd, make 6 picots, join to the center tip of the next petal; repeat from * around. Fasten off.
Rnd 3 Rejoin yarn between the 3rd and 4th picots of any picot strand. *Make 6 picots, join between the 3rd and

4th picots of the next picot strand; repeat from * around. Fasten off.

OUTER FLOWERS
Using MC, make 8 Centers with Petals using a needle 2 sizes smaller. *Sew the tip of the 3rd petal of one flower to the tip of the 6th petal of another flower; repeat from * until all flowers are sewn together to form a ring. Sew the tips of the 2 inner petals of each flower to rnd 3 of the Body.

....

AUREOLE

Worked in the round from the center to the outer edge

Cast on 8 stitches (2 stitches each on 4 dpns); mark the beginning of the round and join without twisting.
Rnd 1 *Yo, k1, pm; repeat from * around (2 stitches each section/16 stitches total).
Rnds 2–4 Knit.
Rnd 5 *Yo, k1; repeat from * around (4/32 stitches).
Rnds 6–8 Knit.
Rnd 9 *K2tog, [yo] 7 times, k2tog; repeat from * around (9/72 stitches).
Rnd 10 *K1, [k1 tbl] 7 times in 7yo, k1; repeat from * around.
Rnds 11–16 Knit.
Rnd 17 *Yo, k9; repeat from * around (10/80 stitches).
Rnds 18, 20, 22, 24, 26, and 28 Knit.
Rnd 19 *Yo, k1, yo, k9; repeat from * around (12/96 stitches).
Rnd 21 *Yo, k3, yo, k3, SK2P, k3; repeat from * around.
Rnd 23 *Yo, k1, yo, SK2P, yo, k1, yo, k2, SK2P, k2; repeat from * around.
Rnd 25 *Yo, k3, yo, k1, yo, k3, yo, k1, SK2P, k1; repeat from * around (14/112 stitches).
Rnd 27 *Yo, k1, yo, SK2P, yo, k3, yo, SK2P, yo, k1, yo, SK2P; repeat from * around.
Rnd 29 *K13, yo, k1, yo; repeat from * around (16/128 stitches).
Rnds 30–32 Knit.
If not working edging, bind off using a needle one size larger.

K2, P2 EDGING
Rnds 1–3 P1, *k2, p2; repeat from * to the last 3 stitches, k2, p1.
Bind off in pattern using a needle one size larger.

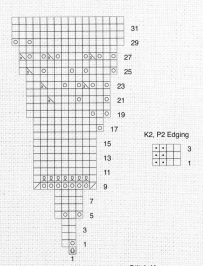

31
29
27
25
23
21
19
17
15
13
11
9
7
5
3
1
1

K2, P2 Edging

3
1

Stitch Key
	Knit on RS, Purl on WS
:	Purl on RS, Knit on WS
O	Yo
⊻	K1 tbl
╱	K2tog
╲	SK2P
⊙	CO 1 st
⌒	BO 1 st
	Repeat

Flower

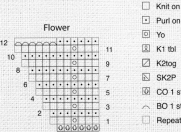

12
10
8
6
4
2
11
9
7
5
3
1
6 5 1

FLOWER
Cast on 6 stitches.
Row 1 (RS) K3, yo, k3 (7 stitches).
Row 2 and all WS rows Knit.
Row 3 K3, yo, k4 (8 stitches).
Row 5 K3, yo, k5 (9 stitches).
Row 7 K3, yo, k6 (10 stitches).
Row 9 K3, yo, k7 (11 stitches).
Row 11 K3, yo, k8 (12 stitches).
Row 12 Bind off 6 stitches, knit to end (6 stitches).
Repeat rows 1–12 four more times (5 petals total). Bind off the remaining 6 stitches.
Sew the bound-off edge to the cast-on edge. Weave yarn through eyelets, pull tight, and secure.
Sew a bead to the center of the flower. Sew the flower to the center of the circle.

CELESTIAL BLOOM

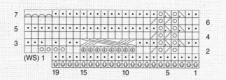

Worked as sideways edging, then gathered into a circle

Stitch Key

☐	K on RS, P on WS
·	P on RS, K on WS
○	Yo
⊕	Knit, wrapping yarn around needle 4 times
╱	Ssk
╲	K2tog on WS
◎	CO 1 st
⌢	BO 1 st
▨	Slip 8 sts, dropping extra wraps, pass first 4 elongated sts over last 4 sts and to left-hand needle, slip last 4 sts to left-hand needle, knit 8
☐	Repeat

Cast on 21 stitches.

Row 1 (WS) Knit.

Row 2 K3, [yo, k2tog] twice, k2, k8 wrapping yarn around each stitch 4 times, k2, [yo] 4 times, k2.

Row 3 K2, [k1, p1] twice into 4yo of the previous row, k2, sl 8 (dropping extra wraps); pass the first 4 elongated stitches over the last 4 stitches and onto the left-hand needle, then slip the last 4 stitches onto the left-hand needle; k8, k3, [yo, k2tog] twice, k2 (25 stitches).

Rows 4 and 6 K3, [yo, k2tog] twice, k18.

Row 5 K19, [yo, k2tog] twice, k2.

Row 7 Bind off 4 stitches, k14, [yo, k2tog] twice, k2 (21 stitches).

Repeat rows 2–7 twenty more times (21 repeats). Bind off. Break the yarn, leaving a long tail. Sew the bound-off edge to the cast-on edge.

Thread the yarn through the first yo column. Pull tight to form a rosette at the center and secure.

FANFARE

Worked in the round from the outer edge to the center, then wide edging is added

STOCKINETTE ST CENTER

Cast on 70 stitches. Mark the beginning of the round and join without twisting.

Rnd 1 *K2tog, k5; repeat from * to end (60 stitches).

Rnds 2, 4, 6, 8, and 10 Knit.

Rnd 3 *K2tog, k4; repeat from * to end (50 stitches).

Rnd 5 *K2tog, k3; repeat from * to end (40 stitches).

Rnd 7 *K2tog, k2; repeat from * to end (30 stitches).

Rnd 9 *K2tog, k1; repeat from * to end (20 stitches).

Rnd 11 *K2tog; repeat from * to end (10 stitches).

Break off the yarn. Thread the tail through the remaining stitches, tighten, and secure.

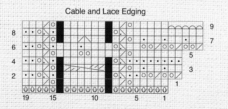
Cable and Lace Edging

Stockinette Stitch Center

Stitch Key

☐	K on RS, P on WS
·	P on RS, K on WS
○	Yo
╱	K2tog
╲	Ssk
◢	K2tog on WS
◎	CO 1 st
⌢	BO 1 st
▨	3/3 LC
■	No stitch
☐	Repeat

CABLE AND LACE EDGING

Cast on 19 stitches.

Row 1 (RS) K5, yo, k2tog, k7, yo, k2tog, k3.

Row 2 K2, yo, k2tog, k1, p6, yo, k2tog, k2, [yo] twice, k2tog, [yo] twice, k2tog (21 stitches).

Row 3 [K1, (k1, p1) in double yo of previous row] twice, k1, yo, k2tog, k1, 3/3 LC, yo, k2tog, k3.

Row 4 K2, yo, k2tog, k1, p6, yo, k2tog, k8.

Row 5 K7, yo, k2tog, k4, [yo] twice, k3, yo, k2tog, k3 (23 stitches).

Row 6 K2, yo, k2tog, k1, p3, (k1, p1) in double yo, p3, yo, k2tog, k2 ([yo] twice, k2tog) 3 times (26 stitches).

Row 7 [K1, (k1, p1) in double yo] 3 times, k1, yo, k2tog, k3, ssk, k2tog, k2, yo, k2tog, k3 (24 stitches).

Row 8 K2, yo, k2tog, k1, p6, yo, k2tog, k11.

Row 9 Bind off 5 stitches, k4, yo, k2tog, k7, yo, k2tog, k3 (19 stitches).

Repeat rows 2–9 twenty-two more times (23 repeats). Bind off. Break the yarn, leaving a long tail. Sew the bound-off edge to the cast-on edge.

Thread the yarn through the bumps along the Garter st edge. Lightly gather until the edge fits the Stockinette St Center. Pin in place and sew together using whipstitch.

WHEEL WEB

Worked from the bottom

W3 Sl 3 wyib, bring yarn to front, slip these 3 stitches back onto the left-hand needle, bring yarn to the back, k3.

CDI Insert right-hand needle from top down into the purled head of the first stitch in the row below, knit into the back loop of this stitch and knit into the back loop of the stitch on the left-hand needle. Then, with the left-hand needle, lift the left-side strand of the same stitch in the row below, and knit into the back loop to make a 3rd stitch.

Dec4 Sl 3 stitches wyib onto the right-hand needle, *pass the 2nd stitch onto the right-hand needle over the first stitch, slip the first stitch back onto the left-hand needle and pass the 2nd stitch onto the left-hand needle over it*. Slip the first stitch back onto the right-hand needle; repeat from * to * once more, k1.

Kbf Knit in back then front of the next stitch.

Cast on 13 stitches.

Setup row P13.

Row 1 (RS) K1, m1, knit to the last stitch, m1, p1 (15 stitches).

Row 2 P1, m1P, purl to the last stitch, m1P, p1 (17 stitches).

Rows 3–6 Repeat rows 1 and 2 (25 stitches).

Row 7 K1, m1, k2, W3, k13, W3, k2, m1, k1 (27 stitches).

Rows 8 and 10 Repeat row 2.

Row 9 K1, m1, k2, *k3tog, yo, CDI, yo, k3tog tbl*, k9; repeat from * to *, k2, m1, k1 (31 stitches).

Row 11 K1, m1, k2, *k3tog, yo, k2tog, yo, CDI, yo, ssk yo, k3tog tbl*, k5; repeat from * to *, k2, m1, k1 (35 stitches).

Row 12 and all WS rows through row 36 Purl.

Row 13 K1, m1, k2, *[k2tog, yo] 3 times, k1 tbl, [yo, ssk] 3 times*, k3; repeat from * to *, k2, m1, k1 (37 stitches).

Row 15 K1, m1, k4, *[yo, k2tog] twice, yo, SK2P, yo, *[ssk, yo] twice, k5*; repeat from * to *, k3, m1, k1 (39 stitches).

Row 17 K1, m1, k4, *[ssk, yo] 3 times, k1 tbl, [yo, k2tog] 3 times*, k3, repeat from * to *, k4, m1, k1 (41 stitches).

Row 19 K7, * kbf, yo, ssk, yo, Dec4, yo, k2tog, yo, kfb*, k5; repeat from * to *, k7.

Row 21 K1, m1, k8, *kbf, yo, Dec4, yo, kfb*, k9; repeat from * to *, k8, m1, k1 (43 stitches).

Row 23 *K5, W3, k4, W3, k5*, W3; repeat from * to *.

Row 25 K1, m1, k2, [*k3tog, yo, CDI, yo, k3tog tbl*, k8] twice; repeat from * to *, k2, m1, k1 (45 stitches).

Picot Chain Edging

Stitch Key

☐	K on RS, P on WS
·	P on RS, K on WS
○	Yo
╱	K2tog on RS, p2tog on WS
╲	Ssk on RS, p2tog tbl on WS
⋀	SK2P
⟋	K3tog
⟍	K3tog tbl
⟁	D4
M	M1 on RS, M1P on WS
ℓ	Kfb
⟋	Kbf
⊔⊔⊔	CDI
ℓ	k1 tbl
⟨3⟩	W3
■	no stitch
⌒	BO 1 st
●	Slip st on right-hand needle onto left-hand needle, CO 3 sts using cable method, BO 4 sts
☐	Repeat

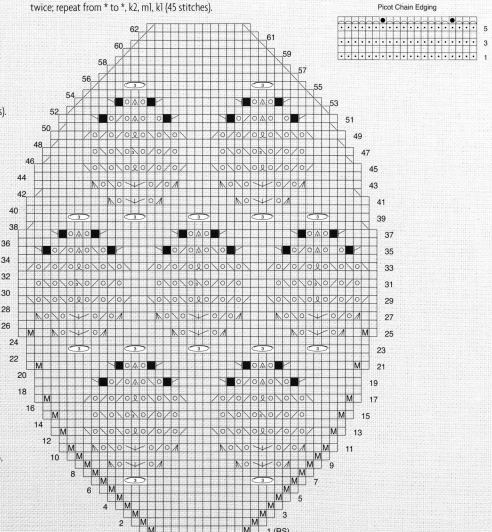

Row 27 K2, [*k3tog, yo, k2tog, yo, CDI, yo, ssk, yo, k3tog tbl*, k4] twice; repeat from * to *, k2.

Row 29 K1, [*(k2tog, yo) 3 times, k1 tbl, (yo, ssk) 3 times*, k2] twice, repeat from * to *, k1.

Row 31 K2, [*(yo, k2tog) twice, yo, SK2P, yo, (ssk, yo) twice*, k4] twice; repeat from * to *, k2.

Row 33 K1, [*(ssk, yo) 3 times, k1 tbl, (yo, k2tog) 3 times*, k2] twice; repeat from * to *, k1.

Row 35 K2, (*kbf, yo, ssk, yo, Dec4, yo, k2tog, yo, kfb*, k4) twice; repeat from * to *, k2.

Row 37 K4, (kfb, yo, Dec4, yo, kfb*, k8) twice; repeat from * to *, k4.

Rows 38 and 42 P2tog, purl to the last 2 stitches, p2tog tbl (41 stitches after row 43).

Row 39 Repeat row 23.

Rows 40 and 44 Purl.

Row 41 K10, *k3tog, yo, CDI, yo, k3tog tbl*, k9; repeat from * to *, k10.

Row 43 K7, *k3tog, yo, k2tog, yo, CDI, yo, ssk, yo, k2tog tbl*, k5; repeat from * to *, k7.

Row 45 K6, *[k2tog, yo] 3 times, k1 tbl, [yo, ssk] 3 times*, k3; repeat from * to *, k6.

Row 46 and all WS rows through row 60 P2tog, purl to the last 2 stitches, p2tog tbl.

Row 47 K6, *[yo, k2tog] twice, yo, SK2P, yo, [ssk, yo] twice*, k5; repeat from * to *, k6 (39 stitches).

Row 49 K4, *[ssk, yo] 3 times, k1 tbl, [yo, k2tog] 3 times*, k3; repeat from * to *, k4 (37 stitches).

Row 51 K4, *kbf, yo, ssk, yo, Dec4, yo, k2tog, yo, kfb*, k5; repeat from * to *, k4 (35 stitches).

Row 53 Ssk, k3, kbf, yo, Dec4, yo, kfb*, k9; repeat from * to *, k3, k2tog (31 stitches).

Row 55 Ssk, k3, W3, k13, W3, k3, k2tog (27 stitches).

Rows 57, 59, and 61 Ssk, knit to the last 2 stitches, k2tog (17 stitches after row 61).

Row 62 P2tog, purl to the last 2 stitches, p2tog tbl (15 stitches).

Bind off.

PICOT CHAIN EDGING (MULTIPLE OF 7 STITCHES)

With RS facing, pick up and knit 175 stitches evenly around the perimeter of the circle.

Rnds 1, 3, and 5 Purl.

Rnds 2 and 4 Knit.

Rnd 6 Bind off 6 stitches, *slip stitch on the right-hand needle onto the left-hand needle; using the cable cast on method, cast on 3 stitches; bind off 9 stitches; repeat from * to the last stitch, cast on 3 stitches, bind off 4 stitches.

Fasten off.

....

STAR BRIGHT

Worked in the round from the center to the outer edge

Cast on 10 stitches and divide over 3 needles (4-2-4); mark the beginning of the round and join without twisting.

Rnds 1 and 3 Knit.

Rnd 2 *K1, yo, k1, pm; repeat from * around (3 stitches each section/15 stitches total).

Rnd 4 *K1, yo, k1, [yo] twice, k1, yo; repeat from * around (7/35 stitches).

Rnd 5 *K3, (p1, k1) in double yo of the previous round, k2; repeat from * around.

Rnd 6 *[K1, yo] twice, k2tog, ssk, yo, k1, yo; repeat from * around (9/45 stitches).

Rnd 7 and all odd-numbered rnds Knit.

Rnd 8 *K1, [yo, k1] twice, k2tog, ssk, [k1, yo] twice; repeat from * around (11/55 stitches).

Rnd 10 *[K1, yo] twice, k2, k2tog, ssk, k2, yo, k1, yo; repeat from * around (13/65 stitches).

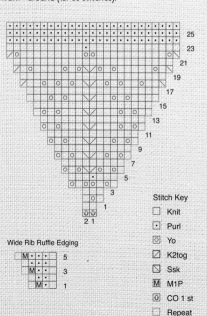

Wide Rib Ruffle Edging

Stitch Key
- ☐ Knit
- · Purl
- ⊙ Yo
- ╲ K2tog
- ╱ Ssk
- M M1P
- Ⓞ CO 1 st
- ☐ Repeat

Rnd 12 *[K1, yo] twice, k3, k2tog, ssk, k3, yo, k1, yo; repeat from * around (15/75 stitches).

Rnd 14 *K2, yo, k1, yo, k3, k2tog, ssk, k3, yo, k1, yo, k1; repeat from * around (17/85 stitches).

Rnd 16 *K4, yo, k1, yo, k2, k2tog, ssk, k2, yo, k1, yo, k3; repeat from * around (19/95 stitches).

Rnd 18 *Ssk, [k2, yo] twice, k1, yo, k1, k2tog, ssk, [k1, yo] 3 times, k2, k2tog; repeat from * around (21/105 stitches).

Rnd 20 *Ssk, k1, yo, k5, yo, k1, yo, k2tog, ssk, yo, k1, yo, k4, yo, k1, k2tog; repeat from * around (23/115 stitches).

Rnd 22 *Ssk, yo, k10, [yo] twice, k9, yo, k2tog; repeat from * around (25/125 stitches).

Rnd 23 *K12, (k1, p1) in double yo, k11; repeat from * around.

Rnds 24, 25, and 26 Purl.

If not working the edging, bind off using a needle one size larger.

WIDE RIB RUFFLE EDGING

Rnd 1 K1, *p1, m1P, k1; repeat from * around (187 stitches).

Rnd 2 K1, *p2, k1; repeat from * around.

Rnd 3 K1, *p2, m1P, k1; repeat from * around (249 stitches).

Rnd 4 K1, *p3, k1; repeat from * around.

Rnd 5 K1, *p3, m1P, k1; repeat from * around (311 stitches).

Bind off in pattern using a needle one size larger.

MORNING BLOOM

Worked in the round from the center to the outer edge
Colors MC and CC

MB (make bobble) Knit in front, back, front of next stitch, turn; [k3, turn] twice, SK2P.

With CC, cast on 8 stitches (2 stitches each on 4 dpns); mark the beginning of the round and join without twisting.
Rnd 1 Knit.
Rnd 2 *Yo, k1; repeat from * around (16 stitches).
Rnds 3 and 5 Knit.
Rnd 4 *Yo, k3, yo, k1 tbl; repeat from * around (24 stitches).
Rnd 6 *Yo, k5, yo, k1 tbl; repeat from * around (32 stitches).
Rnd 7 *K3, MB, pm; repeat from * around (4 stitches each section/32 stitches total).
Change to MC.
Rnd 8 *Yo, k7, yo, k1; repeat from * around (5/40 stitches).
Rnd 9 and all odd-numbered rnds Knit.
Rnd 10 *Yo, ssk, k2tog, yo, k1; repeat from * around.
Rnd 12 *K1, yo, k2tog, yo, k2; repeat from * around (6/48 stitches).
Rnd 14 *K2, yo, k1 tbl, yo, k3; repeat from * around (8/64 stitches).
Rnd 16 *K3, yo, k1 tbl, yo, k4; repeat from * around (10/80 stitches).
Rnd 18 *K4, yo, k1 tbl, yo, k5; repeat from * around (12/96 stitches).
Rnd 20 *K5, yo, k1 tbl, yo, k6; repeat from * around (14/112 stitches).
Rnd 22 *K6, yo, k1 tbl, yo, k7; repeat from * around (16/128 stitches).
Rnd 24 *K7, yo, k1 tbl, yo, k8; repeat from * around (18/144 stitches).

Rnd 26 *Ssk, k5, yo, k3, yo, k5, k2tog, p1; repeat from * around.
Rnd 28 *Ssk, k4, yo, k5, yo, k4, k2tog, p1; repeat from * around.
Rnd 30 *Ssk, k3, yo, k1, yo, ssk, k1, k2tog, yo, k1, yo, k3, k2tog, p1; repeat from * around.
Rnd 32 *Ssk, k2, yo, k3, yo, SK2P, yo, k3, yo, k2, k2tog, p1; repeat from * around.
Rnd 34 *Ssk, k1, yo, k11, yo, k1, k2tog, p1; repeat from * around.
Rnd 36 *Ssk, yo, k1, [yo, ssk, k1, k2tog, yo, k1] twice, yo, k2tog, p1; repeat from * around.
Rnd 38 Remove marker and k1, pm for new end of rnd.
*Yo, [k3, yo, SK2P, yo] 5 times, k3, yo, SK2P; repeat from * around.
Bind off using a needle one size larger.

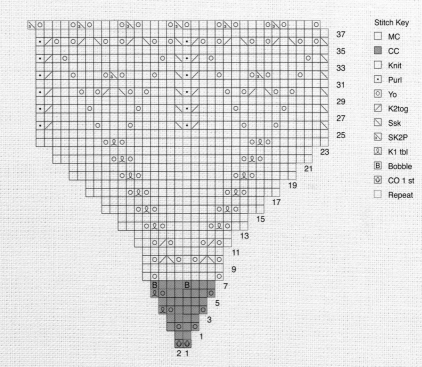

Stitch Key
- ☐ MC
- ■ CC
- ☐ Knit
- · Purl
- ○ Yo
- ╱ K2tog
- ╲ Ssk
- ╲ SK2P
- ℓ K1 tbl
- Ⓑ Bobble
- Ⓞ CO 1 st
- ☐ Repeat

LACY SWIRL

Worked in the round from the center to the outer edge

Cast on 8 stitches (2 stitches each on 4 dpns); mark the beginning of the round and join without twisting.

Rnds 1, 2, 4, and 8 Knit.

Rnd 3 *Yo, k1, pm; repeat from * around (2 stitches each section/16 stitches total).

Rnd 5 *Yo, k1; repeat from * around (4/32 stitches).

Rnd 6 *K2, k2tog; repeat from * around (3/24 stitches).

Rnd 7 *Yo, k1, yo, k2tog; repeat from * around (4/32 stitches).

Rnd 9 *[Yo, k1] twice, yo, k2tog; repeat from * around (6/48 stitches).

Rnd 10 *K4, k2tog; repeat from * around (5/40 stitches).

Rnd 11 *[Yo, k1] 3 times, k2tog; repeat from * around (7/56 stitches).

Rnd 12 *K5, k2tog; repeat from * around (6/48 stitches).

Rnd 13 *[Yo, k1] twice, yo, k2, k2tog; repeat from * around (8/64 stitches).

Rnd 14 *K6, k2tog; repeat from * around (7/56 stitches).

Rnd 15 *[Yo, k1] twice, yo, k3, k2tog; repeat from * around (9/72 stitches).

Rnd 16 *K7, k2tog; repeat from * around (8/64 stitches).

Rnd 17 *[Yo, k1] twice, yo, k4, k2tog; repeat from * around (10/80 stitches).

Rnd 18 *K8, k2tog; repeat from * around (9/72 stitches).

Rnd 19 *[Yo, k1] twice, yo, k5, k2tog; repeat from * around (11/88 stitches).

Rnd 20 *K9, k2tog; repeat from * around (10/80 stitches).

Rnd 21 *[Yo, k1] twice, yo, k6, k2tog; repeat from * around (12/96 stitches).

Rnd 22 *K10, k2tog; repeat from * around (11/88 stitches).

Rnd 23 *[Yo, k1] twice, yo, k7, k2tog; repeat from * around (13/104 stitches).

Rnd 24 *K11, k2tog; repeat from * around (12/96 stitches).

Rnd 25 *[Yo, k1] twice, yo, k8, k2tog; repeat from * around (14/112 stitches).

Rnd 26 *K12, k2tog; repeat from * around (13/104 stitches).

Rnd 27 *[Yo, k1] twice, yo, k9, k2tog; repeat from * around (15/120 stitches).

Rnd 28 *K13, k2tog; repeat from * around (14/112 stitches).

Rnd 29 *[Yo, k1] twice, yo, k10, k2tog; repeat from * around (16/128 stitches).

Rnd 30 *K14, k2tog; repeat from * around (15/120 stitches).

Rnd 31 *[Yo, k1] twice, yo, k11, k2tog; repeat from * around (17/136 stitches).

Rnd 32 *K15, k2tog; repeat from * around (16/128 stitches).

Rnd 33 *[Yo, k1] twice, yo, k12, k2tog; repeat from * around (18/144 stitches).

Rnd 34 *K16, k2tog; repeat from * around (17/136 stitches).

If not working edging, bind off using a needle one size larger.

REVERSE STOCKINETTE ST EDGING

Rnds 1 and 2 Purl.

Bind off using a needle one size larger.

Note For a smaller circle, work to desired size, end on an odd-numbered row, and bind off. For a larger circle, continue increasing and decreasing as established, working one more stitch before the increase or decrease on each round.

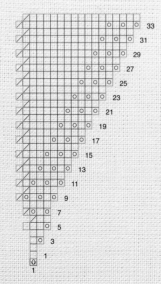

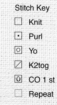

Stitch Key

☐ Knit
· Purl
◯ Yo
◿ K2tog
◙ CO 1 st
☐ Repeat

Reverse Stockinette Stitch Edging

STELLA LUNA

Worked in the round from the outer edge to the center

MB (make bobble) [Kfb] twice in the same stitch, turn; p4, turn; k4, turn; p4tog.

Cast on 168 stitches. Mark the beginning of the round and join without twisting.

Rnds 1, 3, 5, 7, 9, and 11 Knit.

Rnds 2, 4, 6, 8 10, and 12 *K1, yo, k3, ssk, yo, SK2P, yo, k2tog, k3, yo, pm; repeat from * around (14 stitches each section/168 stitches total). **Note** Slip markers after rnd 2.

Rnd 13 Knit to the last stitch, slip the last stitch onto the first dpn for a new beginning of rnd; move other markers 1 stitch over when you come to them or remove them.

Rnd 14 *SK2P, [k2tog] twice; repeat from * around (6/72 stitches).

Stitch Key

□	Knit
·	Purl
○	Yo
╱	K2tog
╲	Ssk
╲	Sk2p
B	Bobble
□	Repeat
□	Knit in each rep until last rep, then end last rep before this st; it is worked with the dec at the beg of the next rnd

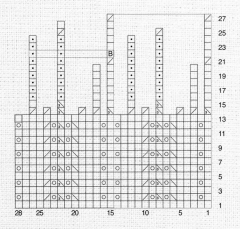

Rnd 15 *K2, SK2P, k1; repeat from * around (4/48 stitches).

Rnds 16–20 *K2, p2; repeat from * around.

Rnd 21 *K2tog, p2; repeat from * around (3/36 stitches).

Rnd 22 *K1, p2, MB, p2; repeat from * around.

Rnds 23 and 24 *K1, p2; repeat from * around.

Rnd 25 *K1, k2tog; repeat from * around (2/24 stitches).

Rnd 26 Knit.

Rnd 27 *K2tog; repeat from * around (12 stitches).

Break the yarn. Thread tail through the remaining stitches, pull tight, and secure.

ILLUMINATOR

Worked with short rows

Loosely cast on 15 sts.

Row 1 (RS) Sl 1, k9, yo, p2tog, k1, yo, k2 (16 stitches).

Row 2 K4, yo, p2tog, p8. Turn, leaving last 2 stitches unworked.

Row 3 Sl 1, k7, yo, p2tog, k2, yo, k2 (17 stitches).

Row 4 K5, yo, p2tog, p6. Turn, leaving last 4 stitches unworked.

Row 5 Sl 1, k5, yo, p2tog, k3, yo, k2 (18 stitches).

Row 6 K6, yo, p2tog, p4. Turn, leaving last 6 stitches unworked.

Row 7 Sl 1, k3, yo, p2tog, k2tog, [yo] twice, k2, yo, k2 (20 stitches).

Row 8 K5, [p1, k1] in double yo of previous row, k1, yo, p2tog, p2. Turn, leaving last 8 stitches unworked.

Row 9 Sl 1, k1, yo, p2tog, k8.

Row 10 Loosely bind off 5 stitches (1 stitch on right-hand needle), k2, [yo, p2tog] 5 times, p2.

Repeat rows 1–10 fifteen more times.

Bind off. Sew bound off edge to cast-on edge.

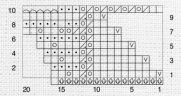

Stitch Key

□	K on RS, P on WS
·	Knit on WS
⓪	CO 1 st
○	Yo
╱	K2tog on RS, P2tog on WS
╱	P2tog on RS
∨	Slip 1 wyib
⌢	Bind off
□	Repeat

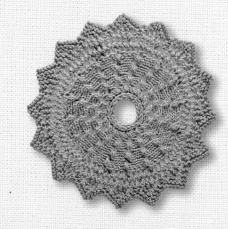

Optional To close circle, thread yarn through end stitches at center, pull tightly to gather, and secure.

COLORWORK

Colorwork ttechniques can make any basic circle interesting and unique. I've enhanced some of the circles we
learned in Round I with intarsia, stripes, motifs, duplicate
stitch, and two-color medallions. Again, make sure to note
some of the color edgings and textures that finish off the
circles as you can decide to use them as a design detail for a
different circle. Feel inspired to make your own colorwork
designs and add a little (or a lot) of color to your life.

Examples of these techniques used in projects are the
Hoopla Bag on page 202, Kaleidoscope Afghan on page
200, and Circle Sampler Afghan on page 198.

orbit (bi-color)
page 134

rotunda
page 135

dots
page 136

karma
page 136

yin/yang
page 137

*fair isle
image*
page 139

*fractal
fair isle*
page 139

sailing
page 140

spheroid
page 140

stallion
(textures)
page 141

kismet
page 141

western hemisphere (North and South America)
page 142

starry night
page 143

jacobean bluebird

page 144

halo color orb
page 144

rosey
page 145

queen of
hearts
page 146

tick tock
clock
page 147

ORBIT (*bi-color*)

Worked in short rows

Colors MC and CC

With MC, cast on 22 stitches.

Row 1 (RS) Knit.

Row 2 [K1, p1] 9 times, k1, W&T, leaving 3 stitches unworked (including wrapped stitch).

Row 3 and all RS rows Knit.

Row 4 [K1, p1] 8 times, k1, W&T, leaving 5 stitches unworked.

Row 6 [K1, p1] 7 times, k1, W&T, leaving 7 stitches unworked.

Row 8 [K1, p1] 6 times, k1, W&T, leaving 9 stitches unworked.

Row 10 [K1, p1] 5 times, k1, W&T, leaving 11 stitches unworked.

Row 12 [K1, p1] 4 times, k1, W&T, leaving 13 stitches unworked.

Row 14 [K1, p1] 3 times, k1, W&T, leaving 15 stitches unworked.

Row 16 [K1, p1] twice, k1, W&T, leaving 17 stitches unworked.

Row 18 K1, p1, k1, W&T, leaving 19 stitches unworked.

Row 20 K1, W&T, leaving 21 stitches unworked.

Row 22 *K1, p1; repeat from * to end, lifting each wrap and working it together with its wrapped stitch.

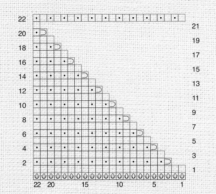

Break off MC and join CC. Work rows 1–22 with CC. Work 6 more sections alternating colors MC and CC for 8 sections total.

Bind off and sew cast-on edge to bound-off edge.

2-COLOR STRIPED RIBBED EDGING

With RS facing and CC, pick up and knit 116 stitches evenly around circumference of circle, pm.

Rnds 1 and 2 *K1, p1; repeat from * around.

Change to MC.

Rnd 3 Knit.

Bind off using a needle one size larger.

Optional Sew a decorative button at the center of the circle.

Stitch Key

☐ MC

▨ CC

⊑ K on RS, P on WS

⊡ P on RS, K on WS

◗ W&T on WS

⊙ CO 1 st

☐ Repeat

2-Color Ribbed Edging

HOOPS (*circle ridges*)

Worked in the round from the center to the outer edge

Colors MC and CC

With MC, cast on 12 stitches (4 stitches each on 3 dpns). Mark the beginning of the round and join without twisting.

Rnd 1 Knit.

Rnd 2 *Kfb, pm; repeat from * around (2 stitches each section/24 stitches total).

Rnd 3 Knit.

Change to CC.

Rnds 4–6 Purl.

Change to MC.

Rnd 7 Knit.

Rnd 8 *K1, kfb; repeat from * around (3/36 stitches).

Rnd 9 Knit.

Change to CC.

Rnds 10–12 Purl.

Change to MC.

Rnd 13 Knit.

Rnd 14 *Knit to 1 stitch before marker, kfb; repeat from * around (4/48 stitches).

Rnd 15 Knit.

Continue working the last 6 rnds in pattern as established, changing colors every 3 rnds, until there are 10 stitches in each section (120 stitches) or to desired size. End with a knit round after an increase round with MC.

GARTER ST EDGING

Change to CC.

Rnds 1, 3, and 5 Purl.

Rnds 2 and 4 Knit.

Bind off using a needle one size larger.

Stitch Key

☐ MC

▨ CC

☐ Knit

⊡ Purl

◺ Kfb

☐ Repeat

Garter Stitch Edging

ROTUNDA

Worked back and forth from the outer edge to the center

Colors A, B, C, and D

Note Work the colors with the intarsia method, using separate balls of yarn for each section and twisting yarns on the wrong side to prevent holes from forming when changing colors. Maintain color changes as established throughout unless noted otherwise.

MB (make bobble) [K1, p1] twice, in the same stitch, turn; p4, turn; k4, turn; p4, turn; k4, pass the 2nd, 3rd, and 4th stitches, one at a time, over the first stitch. Slip the bobble stitch onto the right-hand needle.

With A, cast on 158 stitches.
Work 3 rows in K1, P1 Rib.
Setup row (WS) With A, p27; with B, *p26; repeat from * with A, C, A, and D, ending p1 with D.
Row 1 With A, k1, *ssk, k22, k2tog; repeat from * with each color as established, k1 (24 stitches each section plus 2 selvedge stitches/146 stitches total).
Row 2 and all WS rows Purl, maintaining color changes.
Rows 3, 9, 21, and 27 Knit, maintaining color changes.
Row 5 With A, k1, *ssk, k20, k2tog; repeat from * with each color as established, k1 (22/134 stitches).
Row 7 With A, k1, *ssk, k7, MB, k2, MB, k7, k2tog; repeat

from * with each color as established, k1 (20/122 stitches).
Row 11 With A, k1, *ssk, k16, k2tog; repeat from * with each color as established, k1 (18/110 stitches).
Row 13 With A, k1, *ssk, k14, k2tog; repeat from * with each color as established, k1 (16/98 stitches).
Row 14 With A only, purl.
Row 15 With A only, knit.
Row 17 With A, k1, *ssk, k12, k2tog; repeat from * with each color as established, k1 (14/86 stitches).
Row 19 With A, k1, *ssk, k10, k2tog; repeat from * with each color as established, k1 (12/74 stitches).
Row 23 With A, k1, *ssk, [k2, MB] twice, k2, k2tog; repeat from * with each color as established, k1 (10/62 stitches).
Row 25 With A, k1, *ssk, k6, k2tog; repeat from * with each color as established, k1 (8/50 stitches).
Row 29 With A, k1, *ssk, k4, k2tog; repeat from * with each color as established, k1 (6/38 stitches).
Row 31 With A, k1, *ssk, k2, k2tog; repeat from * with each color as established, k1 (4/26 stitches).
Row 33 With A, k1, *ssk, k2tog; repeat from * with each color as established, k1 (2/14 stitches).
Row 34 With A, p1, *p2tog; repeat from * with each color as established, p1 (8 stitches).
Bind off and break off yarns, leaving a long tail of A or D. Thread the tail through the remaining stitches and sew the cast-on edge to the bound-off edge.

K1, P1 EDGING

With RS facing and A, pick up and knit 150 stitches evenly around the circumference of the circle, pm.
Rnds 1–3 *K1, p1; repeat from * around.
Bind off in pattern using a needle one size larger.

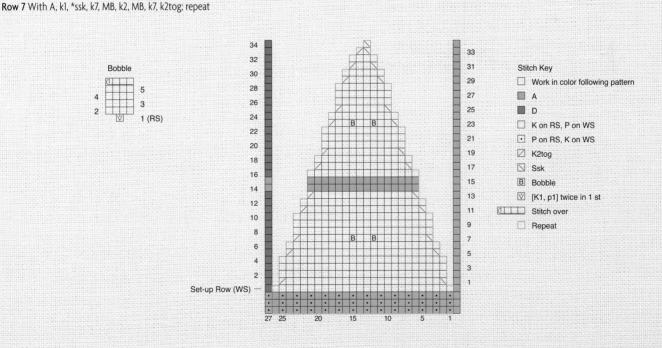

Bobble

Stitch Key

☐ Work in color following pattern
▨ A
▨ D
☐ K on RS, P on WS
⊡ P on RS, K on WS
▧ K2tog
◺ Ssk
Ⓑ Bobble
Ⓥ [K1, p1] twice in 1 st
▭ Stitch over
☐ Repeat

DOTS

Worked from the bottom
Colors MC and CC

With MC, make a Stockinette St Circle (see page 52).

2-COLOR GARTER ST EDGING

With RS facing and CC, pick up and knit 120 stitches evenly around the edge of the circle, pm.
Rnd 1 Purl.

Change to MC.
Rnd 2 Knit.
Rnd 3 Purl.
Change to CC.
Rnds 4 and 5 Repeat rnds 2 and 3.
Bind off knitwise with a needle one size larger.

DOTS (MAKE 10)

With CC, loosely cast on 20 stitches.
Knit 3 rows.
Pass all stitches, one at a time, over the first stitch.
Fasten off.
Sew dots to the circle as shown.

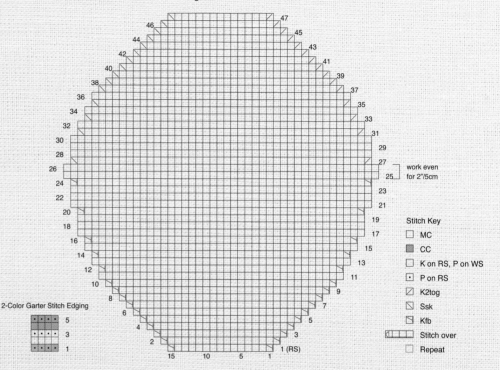

work even for 2"/5cm

Stitch Key
☐ MC
▨ CC
☐ K on RS, P on WS
• P on RS
◪ K2tog
◩ Ssk
◪ Kfb
▥ Stitch over
☐ Repeat

KARMA

Worked in the round from the outer edge to the center
Colors MC and CC

LOOP EDGING

With CC, cast on 200 stitches.
Row 1 Bind off 3 stitches, *k1, bind off the next 3 stitches; repeat from * to end (50 stitches).
Row 2 *K1, cast on 2 stitches; repeat from * to end (150 stitches).
Mark the beginning of the rnd and join without twisting.
BODY
Setup rnd *Work 25 stitches of the Karma chart, pm; repeat from * around.
Complete 24 rnds of chart, working decreases in colors as charted.
Dec rnds 3, 5, 7, 9, 11, 13, 15, 17, 19, 21, and 23 *K2tog, work to last 2 stitches of chart, ssk; repeat from * around (18 stitches after rnd 23).
Rnd 25 With CC, *k2tog; repeat from * around (9 stitches). Break the yarn. Thread the tail through the remaining 9 stitches, pull tight, and secure.

Stitch Key
☐ MC
▨ CC
☐ K on RS, P on WS
• P on RS, K on WS
◪ K2tog
◩ Ssk
◎ Cast on 1 st
⌒ Bind off 1 st
■ No stitch
☐ Repeat

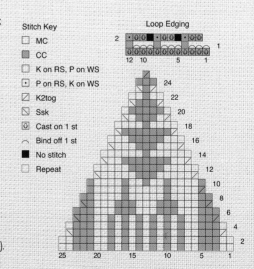

YIN/YANG

Worked from the bottom

Colors A and B

Note Work the colors with the intarsia method, using separate balls of yarn for each section and twisting yarns on wrong side to prevent holes when changing colors.

With MC, cast on 13 stitches.
Work 62 rows of the Yin / Yang chart. Bind off.

K2, P2 EDGING

With RS facing and MC, pick up and knit 144 stitches evenly around the circumference of the circle, pm.

Rnds 1–3 *K2, p2; repeat from * around.

Bind off in pattern using a needle one size larger.

K2, P2 Edging

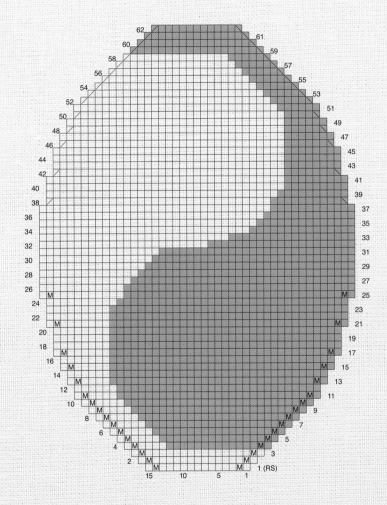

Stitch Key

☐ MC

▨ CC

☐ K on RS, P on WS

· Purl

◩ K2tog on RS, p2tog on WS

◪ Ssk on RS, ssp on WS

Ⓜ M1 on RS, M1P on WS

☐ Repeat

MODERN FAIR ISLE

GARTER ST EDGING

With RS facing and CC, pick up and knit 140 stitches evenly around the circumference of the circle, pm.

Rnd 1 Knit.

Rnd 2 Purl.

Change to MC.

Rnds 3 and 4 Repeat rnds 1 and 2.

Bind off using a needle one size larger.

Worked from the bottom

Colors MC and CC

With MC, cast on 13 stitches.

Work 64 rows of the Modern Fair Isle chart. Bind off.

Note Floats should be caught up every other stitch.

Stitch Key
- ☐ MC
- ▨ CC
- ☐ K on RS, P on WS
- ⬚ Purl
- ▨ K2tog on RS, p2tog on WS
- ◹ Ssk on RS, ssp on WS
- ⋈ M1 on RS, M1P on WS
- ☐ Repeat

Garter Stitch Edging

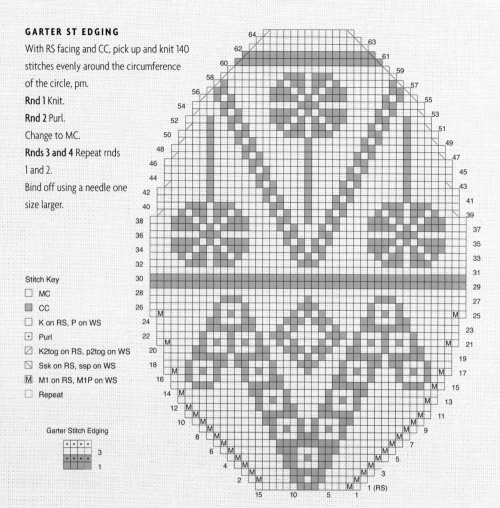

RETRO BOUQUET

Worked from the bottom with embroidery

Colors A, B, C, D, and E

With A, make a Stockinette St Circle (see page 52).

EMBROIDERY

Following the diagram, use French knots to make border flowers and centers.

Use Stem stitch to make stems of border flowers.

Use long and short stitches to make flowers at the center.

Stitch Key
- ☐ Yellow (B)
- ▨ Gold (C)
- ☐ Pink (D)
- ■ Brown (E)

Border Flowers and Centers = French Knots

Stems = Stem Stitch

Center Flower = Long and Short Stitches

FAIR ISLE IMAGE

Worked from the bottom

Colors A, B, and C

With B, cast on 13 stitches.
Work 32 rows of the Fair Isle Image chart, then work in reverse from rows 31 to 1. Bind off.

GARTER ST EDGING

With RS facing and A, pick up and knit 140 stitches evenly around the circumference of the circle, pm.

Rnd 1 Purl.

Change to C.

Rnd 2 Knit.

Rnd 3 Purl.

Bind off using a needle one size larger.

Stitch Key
- A
- B
- C
- K on RS, P on WS
- P on RS
- Repeat

Work Rows 1-32 once, then work in reverse from Row 31 to Row 1.

Garter Stitch Edging

FRACTAL FAIR ISLE

Worked in the round from the outer edge to the center

Colors A, B, C, and D

DOUBLE ROLLED STOCKINETTE ST EDGE

With A and a circular needle, cast on 144 stitches; pm and join without twisting.

Rnds 1–6 Knit.

Put aside.

With B and a second circular needle, cast on 144 stitches; pm and join without twisting.

Rnds 1–4 Knit.

Place the needle with A behind the needle with B; *with B, knit one stitch B together with one stitch A; repeat from * around.

BODY

Setup rnd *Work 12 stitches of the Fractal chart, pm; repeat from * around.

Complete 17 rnds of the chart, working decreases in colors as charted.

Dec rnds 6, 8, 10–16 *Ssk, work to the end of the chart; repeat from * around.

Rnds 17 and 18 With A, *k2tog; repeat from * around (9 stitches after rnd 18).

Break the yarn. Thread the tail through the remaining 9 stitches, pull tight, and secure.

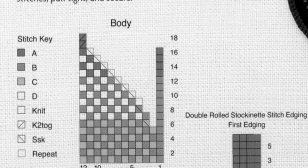

Body

Stitch Key
- A
- B
- C
- D
- Knit
- K2tog
- Ssk
- Repeat

Double Rolled Stockinette Stitch Edging
First Edging

Double Rolled Stockinette Stitch Edging
Second Edging

SAILING

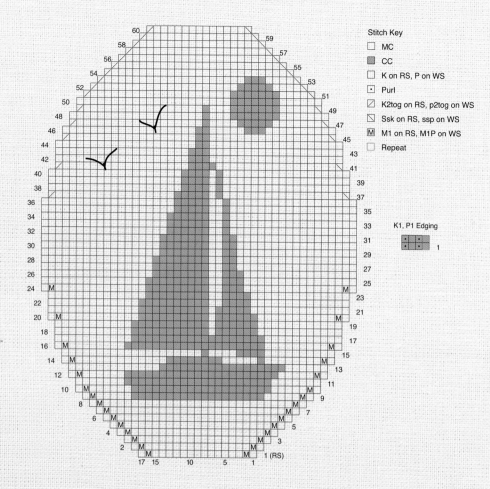

Stitch Key

☐ MC
▨ CC
☐ K on RS, P on WS
· Purl
▨ K2tog on RS, p2tog on WS
◩ Ssk on RS, ssp on WS
Ⓜ M1 on RS, M1P on WS
☐ Repeat

K1, P1 Edging

Worked from the bottom

Colors MC and CC

With MC, cast on 15 stitches.

Make a solid circle, following the Sailing chart, working increase and decrease rows the same as for the Stockinette St Circle (see page 52). With CC, use Duplicate stitch for the sailboat and sun, and Long stitch with a twist for the birds.

K1, P1 EDGING

With RS facing and CC, pick up and knit 140 stitches evenly around the circumference of the circle, pm.

Rnds 1 and 2 *K1, p1; repeat from * around.

Bind off in pattern using a needle one size larger.

SPHEROID

Worked in the round from the outer edge to the center

Colors MC and CC

PICOT HEM

With MC, cast on 150 stitches. Mark the beginning of the round and join without twisting.

Picot Hem

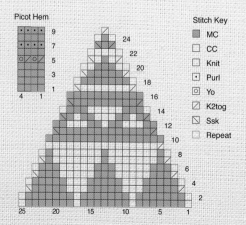

Stitch Key

▨ MC
☐ CC
▨ Knit
· Purl
◎ Yo
▨ K2tog
◩ Ssk
☐ Repeat

Rnds 1–4 Knit.

Rnd 5 *K2tog, yo; repeat from * around.

Rnds 6 and 8 Knit.

Rnds 7 and 9 Purl.

BODY

Setup rnd *Work 25 stitches of the Spheroid chart, pm; repeat from * around.

Complete 24 rnds of chart, working decreases in colors as charted.

Dec rnds 3, 5, 7, 9, 11, 13, 15, 17, 19, 21, and 23 *K2tog, work to last 2 stitches of chart, ssk; repeat from * around (18 stitches on last rnd).

Rnd 25 With CC, *k2tog; repeat from * around (9 stitches). Break the yarn. Thread the tail through the remaining 9 stitches, pull tight, and secure.

Fold the picot hem to the WS and sew in place.

STALLION

Worked from the bottom
Colors MC and CC

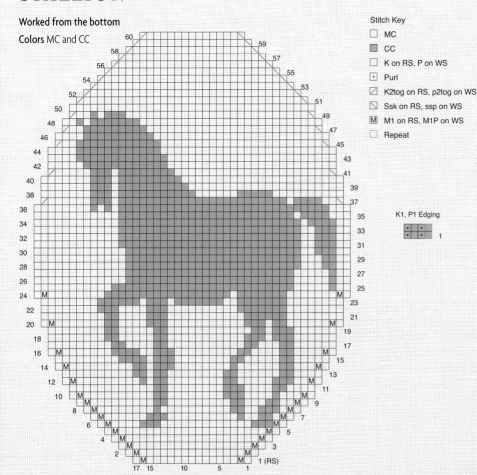

K1, P1 Edging

With MC, cast on 15 stitches.

Make a solid circle following the Stallion chart, working increase and decrease rows the same as for the Stockinette St Circle (see page 52). With CC, use Duplicate stitch for the horse.

K1, P1 EDGING

With RS facing and CC, pick up and knit 140 stitches evenly around the circumference of the circle, pm.
Rnds 1 and 2 *K1, p1; repeat from * around.
Bind off in pattern using a needle one size larger.

KISMET

Worked in the round from the outer edge to the center
Colors MC and CC

LOOP EDGING

With CC, cast on 200 stitches.
Row 1 Bind off 3 stitches, *k1, bind off the next 3 stitches; repeat from * to end (50 stitches).
Row 2 *K1, cast on 2 stitches; repeat from * to end (150 stitches).

BODY

Setup row (RS) *Work 25 stitches of the Kismet chart, pm; repeat from * around; mark the beginning of the rnd and join without twisting.
Complete 24 rnds of the chart, working decreases in colors as charted.

Dec rnds 3, 5, 7, 9, 11, 13, 15, 17, 19, 21, and 23 *K2tog, work to the last 2 stitches of the chart, ssk; repeat from * around (18 stitches after rnd 23).

Loop Edging

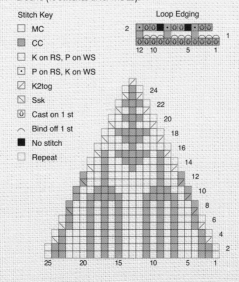

Rnd 25 With MC, *k2tog; repeat from * around (9 stitches).
Break the yarn. Thread the tail through the remaining 9 stitches, pull tight, and secure.

WESTERN HEMISPHERE (*North and South America*)

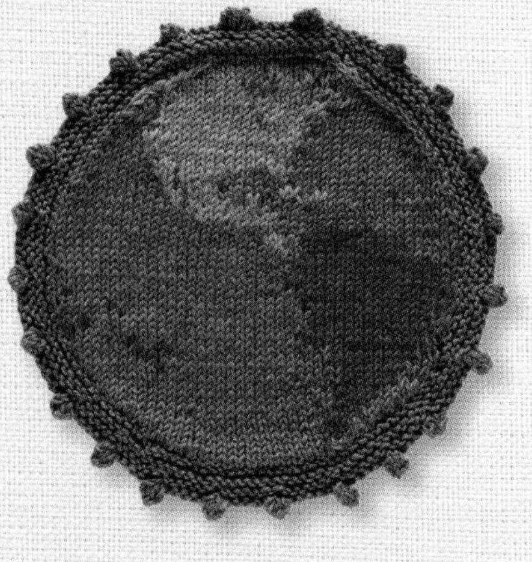

Worked from the bottom

Colors A, B, and C

Note Work the colors with the intarsia method, using separate balls of yarn for each section and twisting yarns on wrong side to prevent holes when changing colors.

With A, cast on 15 stitches.

Work 60 rows of the Western Hemisphere chart, working increase and decrease rows the same as for the Stockinette St Circle (see page 52). Bind off.

GARTER ST BOBBLE EDGING

MB (make bobble) [K1, p1] twice in the next stitch, turn; p4, turn; k4, turn; [p2tog] twice, turn; k2tog.

With MC, cast on 157 stitches.

Row 1 (WS) Knit.

Row 2 (RS) K3, *MB, k5; repeat from * to the last 4 stitches, MB, k3.

Rows 3–8 Knit.

Bind off. Sew the edging around the circle. Sew the ends of the edging together.

Stitch Key

- A
- B
- C
- K on RS, P on WS
- K on WS
- K2tog on RS, p2tog on WS
- Ssk on RS, ssp on WS
- M1 on RS, M1P on WS
- Bobble
- [K1, p1] twice in 1 st
- Repeat

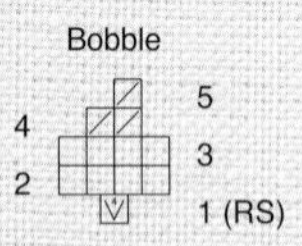

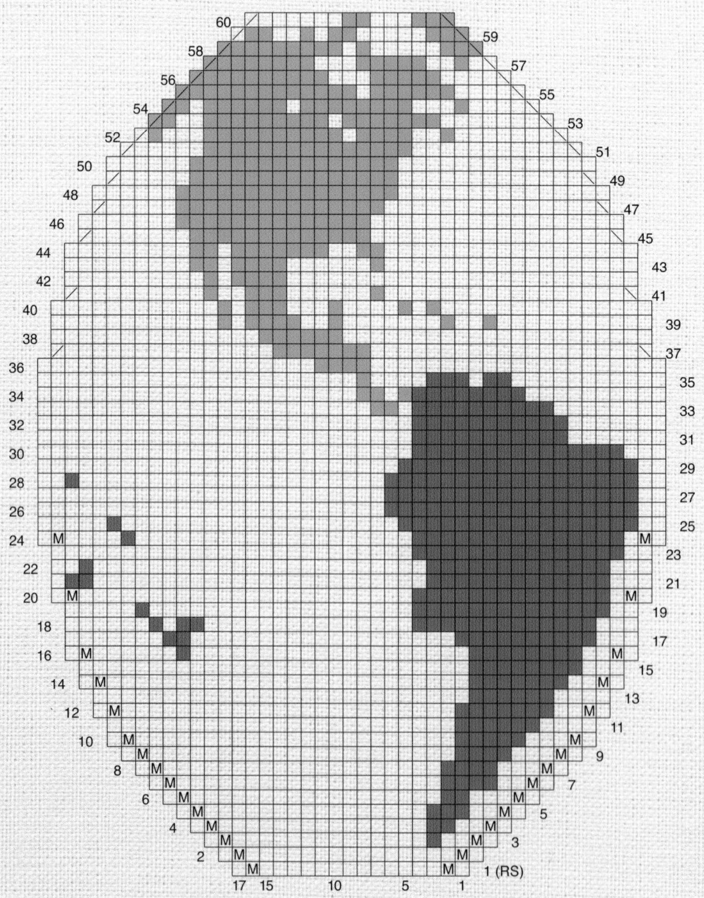

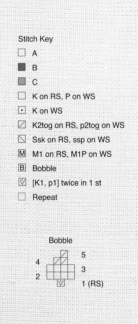

STARRY NIGHT

Worked from the bottom

Colors A, B, and C

Note Work the colors with the intarsia method, using separate balls of yarn for each section and twisting yarns on wrong side to prevent holes when changing colors.

With A, cast on 13 stitches.

Work 62 rows of the Starry Night chart, working increase and decrease rows the same as for the Stockinette St Circle (see page 52). **Note** Work decreases one stitch from edge along the side of the moon. Bind off.

SHELL EDGING

With B, cast on 162 stitches.

Row 1 (RS) K1, yo, *k5, slip the 2nd, 3rd, 4th, and 5th stitches over the first stitch, yo; repeat from * to the last stitch, k1.

Row 2 P1, *(p1, yo, k1 tbl) in the next stitch, p1; repeat from * to end.

Row 3 K2, k1 tbl, *k3, k1 tbl; repeat from * to the last 2 stitches, k2.

Rows 4–6 Knit.

Bind off. Sew edging around circle. Sew ends of edging together.

Stitch Key

- ▨ A
- ☐ B
- ▨ C
- ☐ K on RS, P on WS
- · P on RS, K on WS
- ⊙ Yo
- ◸ K2tog on RS, p2tog on WS
- ◺ Ssk on RS, ssp on WS
- Ⓜ M1 on RS, M1P on WS
- ℓ K1 tbl
- ℣ (p1, yo, k1 tbl) in same st
- ⊏⊥⊥⊥⊐ K5, slip 2nd, 3rd, 4th, and 5th sts over first st
- ■ No stitch
- ☐ Repeat

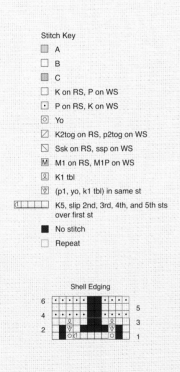

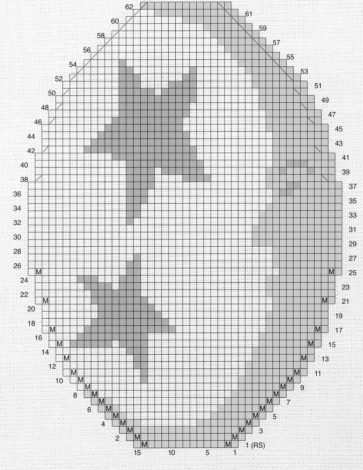

JACOBEAN BLUEBIRD

Worked from the bottom
Colors A, B, C, D, E, F, G, and H

With A, cast on 13 stitches. Make a solid circle following the Bluebird Jacobean chart, working increase and decrease rows the same as for the Stockinette St Circle (see page 52). Use Duplicate stitch for the bird, flowers, leaves, and branches. Use French knots for the bird's eye and flower centers. Use Straight stitch for the stamens.

SEED ST EDGING

With B, pick up and knit 141 stitches evenly around the circumference of the circle, pm.
Rnds 1 and 3 K1, *p1, k1; repeat from * around.
Rnd 2 P1, *k1, p1; repeat from * around.
Bind off in pattern using a needle one size larger.

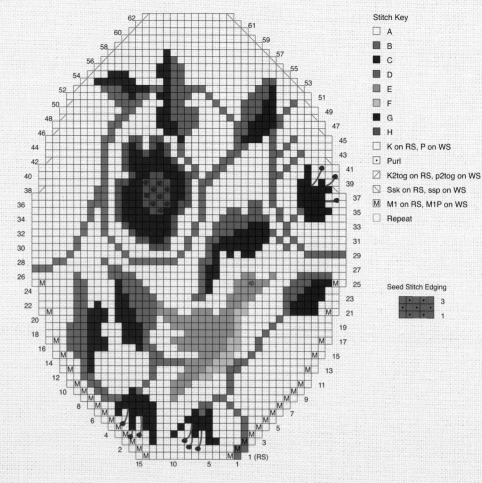

Stitch Key

☐	A
▨	B
■	C
▨	D
▨	E
▨	F
■	G
▨	H
☐	K on RS, P on WS
·	Purl
⧄	K2tog on RS, p2tog on WS
⧅	Ssk on RS, ssp on WS
M	M1 on RS, M1P on WS
☐	Repeat

Seed Stitch Edging

HALO COLOR ORB

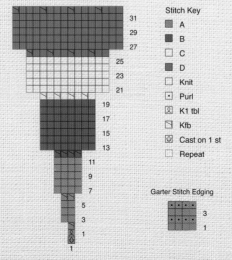

Stitch Key

▨	A
▨	B
☐	C
▨	D
☐	Knit
·	Purl
⊠	K1 tbl
⧖	Kfb
⊍	Cast on 1 st
☐	Repeat

Garter Stitch Edging

Worked in the round from the center to the outer edge
Colors A, B, C, and D

With A, cast on 8 stitches (2 stitches each on 4 dpns); mark the beginning of the round and join without twisting.
Rnd 1 *K1 tbl; repeat from * around.
Rnd 2 *Kfb; repeat from * around (16 stitches).
Rnds 3–5 Knit.
Rnd 6 *Kfb; repeat from * to end (32 stitches).
Rnds 7–11 Knit.
Change to B.
Rnd 12 *Kfb; repeat from * to end (64 stitches).

Rnds 13–19 Knit.

Change to C.

Rnd 20 *K1, kfb; repeat from * to end (96 stitches).

Rnds 21–25 Knit.

Change to D.

Rnd 26 *K2, kfb; repeat from * to end (128 stitches).

Rnds 27–31 Knit.

Rnd 32 *K3, kfb; repeat from * to end (160 stitches).

If not working edging, bind off using a needle one size larger.

GARTER ST EDGING

Change to A.

Rnds 1 and 3 Knit.

Rnds 2 and 4 Purl.

Bind off using a needle one size larger.

ROSEY

Worked from the bottom

Colors MC and CC

With MC, make a Stockinette St Circle (see page 52) as charted, beginning with 13 stitches.
Following the Rosey chart, use Duplicate stitch for the rose and bars.

SCALLOPED EDGING

With CC, cast on 5 stitches.

Row 1 (RS) K2, yo, k1, yo, k2 (7 stitches).

Row 2 P6, m1, k1 (8 stitches).

Row 3 K1, p1, k2, yo, k1, yo, k3 (10 stitches).

Row 4 P8, m1, k2 (11 stitches).

Row 5 K1, p2, k3, yo, k1, yo, k4 (13 stitches).

Row 6 P10, m1, k3 (14 stitches).

Row 7 K1, p3, k4, yo, k1, yo, k5 (16 stitches).

Row 8 P12, m1, k4 (17 stitches).

Row 9 K1, p4, ssk, k7, k2tog, k1 (15 stitches).

Row 10 P10, m1, k5 (16 stitches).

Row 11 K1, p5, ssk, k5, k2tog, k1 (14 stitches).

Row 12 P8, m1, k2, p1, k3 (15 stitches).

Row 13 K1, p1, k1, p4, ssk, k3, k2tog, k1 (13 stitches).

Row 14 P6, m1, k3, p1, k3 (14 stitches).

Row 15 K1, p1, k1, p5, ssk, k1, k2tog, k1 (12 stitches).

Row 16 P4, m1, k4, p1, k3 (13 stitches).

Row 17 K1, p1, k1, p6, SK2P, k1 (11 stitches).

Row 18 P2tog, bind off the next 5 stitches, purl to the last stitch, k1 (5 stitches).

Repeat rows 1–18 ten more times (11 leaves).

Bind off. Break the yarn, leaving a long tail. Sew the bound-off edge to the cast-on edge. With RS facing, sew the Reverse Stockinette st edge of the edging to the outer edge of the circle.

Stitch Key

☐	MC
■	CC
☐	K on RS, P on WS
·	P on RS, K on WS
◯	Yo
╱	K2tog on RS, p2tog on WS
╲	Ssk on RS, ssp on WS
◣	SK2P
M	M1 on RS, M1P on WS
◎	Cast on 1 st
⌒	Bind off 1 st
☐	Repeat

Scalloped Edging

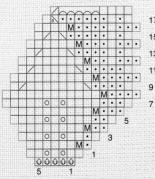

QUEEN OF HEARTS

Worked back and forth from the outer edge to the center

Colors A, B, C, D, E, and F

Note Work the colors with the intarsia method, using separate balls of yarn for each section and twisting yarns on the wrong side to prevent holes when changing colors. Maintain color changes as established throughout, unless noted otherwise.

With A, cast on 158 stitches.
Knit 4 rows for Garter St Edging.
Setup row (WS) With F, p27; with E, *p26; repeat from *
with D, C, B, and A, ending p1 with A.

Row 1 With A, k1, *ssk, k22, k2tog; repeat from * with each color as established, k1 (24 stitches each section plus 2 selvedge stitches/146 stitches total).

Row 2 and all WS rows Purl, maintaining color changes.

Rows 3, 9, 15, 21, and 27 Knit, maintaining color changes.

Row 5 With A, k1, *ssk, k20, k2tog; repeat from * with each color as established, k1 (22/134 stitches).

Row 7 With A, k1, *ssk, k18, k2tog; repeat from * with each color as established, k1 (20/122 stitches).

Row 11 With A, k1, *ssk, k16, k2tog; repeat from * with each color as established, k1 (18/110 stitches).

Row 13 With A, k1, *ssk, k14, k2tog; repeat from * with each color as established, k1 (16/98 stitches).

Row 17 With A, k1, *ssk, k12, k2tog; repeat from * with each color as established, k1 (14/86 stitches).

Row 19 With A, k1, *ssk, k10, k2tog; repeat from * with each color as established, k1 (12/74 stitches).

Row 23 With A, k1, *ssk, k8, k2tog; repeat from * with each color as established, k1 (10/62 stitches).

Row 25 With A, k1, *ssk, k6, k2tog; repeat from * with each color as established, k1 (8/50 stitches).

Row 29 With A, k1, *ssk, k4, k2tog; repeat from * with each color as established, k1 (6/38 stitches).

Row 31 With A, k1, *ssk, k2, k2tog; repeat from * with each color as established, k1 (4/26 stitches).

Row 33 With A, k1, *ssk, k2tog; repeat from * with each color as established, k1 (2/14 stitches).

Row 34 With A, p1, *p2tog; repeat from * with each color as established, p1 (8 stitches).

Break off the yarns, leaving a long tail of A or F. Thread the tail through the remaining stitches, pull tight, and secure. Sew seam.

HEARTS (MAKE 1 IN EACH COLOR)

Cast on 3 stitches. With a separate ball of yarn, cast 3 stitches onto the same needle (6 stitches).

Row 1 (RS) *[K1, m1] twice, k1; repeat from * on 2nd set of stitches with 2nd ball of yarn (5 stitches each side).

Row 2 Purl.

Row 3 *K1, m1, k3, m1, k1; repeat from * on 2nd set of stitches (7 stitches each side).

Row 4 Join the 2 sets of stitches as follows: P6, p2tog, p6 (13 stitches).

Row 5 K1, m1, k11, m1, k1 (15 stitches).

Rows 6, 8, 10, 12, and 14 Purl.

Row 7 K6, S2KP, k6 (13 stitches).

Row 9 K5, S2KP, k5 (11 stitches).

Row 11 Ssk, k2, S2KP, k2, k2tog (7 stitches).

Row 13 Ssk, S2KP, k2tog (3 stitches).

Row 15 S2KP.

Fasten off. Sew hearts to the circle, as pictured.

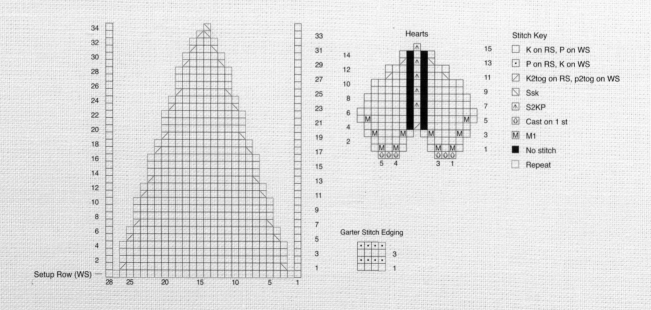

Hearts

Stitch Key

☐	K on RS, P on WS
·	P on RS, K on WS
╱	K2tog on RS, p2tog on WS
╲	Ssk
⅄	S2KP
⓪	Cast on 1 st
M	M1
■	No stitch
☐	Repeat

Garter Stitch Edging

TICK TOCK CLOCK

Worked back and forth from the outer edge to the center

Colors A, B (metallic), C, D, E, F, G, H, I, J, and K (black)

Note Work the colors with the intarsia method, using separate balls of yarn for each section and twisting yarns on wrong side to prevent holes when changing colors. Maintain color changes as established throughout, unless noted otherwise.

With one strand each of A and B held together, cast on 158 stitches.

Rows 1–6 Knit.

Break off B.

Row 7 K14 A, k13 C, k13 D, k13 E, k13 F, k13 G, k13 E, k13 D, k13 H, k13 A, k13 I, k14 J (13 stitches each section plus 2 selvedge stitches/158 stitches total).

Row 8 Purl, maintaining colors as established.

Row 9 K1, *ssk, k9, k2tog; repeat from * to the last stitch, k1 (11 stitches each section/134 stitches total).

Row 10 Purl.

Row 11 Knit.

Row 12 P1, *p2tog, p7, ssp; repeat from * to the last stitch, p1 (9/110 stitches).

Row 13 Knit.

Row 14 Purl.

Row 15 K1, *ssk, k5, k2tog; repeat from * to the last stitch, k1 (7/86 stitches).

Row 16 Purl.

Row 17 Knit.

Row 18 P1, *p2tog, p3, ssp; repeat from * to the last stitch, p1 (5/62 stitches).

Row 19 Knit.

Row 20 Purl.

Row 21 K1, *ssk, k1, k2tog; repeat from * to the last stitch, k1 (3/38 stitches).

Row 22 Purl.

Row 23 Knit.

Row 24 Purl.

Continue to work with one strand each of A and B held together; break off all other colors including yarn for the second A section.

Rows 25–28 Knit.

Break off B.

Row 29 K1, *k2tog, k1; repeat from * to the last stitch, k1 (2/26 stitches).

Row 30 Purl.

Row 31 K1, *k2tog; repeat from * to the last stitch, k1 (14 stitches).

Break off the yarn, leaving a long tail. Thread the tail through the remaining stitches, pull tight, and secure. Sew seam.

With B, embroider inside the Garter stitch edge of the circle, as pictured, using Straight stitch. With K, embroider Roman numerals and clock hands, as pictured, using Stem stitch; points using one Leaf stitch each; center using a 3-wrap French knot.

Stitch Key

- ▨ A
- ■ A + B held tog
- ▦ B
- ▨ J
- ■ K
- ☐ Color A, C, D, E, F, G, H, I, or J as given in instructions
- ☐ K on RS, P on WS
- · P on RS, K on WS
- ▨ K2tog on RS, p2tog on WS
- ◹ Ssk on RS, ssp on WS
- ☐ Repeat

Roman numerals and clock hands = Stem St

Points = Leaf St

Border = Straight St

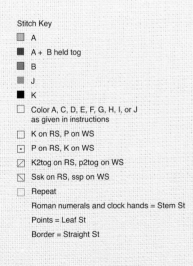

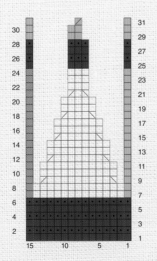

ECLECTIC

I hope by now you are completely addicted to circle knitting and ready to let your creativity run wild. Here you'll find circles that are original, unique, and great fun to make. This may be my favorite chapter. These circles showcase techniques such as cords, appliquéd flowers, embroidery, beads, fabulous edgings, and ruched ruffles. The Celtic knots are made by shaping and appliquéing cords onto a circle background—easy and pretty! These extra flourishes offer a new whirl to your circles.

An example of a project that features the circles in this chapter is the Big Blooms Capelet on page 195.

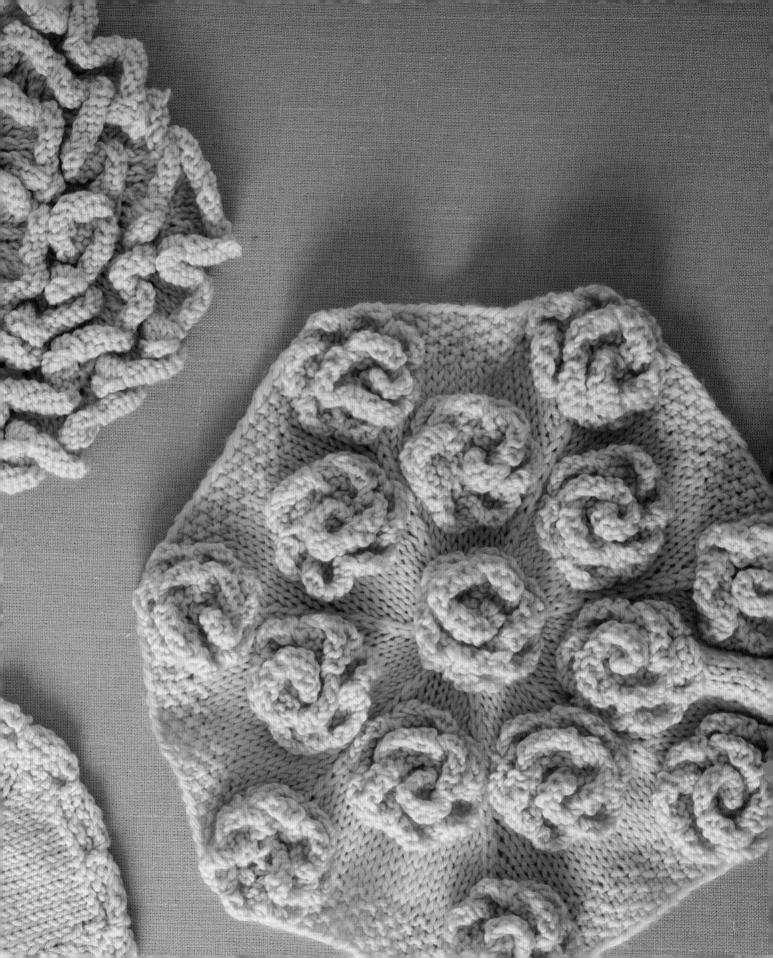

link frame
page 164

camarilla
page 164

small center
(5-spiral)
page 165

victorian parasol
page 166

ringed leaves with beads
page 167

coil and leaf
page 168

circus wheel

page 168

hearts entwined
page 169

*two hearts
together*
page 169

*two hearts
in one*
page 170

bold ruffle floral

page 171

rotate spiral
page 172

nautilus
page 173

ruching round
page 173

round and round
page 174

quatrefoil
page 174

blooming petals
page 175

petite floral
page 176

revolve
page 177

LINK FRAME

Make a Seed St Circle (see page 53).

GARTER ST EDGING

Pick up and knit approximately 144 stitches evenly around edge of circle.

Rnds 1 and 3 Purl.

Rnd 2 Knit.

Bind off knitwise using a needle one size larger.

LINK CORD

Using double-pointed needles, cast on 5 stitches.

*Slide the stitches onto the other end of the needle, k5. Do not turn; repeat from * until cord measures approximately 3½ yards (3.2m).

Follow the diagram for cord shaping. Pin into position and sew in place.

Note on Cords: Before binding off, place stitches onto a safety pin and shape as desired until you're sure that the cord is the right length. Remove or add length as needed.

Garter Stitch Edging

Link Cord

Stitch Key

□	Knit
⊡	Purl
⓪	Cast on 1 st
→	Do not turn
□	Repeat

CAMARILLA

Make a Stockinette St Circle (see page 52).

String approximately 150 size 6/0 beads onto yarn.

K3, P3 RIB EDGING

Pick up and knit 174 stitches evenly around the edge of the circle. Pm.

Rnds 1 and 2 *K3, p3; repeat from * around.

Rnd 3 *K1, slide bead up to the needle, sl 1 wyif, k1, p3; repeat from * around.

Bind off in pattern using a needle one size larger.

CAMARILLA CORD

Using double-pointed needles, cast on 5 stitches.

Rows 1–3 K5, do not turn, slide stitches onto the other end of the needle.

Row 4 K2, slide bead up to the needle, sl 1 wyif, k2, do not turn, slide stitches onto the other end of the needle.

Repeat rows 1–4 until cord measures approximately 56" (142cm).

Follow the diagram for cord shaping. Pin in position and sew in place, making sure the beads face front.

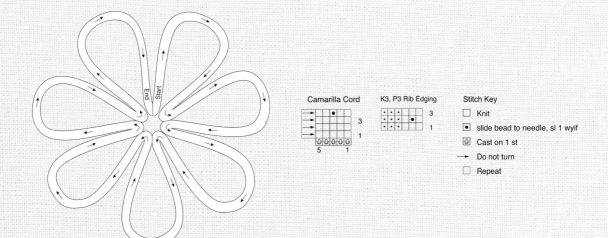

Camarilla Cord

K3, P3 Rib Edging

Stitch Key
- ☐ Knit
- • slide bead to needle, sl 1 wyif
- ⓪ Cast on 1 st
- → Do not turn
- ☐ Repeat

SMALL CENTER (5-spiral)

Worked back and forth from the outer edge to the center

Cast on 102 stitches.

Row 1 (RS) K1, pm, *SK2P, k17, pm; repeat from * to the last stitch, k1 (18 stitches each section plus 2 selvedge stitches/92 stitches total).

Row 2 and all WS rows Purl.

Row 3 K1, *SK2P, k15; repeat from * to the last stitch, k1 (16/82 stitches).

Row 5 K1, *SK2P, k13; repeat from * to the last stitch, k1 (14/72 stitches).

Row 7 K1, *SK2P, k11; repeat from * to the last stitch, k1 (12/62 stitches).

Row 9 K1, *SK2P, k9; repeat from * to the last stitch, k1 (10/52 stitches).

Row 11 K1, *SK2P, k7; repeat from * to the last stitch, k1 (8/42 stitches).

Row 13 K1, *SK2P, k5; repeat from * to the last stitch, k1 (6/32 stitches).

Row 15 K1, *SK2P, k3; repeat from * to the last stitch, k1 (4/22 stitches).

Row 17 K1, *SK2P, k1; repeat from * to the last stitch, k1 (2/12 stitches).

Row 18 Purl.

Break the yarn, leaving a long tail. Thread the tail through the remaining 12 stitches, pull tight, and secure. Sew seam.

Note This circle can be used as a "filler" circle when putting large circles together.

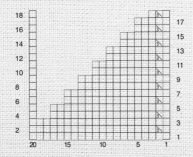

Stitch Key
- ☐ Knit
- • Purl
- ⟍ SK2P
- ☐ Repeat

VICTORIAN PARASOL

Worked back and forth from the outer edge to the center

Colors MC and CC

With MC, cast on 164 stitches.

Garter St Twist Edging

Rows 1–4 Knit.

Row 5 (RS) K4, rotate the left-hand needle counter-clockwise 360 degrees, *k6, rotate the left-hand needle counterclockwise 360 degrees; repeat from * to the last 4 stitches, k4.

Row 6 Knit, decreasing 2 stitches evenly across (162 stitches).

BODY

Row 1 (RS) K1, *k2tog, k14, pm; repeat from * to the last stitch, k1 (15 stitches each section plus 2 selvedge stitches/152 stitches total).

Row 2 and all WS rows Purl.

Row 3 K1, *k2tog, k13; repeat from * to the last stitch, k1 (14/142 stitches).

Row 5 K1, *k2tog, k12; repeat from * to the last stitch, k1 (13/132 stitches).

Row 7 K1, *k2tog, k11; repeat from * to the last stitch, k1 (12/122 stitches).

Row 9 K1, *k2tog, k10; repeat from * to the last stitch, k1 (11/112 stitches).

Row 11 K1, *k2tog, k9; repeat from * to the last stitch, k1 (10/102 stitches).

Row 13 K1, *k2tog, k8; repeat from * to the last stitch, k1 (9/92 stitches).

Row 15 K1, *k2tog, k7; repeat from * to the last stitch, k1 (8/82 stitches).

Row 17 K1, *k2tog, k6; repeat from * to the last stitch, k1 (7/72 stitches).

Row 19 K1, *k2tog, k5; repeat from * to the last stitch, k1 (6/62 stitches).

Row 21 K1, *k2tog, k4; repeat from * to the last stitch, k1 (5/52 stitches).

Row 23 K1, *k2tog, k3; repeat from * to the last stitch, k1 (4/42 stitches).

Row 25 K1, *k2tog, k2; repeat from * to the last stitch, k1 (3/32 stitches).

Row 27 K1, *k2tog, k1; repeat from * to the last stitch, k1 (2/22 stitches).

Row 29 K1, *k2tog; repeat from * to the last stitch, k1 (12 stitches).

Break off the yarn and thread the tail through the remaining 12 stitches, pull tightly to gather, and secure. Sew seam.

For a smaller (larger) circle, begin with a smaller (larger) multiple of 10 stitches, plus 2 selvedge stitches; divide into 10 sections (with a selvedge stitch at each end) and decrease every other row at the beginning of each section.

ROSE

With MC, cast on 62 stitches.

Rows 1–6 Knit.

Row 7 (RS) Work row 5 of Garter St Twist Edging (above).

Row 8 *K2tog; repeat from * to end (31 stitches).

Row 9 *K2tog; repeat from * to the last stitch, k1 (16 stitches).

Row 10 *K2tog; repeat from * to end (8 stitches).

Pass all the stitches, one at a time, over the first stitch. Fasten off.

Form into a spiral and secure at bottom. Sew to the center of the circle.

LEAF (MAKE 5)

With CC, cast on 9 stitches.

Rows 1, 3, and 5 K3, S2KP, k3 (7 stitches).

Rows 2 and 4 K1, m1, k2, p1, k2, m1, k1 (9 stitches).

Row 6 K3, p1, k3.

Row 7 K2, S2KP, k2 (5 stitches).

Row 8 K2, p1, k2.

Row 9 K1, S2KP, k1 (3 stitches).

Row 10 K1, p1, k1.

Row 11 S2KP (1 stitch).

Fasten off.

Sew leaves around the rose, as pictured.

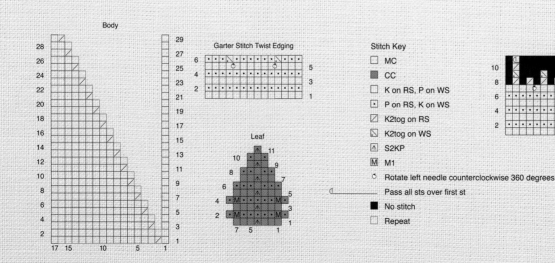

Stitch Key

☐	MC
▨	CC
☐	K on RS, P on WS
·	P on RS, K on WS
╱	K2tog on RS
╲	K2tog on WS
⋀	S2KP
M	M1
ᵒ	Rotate left needle counterclockwise 360 degrees
⟜	Pass all sts over first st
■	No stitch
☐	Repeat

RINGED LEAVES WITH BEADS

Worked in short rows
250 size 6/0 glass beads
Steel crochet hook for adding beads

AB (add bead) Pick up a bead with the crochet hook and slip the next stitch behind it, draw the loop through the bead and slip the stitch back onto the needle, knit this stitch.

Cast on 26 stitches.
Row 1 (RS) Sl 1, k20, pm, k2, yo, AB, yo, k2 (28 stitches).
Row 2 P6, kfb, k19, sl 1, bring yarn to the front and turn, leaving 1 stitch unworked.
Row 3 Knit the slipped stitch, AB, *k1, AB; repeat from * to marker, k1, p1, k2, yo, AB, yo, k3 (31 stitches).
Row 4 P8, kfb, k1, k18, sl 1, bring yarn to front and turn, leaving 2 stitches unworked.
Row 5 Knit the slipped stitch, knit to marker, k1, p2, k3, yo, AB, yo, k4 (34 stitches).
Row 6 P10, kfb, k2, k17, sl 1, bring yarn to the front and turn, leaving 3 stitches unworked.
Row 7 Knit the slipped stitch, knit to marker, k1, p3, k4, yo, AB, yo, k5 (37 stitches).
Row 8 P12, kfb, k3, k16, sl 1, bring yarn to the front and turn, leaving 4 stitches unworked.
Row 9 Knit the slipped stitch, knit to marker, k1, p4, ssk, k7, k2tog, k1 (36 stitches).
Row 10 P10, kfb, k4, k15, sl 1, bring yarn to the front and turn, leaving 5 stitches unworked.
Row 11 Knit the slipped stitch, knit to marker, k1, p5, ssk, k5, k2tog, k1 (35 stitches).
Row 12 P8, kfb, k2, p1, k2, k14, sl 1, bring yarn to the front and turn, leaving 6 stitches unworked.
Row 13 Knit the slipped st, knit to marker, k1, p1, AB, p4, ssk, k3, k2tog, k1 (34 stitches).
Row 14 P6, kfb, k3, p1, k2, k13, sl 1, bring yarn to the front and turn, leaving 7 stitches unworked.
Row 15 Knit the slipped stitch, AB, *k1, AB; repeat from * to marker, k1, p1, AB, p5, ssk, k1, k2tog, k1 (33 stitches).
Row 16 P4, kfb, k4, p1, k2, k12, sl 1, bring yarn to the front and turn, leaving 8 stitches unworked.

Row 17 Knit the slipped stitch, knit to marker, k1, p1, AB, p6, SK2P, k1 (32 stitches).
Row 18 P2tog, bind off 5 stitches, p3, k1, k11, sl 1, bring yarn to the front and turn, leaving 9 stitches unworked.
Row 19 Knit the slipped stitch, knit to marker, k2, yo, AB, yo, k2 (28 stitches).
Row 20 P6, kfb, k10, sl 1, bring yarn to the front and turn, leaving 10 stitches unworked.
Row 21 Knit the slipped stitch, knit to marker, k1, p1, k2, yo, AB, yo, k3 (31 stitches).
Row 22 P8, kfb, k1, k9, sl 1, bring yarn to the front and turn, leaving 11 stitches unworked.
Row 23 Knit the slipped stitch, knit to marker, k1, p2, k3, yo, AB, yo, k4 (34 stitches).
Row 24 P10, kfb, k2, k8, sl 1, bring yarn to the front and turn, leaving 12 stitches unworked.
Row 25 Knit the slipped stitch, knit to marker, k1, p3, k4, yo, AB, yo, k5 (37 stitches).
Row 26 P12, kfb, k3, k7, sl 1, bring yarn to the front and turn, leaving 13 stitches unworked.
Row 27 Knit the slipped stitch, AB, *k1, AB; repeat from * to marker, k1, p4, ssk, k7, k2tog, k1 (36 stitches).
Row 28 P10, kfb, k4, k6, sl 1, bring yarn to the front and turn, leaving 14 stitches unworked.
Row 29 Knit the slipped stitch, knit to marker, k1, p5, ssk, k5, k2tog, k1 (35 stitches).
Row 30 P8, kfb, k2, p1, k2, k5, sl 1, bring yarn to the front and turn, leaving 15 stitches unworked.

Row 31 Knit the slipped stitch, knit to marker, k1, p1, AB, p4, ssk, k3, k2tog, k1 (34 stitches).
Row 32 P6, kfb, k3, p1, k2, k4, sl 1, bring yarn to the front and turn, leaving 16 stitches unworked.
Row 33 Knit the slipped stitch, knit to marker, k1, p1, AB, p5, ssk, k1, k2tog, k1 (33 stitches).
Row 34 P4, kfb, k4, p1, k2, k3, sl 1, bring yarn to the front and turn, leaving 17 stitches unworked.
Row 35 Knit the slipped stitch, knit to marker, k1, p1, AB, p6, SK2P, k1 (32 stitches).
Row 36 P2tog, bind off 5 stitches, p3, k1, knit to end, bring yarn to the front and turn (26 stitches).
Repeat rows 1–36 six more times (7 sections/14 leaves).
Sew the last row to the cast-on edge.

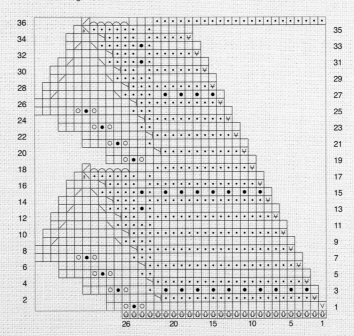

Stitch Key
- ☐ K on RS, P on WS
- ⊡ P on RS, K on WS
- ○ Yo
- ◪ K2tog
- ◩ Ssk
- ◪ SK2P
- ◩ Kfb
- ● Add bead
- ⊻ Sl 1 st wyib on RS
- ⊻ Sl 1 st wyib on WS
- ◎ Cast on 1 st
- ⌒ Bind off 1 st
- ☐ Repeat

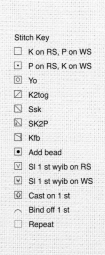

COIL AND LEAF

Worked in an I-cord

LEAF

Cast on 5 stitches.

Row 1 (RS) K2, yo, k1, yo, k2 (7 stitches).

Rows 2, 4, 6, 8, and 10 Purl.

Row 3 K3, yo, k1, yo, k3 (9 stitches).

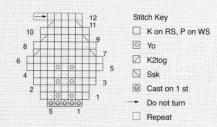

Stitch Key
- ☐ K on RS, P on WS
- ⊙ Yo
- ☑ K2tog
- ☒ Ssk
- ⑴ Cast on 1 st
- → Do not turn
- ☐ Repeat

Row 5 K4, yo, k1, yo, k4 (11 stitches).

Row 7 Ssk, k7, k2tog (9 stitches).

Row 9 Ssk, k5, k2tog (7 stitches).

Row 11 Ssk, k3, k2tog; do not turn (5 stitches).

Row 12 Slide the stitches onto the other end of the needle, k5, do not turn.

Repeat row 12 until the cord measures approximately 8 feet (2.4m).

Starting at the center with the leaf, wind the cord into a flat spiral. Sew cord in place.

For a smaller or larger circle, make a shorter or longer cord.

CIRCUS WHEEL

Worked in the round from the center to the outer edge

Cast on 8 stitches (2 stitches each on 4 dpns). Mark the beginning of the round and join without twisting.

Rnd 1 *K1 tbl; repeat from * around.

Rnd 2 *Kfb; repeat from * around (16 stitches).

Rnds 3–5 Knit.

Rnd 6 *Kfb; repeat from * around (32 stitches).

Rnds 7–11 Knit.

Rnd 12 *Kfb; repeat from * around (64 stitches).

Rnds 13–19 Knit.

Rnd 20 *K1, kfb; repeat from * around (96 stitches).

Rnds 21–25 Knit.

Rnd 26 *K2, kfb; repeat from * around (128 stitches).

Rnds 27–31 Knit.

Rnd 32 *K3, kfb; repeat from * around (160 stitches).

If not working edging, bind off using a needle one size larger.

GARTER ST EDGING

Rnds 1 and 3 Purl.

Rnd 2 Knit.

Bind off using a needle one size larger.

BALL SPOKES (MAKE 8)

Using double-pointed needles, cast on 4 stitches.

*Do not turn, slide stitches onto the other end of the needle, k4; repeat from * until cord measures 4" (10cm).

Row 1 (WS) *Pfb; repeat from * to end (8 stitches).

Row 2 *Kfb; repeat from * to end (16 stitches).

Rows 3, 5, 7, and 9 Purl.

Rows 4, 6, and 8 Knit.

Row 10 *K2tog; repeat from * to end (8 stitches).

Break the yarn and thread the tail through the remaining stitches. Pull tight and secure. Stuff with polyfill and sew side seam.

Sew Ball Spokes to the circle, as pictured. Sew a decorative button to the center.

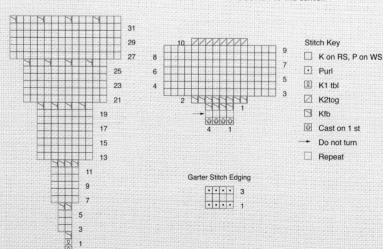

Stitch Key
- ☐ K on RS, P on WS
- · Purl
- ⓫ K1 tbl
- ☑ K2tog
- ◩ Kfb
- ⑴ Cast on 1 st
- → Do not turn
- ☐ Repeat

Garter Stitch Edging

HEARTS ENTWINED

Make a Stockinette St Circle (see page 52).

K2, P2 EDGING

With the WS facing for a Reverse Stockinette stitch base, pick up and knit 170 stitches evenly around edge of circle. Pm.
Rnds 1–3 *K2, p2; repeat from * around.
Bind off in pattern using a needle one size larger.

HEARTS ENTWINED CORD

Make 1 short 12" (30.5cm), 2 medium 24" (61cm), and 1 long 56" (142cm) cords.
Note Lengths are approximate. Make adjustments before binding off.

Using double-pointed needles, cast on 3 stitches.
*Do not turn, slide stitches onto the other end of the needle, k3; repeat from * to desired length.

Follow the diagram for cord placement. Pin and sew in place.

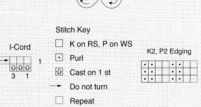

Stitch Key
☐ K on RS, P on WS
· Purl
0 Cast on 1 st
→ Do not turn
☐ Repeat

I-Cord

K2, P2 Edging

TWO HEARTS TOGETHER

Make a Seed St Circle (see page 53).

K3, P3 EDGING

With the RS facing, pick up and knit 186 stitches evenly around edge of circle. Pm.
Rnds 1 and 2 *K3, p3; repeat from * around.
Bind off in pattern using a needle one size larger.

CORD (MAKE 2)

Using double-pointed needles, cast on 3 stitches.
*Do not turn, slide stitches onto the other end of the needle, k3; repeat from * until cord measures approximately 40" (101.5cm).

Follow the diagram for cord placement. Pin and sew in place.

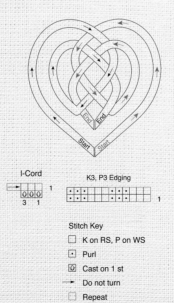

I-Cord

K3, P3 Edging

Stitch Key
☐ K on RS, P on WS
· Purl
0 Cast on 1 st
→ Do not turn
☐ Repeat

TWO HEARTS IN ONE

Make a Seed St Circle (see page 53).

Start here
at center of cord

REVERSE STOCKINETTE ST EDGING

With the RS facing, pick up and knit 170 stitches evenly around edge of circle. Pm.

Rnds 1–3 Purl.

Bind off using a needle one size larger.

CORD

Using double-pointed needles, cast on 5 stitches.

*Do not turn, slide stitches onto the other end of the needle, k5; repeat from * until cord measures approximately 58" (147.5cm).

Follow the diagram for cord placement. Pin and sew in place.

Reverse Stockinette Stitch Edging

				3
				1

I-Cord

					1
0	0	0	0	0	
5				1	

Stitch Key

☐ K on RS, p on WS
· Purl
0 Cast on 1 st
→ Do not turn
☐ Repeat

BOLD PETAL

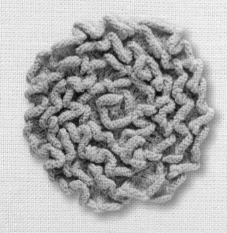

INNER PETAL (MAKE 3)

Cast on 108 stitches.

Rows 1 and 3 Knit.

Rows 2 and 4 Purl.

Row 5 *K6, then rotate the left-hand needle counterclockwise 360 degrees; repeat from * to the end.

Row 6 Purl.

Row 7 *K2tog; repeat from * to end (54 stitches).

Row 8 *P2tog; repeat from * to end (27 stitches).

Bind off.

OUTER PETAL (MAKE 5)

Work the same as for the Inner Petal through row 7.

Row 8 *P2tog, p1; repeat from * to end (36 stitches).

Bind off.

Starting with an Inner Petal, twist into a spiral and sew in place. Continue to add the Inner, then the Outer, Petals in a spiral and sew in place.

For a smaller or larger circle, make fewer or more petals.

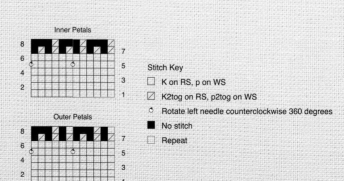

Inner Petals

Outer Petals

Stitch Key

☐ K on RS, p on WS
╱ K2tog on RS, p2tog on WS
↻ Rotate left needle counterclockwise 360 degrees
■ No stitch
☐ Repeat

BOLD RUFFLE FLORAL

Worked back and forth from the outer edge to the center

GARTER ST EDGING
Cast on 162 stitches.
Rows 1–3 Knit.
BODY
Row 1 (RS) K1, pm, *SK2P, k29, pm; repeat from * to the last stitch, k1 (30 stitches each section plus 2 selvedge stitches/152 stitches total).
Row 2 and all WS rows Purl.
Row 3 K1, *SK2P, k27; repeat from * to the last stitch, k1 (28/142 stitches).
Row 5 K1, *SK2P, k25; repeat from * to the last stitch, k1 (26/132 stitches).
Row 7 K1, *SK2P, k23; repeat from * to the last stitch, k1 (24/122 stitches).
Row 9 K1, *SK2P, k21; repeat from * to the last stitch, k1 (22/112 stitches).
Row 11 K1, *SK2P, k19; repeat from * to the last stitch, k1 (20/102 stitches).
Row 13 K1, *SK2P, k17; repeat from * to the last stitch, k1 (18/92 stitches).

Row 15 K1, *SK2P, k15; repeat from * to the last stitch, k1 (16/82 stitches).
Row 17 K1, *SK2P, k13; repeat from * to the last stitch, k1 (14/72 stitches).
Row 19 K1, *SK2P, k11; repeat from * to the last stitch, k1 (12/62 stitches).
Row 21 K1, *SK2P, k9; repeat from * to the last stitch, k1 (10/52 stitches).
Row 23 K1, *SK2P, k7; repeat from * to the last stitch, k1 (8/42 stitches).
Row 25 K1, *SK2P, k5; repeat from * to the last stitch, k1 (6/32 stitches).
Row 27 K1, *SK2P, k3; repeat from * to the last stitch, k1 (4/22 stitches).
Row 29 K1, *SK2P, k1; repeat from * to the last stitch, k1 (2/12 stitches).
Break off the yarn and thread the tail through the remaining 12 stitches, pull tightly to gather, and secure. Sew seam.

For a smaller (larger) circle, begin with a smaller (larger) multiple of 10 stitches plus 2 selvedge stitches. Divide into 5 sections and decrease every other round at the beginning of each section.

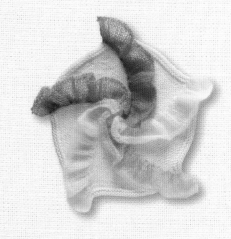

RUFFLES (MAKE 5)
With a lighter-weight yarn, cast on 60 stitches.
Rows 1–3 Knit.
Rows 4, 6, and 8 Purl.
Rows 5, 7, and 9 Knit.
Row 10 Purl.
Bind off as follows: K2tog, *k2tog, pass the first stitch over this stitch; repeat from * to end. Fasten off.
Sew a ruffle to each ridge, as pictured.

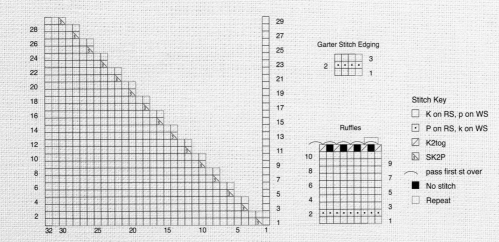

Garter Stitch Edging

Ruffles

Stitch Key

☐ K on RS, p on WS
· P on RS, k on WS
╱ K2tog
◺ SK2P
⌒ pass first st over
■ No stitch
☐ Repeat

ECLIPTIC FLORAL CIRCLE

Worked in the round from the outer edge to the center

SEED ST EDGING

Cast on 140 stitches. Mark the beginning of the round and join without twisting.

Rnds 1, 3, and 5 *K1, p1; repeat from * around.

Rnds 2, 4, and 6 *P1, k1; repeat from * around.

BODY

Rnd 1 *K9, S2KP, k8, pm; repeat from * around (18 stitches each section/126 stitches total).

Rnds 2 and 3 Knit.

Rnd 4 *K8, S2KP , k7; repeat from * around (16/112 stitches).

Rnds 5 and 6 Knit.

Rnd 7 *K7, S2KP, k6; repeat from * around (14/98 stitches).

Rnds 8 and 9 Knit.

Rnd 10 *K6, S2KP, k5; repeat from * around (12/84 stitches).

Rnds 11 and 12 Knit.

Rnd 13 *K5, S2KP, k4; repeat from * around (10/70 stitches).

Rnds 14 and 15 Knit.

Rnd 16 *K4, S2KP , k3; repeat from * around (8/56 stitches).

Rnds 17 and 18 Knit.

Rnd 19 *K3, S2KP, k2; repeat from * around (6/42 stitches).

Rnds 20 and 21 Knit.

Rnd 22 *K2, S2KP, k1; repeat from * around (4/28 stitches).

Rnds 23 and 24 Knit.

Rnd 25 *K1, S2KP; repeat from * around (2/14 stitches).

Rnds 26 and 27 Knit.

Rnd 28 *K2tog; repeat from * around (7 stitches).

Break off the yarn and thread the tail through the remaining stitches. Pull tight and secure.

Stitch Key

☐ K on RS, P on WS

⊡ P on RS, K on WS

◪ K2tog on RS

◩ K2tog on WS

⬔ S2KP

○ Rotate left needle counterclockwise 360 degrees

■ No stitch

⊏ Stitch over

☐ Repeat

ROSES (MAKE 15)

Cast on 60 stitches.

Rows 1–4 Knit.

Row 5 (RS) *K5, rotate the left-hand needle counterclockwise 360 degrees; repeat from * to the end.

Rows 6 and 7 *K2tog; repeat from * to end (15 stitches after row 7).

Row 7 K1, *k2tog; repeat from * to end (8 stitches).

Row 8 Repeat row 6 (4 stitches).

Pass the 2nd, 3rd, and 4th stitches over the first stitch. Twist to shape into a rose and sew to secure. Sew roses to the circle, as pictured.

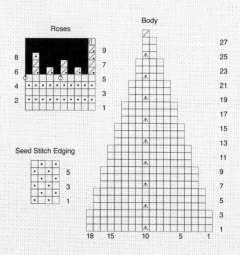

Roses

Body

Seed Stitch Edging

ROTATE SPIRAL

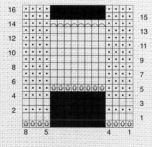

Cast on 172 stitches.

Rows 1–4 Knit.

Row 5 (RS) P4, *turn, cast on 8 stitches, turn, p4; repeat from * to end.

Rows 6, 8, 10, and 12 K4, *p8, k4; repeat from * to end.

Rows 7, 9, 11, and 13 P4, *k8, p4; repeat from * to end.

Row 14 K4, *bind off 8 stitches purlwise, k4; repeat from * to end.

Row 15 Purl.

Row 16 Knit.

Bind off. Form into a spiral, as pictured, and sew in place.

Stitch Key

☐ K on RS, P on WS

⊡ P on RS, K on WS

Ⓤ Cast on 1 st

⌒ Bind off 1 st purlwise on WS

■ No stitch

☐ Repeat

NAUTILUS

Worked back and forth as a strip

Cast on 2 stitches, leaving an extra-long tail for later assembly.

Row 1 (RS) Knit.

Row 2 K2, cast on 1 stitch (3 stitches).

Row 3 Knit.

Row 4 Knit to the end, cast on 1 stitch (4 stitches).

Rows 5–12 Repeat rows 3 and 4 (8 stitches after row 12).

Work even in Garter st for approximately 52" (132cm), ending with a WS row.

Note Assemble circle to determine whether more or less length is needed before finishing.

Dec row (RS) Ssk, knit to end.

Repeat Dec row every 4th row until 1 stitch remains. Fasten off.

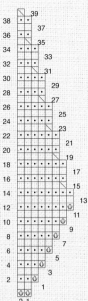

Stitch Key
- ☐ K on RS, P on WS
- ⊡ P on RS, K on WS
- ◹ Ssk
- ⊙ Cast on 1 st
- ☐ Repeat

ASSEMBLY

Thread cast-on tail through every ridge along the straight inner edge of the strip. Gather and ease along this edge to form a spiral, pulling tightly at the center, and sew in place.

RUCHING ROUND

Worked in the round from the outer edge to the center

Yarns A (worsted) and B (lace-weight mohair)

With A, cast on 210 stitches. Mark the beginning of the round and join without twisting.

Change to B.

Rnds 1–12 Knit.

Change to A.

Rnd 13 *K2tog; repeat from * around (105 stitches).

Rnds 14 and 16 Purl.

Rnd 15 Knit.

Change to B.

Rnds 17–28 Knit.

Change to A.

Rnd 29 K1, *k2tog; repeat from * around (53 stitches).

Rnds 30 and 32 Purl.

Rnd 31 Knit.

Change to B.

Rnds 33–44 Knit.

Change to A.

Rnd 45 K2tog, *k3tog; repeat from * around (18 stitches).

Rnd 46 Purl.

Rnd 47 Knit.

Rnd 48 Purl.

Break the yarn. Thread the tail through the remaining 18 stitches, pull tight, and secure.

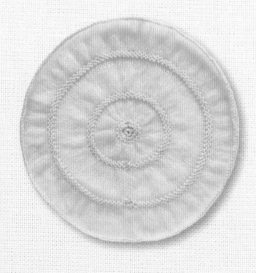

Stitch Key
- ☐ A
- ▨ B
- ☐ K on RS, P on WS
- ⊡ P on RS, K on WS
- ◿ K2tog
- ◺ K3tog
- ⊙ Cast on 1 st
- ☐ Repeat

ROUND AND ROUND

Worked in an I-Cord

MB (make bobble) [Knit into the front and back of stitch] twice (4 stitches), turn; k4; pass the 2nd, 3rd, and 4th stitches, one at a time, over the first stitch.

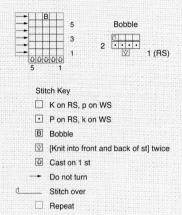

Stitch Key
- ☐ K on RS, p on WS
- ⊡ P on RS, k on WS
- Ⓑ Bobble
- Ⅴ [Knit into front and back of st] twice
- ⑩ Cast on 1 st
- → Do not turn
- ⊏___ Stitch over
- ☐ Repeat

Cast on 5 stitches.
Rows 1–5 K5, do not turn, slide stitches onto the other end of the needle.
Row 6 K2, MB, k2, do not turn, slide stitches onto the other end of the needle.
Repeat rows 1–6 until the cord measures approximately 14 feet (4.2m).
Starting at the center, wind the cord into a flat spiral, making sure the bobbles are on the RS. Sew the cord in place.

For a smaller or larger circle, make a shorter or longer cord.

QUATREFOIL

Make a Seed St Circle (see page 53).

CORD EDGING (MAKE 2)
Using double-pointed needles, cast on 5 stitches.
*Slide the stitches onto the other end of the needle, k5. Do not turn. Repeat from * until cord measures 4" (10cm) more than the circumference of the circle.
Sew the edging to the edge of the circle, leaving the first and last 2" (5cm) of the cord and 2" (5cm) of the circle free. Twist the 2 ends of the cord and sew in place.

QUATREFOIL CORD
Cast on 5 stitches and work cord as above until cord measures approximately 98" (2.5m).
Holding the 2 cords together, follow the diagram for cord shaping. Pin into position and sew in place.

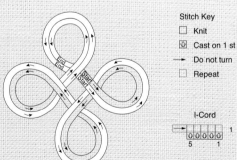

Stitch Key
- ☐ Knit
- ⑩ Cast on 1 st
- → Do not turn
- ☐ Repeat

I-Cord

BLOOMING PETALS

Worked back and forth from the outer edge to the center

BASE CIRCLE

Cast on 152 stitches.

Row 1 (RS) K1, pm, *SK2P, k27, pm; repeat from * to the last stitch, k1 (28 stitches in each section plus 2 selvedge stitches/142 stitches total).

Row 2 and all WS rows Purl.

Row 3 K1, *SK2P, k25; repeat from * to the last stitch, k1 (26/132 stitches).

Row 5 K1, *SK2P, k23; repeat from * to the last stitch, k1 (24/122 stitches).

Row 7 K1, *SK2P, k21; repeat from * to the last stitch, k1 (22/112 stitches).

Row 9 K1, *SK2P, k19; repeat from * to the last stitch, k1 (20/102 stitches).

Row 11 K1, *SK2P, k17; repeat from * to the last stitch, k1 (18/92 stitches).

Row 13 K1, *SK2P, k15; repeat from * to the last stitch, k1 (16/82 stitches).

Row 15 K1, *SK2P, k13; repeat from * to the last stitch, k1 (14/72 stitches).

Row 17 K1, *SK2P, k11; repeat from * to the last stitch, k1 (12/62 stitches).

Row 19 K1, *SK2P, k9; repeat from * to the last stitch, k1 (10/52 stitches).

Row 21 K1, *SK2P, k7; repeat from * to the last stitch, k1 (8/42 stitches).

Row 23 K1, *SK2P, k5; repeat from * to the last stitch, k1 (6/32 stitches).

Row 25 K1, *SK2P, k3; repeat from * to the last stitch, k1 (4/22 stitches).

Row 27 K1, *SK2P, k1; repeat from * to the last stitch, k1 (2/12 stitches).

Break off the yarn and thread the tail through the remaining 12 stitches, pull tightly to gather, and secure. Sew seam.

PETAL (MAKE 19)

Cast on 5 stitches.

Row 1 (RS) K2, yo, k1, yo, k2 (7 stitches).

Row 2 and all WS rows Purl.

Row 3 K3, yo, k1, yo, k3 (9 stitches).

Row 5 K4, yo, k1, yo, k4 (11 stitches).

Row 7 K5, yo, k1, yo, k5 (13 stitches).

Rows 9 and 11 Ssk, k4, yo, k1, yo, k4, k2tog.

Row 13 Ssk, k9, k2tog (11 stitches).

Row 15 Ssk, k7, k2tog (9 stitches).

Row 17 Ssk, k5, k2tog (7 stitches).

Row 19 Ssk, k3, k2tog (5 stitches).

Row 21 Ssk, k1, k2tog (3 stitches).

Row 23 SK2P (1 stitch).

Fasten off.

Sew petals to the base circle, as pictured.

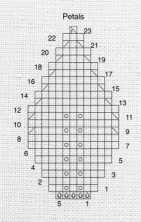

Petals

Stitch Key

☐ K on RS, p on WS
⊙ Yo
◿ K2tog
◺ Ssk
⋀ SK2P
Ⓞ Cast on 1 st
☐ Repeat

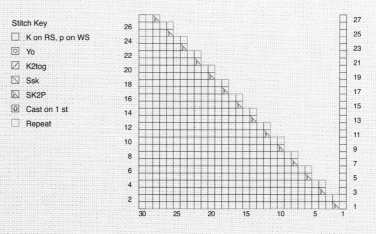

PETITE FLORAL

Worked back and forth from the outer edge to the center

Colors MC and CC, and small amounts for assorted flowers

CENTERED DOUBLE DECREASES

S2KP (RS) Sl 2 as if to k2tog, k1, pass the 2 slipped stitches over.

S2PP (WS) [Sl 1 knitwise] twice, slip these 2 stitches back to the left-hand needle, sl 2 as if to p2tog tbl, p1, pass the 2 slipped stitches over.

K1, P1 EDGING

With CC, cast on 142 stitches.

Rows 1 and 3 (RS) K1, *k1, p1; repeat from * to the last stitch, k1.

Rows 2 and 4: P1, *k1, p1; repeat from * to the last stitch, p1.

BODY

Change to MC.

Row 1 K1, pm, *K9, S2KP, k8, pm; repeat from * to the last stitch, k1 (18 stitches each section plus 2 selvedge stitches/128 stitches total).

Row 2 Purl.

Row 3 Knit.

Row 4 P1, *p7, S2PP, p8; repeat from * to the last stitch, p1 (16/114 stitches).

Row 5 Knit.

Row 6 Purl.

Row 7 K1, *k7, S2KP, k6; repeat from * to the last stitch, k1 (14/100 stitches).

Row 8 Purl.

Row 9 Knit.

Row 10 P1, *p5, S2PP, p6; repeat from * to the last stitch, p1 (12/86 stitches).

Row 11 Knit.

Row 12 Purl.

Row 13 K1, *k5, S2KP, k4; repeat from * to the last stitch, k1 (10/72 stitches).

Row 14 Purl.

Row 15 Knit.

Row 16 P1, *p3, S2PP, p4; repeat from * to the last stitch, p1 (8/58 stitches).

Row 17 Knit.

Row 18 Purl.

Row 19 K1, *k3, S2KP, k2; repeat from * to the last stitch, k1 (6/44 stitches).

Row 20 Purl.

Row 21 Knit.

Row 22 P1, *p1, S2PP, p2; repeat from * to the last stitch, p1 (4/30 stitches).

Row 23 Knit.

Row 24 Purl.

Row 25 K1, *k1, S2KP; repeat from * to the last stitch, k1 (2/16 stitches).

Row 26 Purl.

Row 27 Knit.

Row 28 P1, *p2tog; repeat from * to the last stitch, p1 (9 stitches).

Break off the yarn, leaving a long tail. Thread the tail through the remaining stitches, pull tight, and secure. Sew seam.

FLOWERS (MAKE 14: 2 EACH IN 7 COLORS)

Loosely cast on 25 stitches.

Knit 3 rows.

Pass all the stitches, one at a time, over the first stitch.

Fasten off.

Twist to form the flower. Sew to secure.

Sew one of each color to the end of each spoke. Sew the remainder in a cluster at the center.

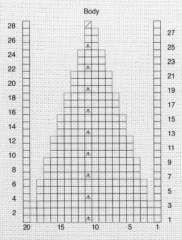

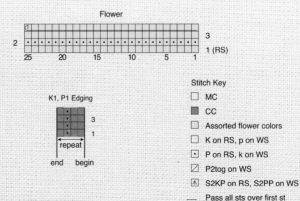

Stitch Key

☐ MC

■ CC

☐ Assorted flower colors

☐ K on RS, p on WS

⊡ P on RS, k on WS

☑ P2tog on WS

⋀ S2KP on RS, S2PP on WS

— Pass all sts over first st

☐ Repeat

REVOLVE

Worked back and forth from the outer edge to the center

Colors MC and CC (solid self-striping)

With CC, cast on 114 stitches.

Rows 1–4 Knit.

Row 5 (RS) P3, *turn, cast on 8 stitches, turn, p4; repeat from * to the last 3 stitches, cast on 8 stitches, p3.

Rows 6, 8, 10, and 12 K3, *p8, k4; repeat from * to the last 11 stitches, p8, k3.

Rows 7, 9, 11, and 13 P3, *k8, p4; repeat from * to the last 11 stitches, k8, p3.

Row 14 K3, *bind off 8 stitches purlwise, k4; repeat from * to the last 11 stitches, bind off 8 stitches purlwise, k3.

Row 15 Purl.

Row 16 Knit, k1, (k36, k2tog) twice, k36, k1 (112 stitches). Change to MC.

Row 17 K1, *SK2P, k19, pm; repeat from * to the last stitch, k1 (20 stitches each section plus 2 selvedge stitches/102 stitches total).

Rows 18, 20, 22, 24, 26, 28, 30, 32, and 34 Purl.

Row 19 K1, *SK2P, k17; repeat from * to the last stitch, k1 (18/92 stitches).

Row 21 K1, *SK2P, k15; repeat from * to the last stitch, k1 (16/82 stitches).

Row 23 K1, *SK2P, k13; repeat from * to the last stitch, k1 (14/72 stitches).

Row 25 K1, *SK2P, k11; repeat from * to the last stitch, k1 (12/62 stitches).

Row 27 K1, *SK2P, k9; repeat from * to the last stitch, k1 (10/52 stitches).

Row 29 K1, *SK2P, k7; repeat from * to the last stitch, k1 (8/42 stitches).

Row 31 K1, *SK2P, k5; repeat from * to the last stitch, k1 (6/32 stitches).

Row 33 K1, *SK2P, k3; repeat from * to the last stitch, k1 (4/22 stitches).

Row 35 K1, *SK2P, k1; repeat from * to the last stitch, k1 (2/12 stitches).

Row 36 Purl.

Break the yarn, leaving a long tail. Thread through remaining 12 stitches, pull tight, and secure. Sew seam.

Stitch Key

☐ K on RS, p on WS

· P on RS, k on WS

Ⓢ SK2P

Ⓜ M1

Ⓞ Cast on 1 st

⌒ Bind off 1 st purlwise on WS

■ No stitch

☐ Repeat

PROJECT
INSTRUCTIONS

STELLA LUNA PULLOVER PAGE 10

Sizes
Small/Medium (Large/XL)

Knitted Measurements
- Bust 41½ (44)" [105.5 (112)cm]
- Length 26 (27)" [66 (68.5)cm]

Materials
- Aslan Trends King Baby Llama and Mulberry Silk (70% llama/30% silk), each approximately 218 yards (200m) and 3.5 oz (100g); 4 (5) skeins of #4075 Grape (MC) and 1 skein of #4090 Lilac (CC)
- Size U.S. 8 (5mm) circular and double-pointed needles or size needed to obtain gauge
- Size U.S. 9 (5.5mm) straight needles
- 24 faceted crystal beads (6mm)
- Stitch marker
- Tapestry needle

Gauge
17 stitches and 20 rows = 4" (10cm) in St st on smaller needles
Take time to check gauge.

BODY
Front
Starting at the lower front with MC and smaller needles, cast on 40 (46) stitches.
Work 2 rows in St st.
Continuing in St st, cast on 4 stitches at the beginning of the next 4 rows, then cast on 2 stitches at the beginning of the next 20 rows [96 (102) stitches].
Inc row (RS) K1, m1, k to the last stitch, m1, k1 [98 (104) stitches].
Repeat Inc row [every 4th row] 3 more times [104 (110) stitches]; [every 6th row] 4 times [112 (118) stitches]; then [every 8th row] 4 times [120 (126) stitches].
Work even in St st until piece measures 23 (24)" [58.5 (61) cm] from beginning, ending with a WS row.

Neck Opening
Next row (RS) K43 (45), attach a second ball of yarn and bind off 34 (36) stitches, k to end. Continuing in St st, work on both sides at the same time.
Next row (WS) Purl.

Dec row Right front: K to the last 3 stitches, ssk, k1; Left front: K1, k2tog, k to end.
Repeat Dec row every RS row twice more [40 (42) stitches each side].
Work 3 rows even.
Next row (RS) Using the same ball of yarn across all stitches, k40 (42), cast on 40 (42) stitches, k40 (42) [120 (126) stitches].

Back
Work even in St st until the back matches the front to the last increase, ending with a WS row.
Dec row (RS) K1, k2tog, k to the last 3 stitches, ssk, k1 [118 (124) stitches].
Repeat Dec row [every 8th row] 3 more times [112 (118) stitches]; [every 6th row] 4 times [104 (110) stitches]; then [every 4th row] 4 times [96 (102) stitches].
Bind off 2 stitches at the beginning of the next 20 rows,

then bind off 4 stitches at the beginning of the next 4 rows [40 (46) stitches]. Work 2 rows in St st. Bind off remaining stitches.

Border
With RS facing, MC, and circular needle, pick up and k546 (568) stitches evenly around the entire body. Place marker. Work in K2, P2 Rib for ¾" (2cm). Bind off loosely in pattern.

Neckband
With RS facing, MC and dpns, pick up and k100 (104) stitches evenly around neck opening. Place marker. Work in K2, P2 Rib for ¾" (2cm). Bind off loosely in pattern.

CIRCLES (MAKE 4)
Make 2 Stella Luna circles (see page 117) each in MC and CC.

FINISHING

Lightly block body and circles.

Sew 6 beads to the center of each circle, as pictured.

Sew circles around the neck opening and shoulders, as pictured. Fold the garment at the shoulder line and mark points 11 (11½)" [28 (29)cm] down from shoulders and 4½" (11.5cm) from the side edges. Following the column of stitches, sew 9½" (24cm) side seams from the marked points down.

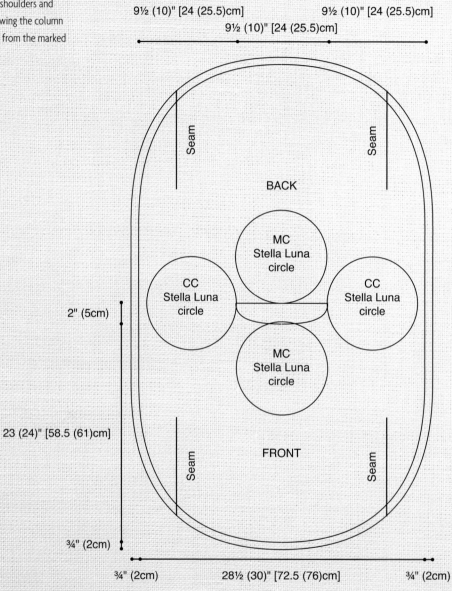

9½ (10)" [24 (25.5)cm]   9½ (10)" [24 (25.5)cm]

9½ (10)" [24 (25.5)cm]

Seam   Seam

BACK

MC
Stella Luna
circle

CC
Stella Luna
circle

CC
Stella Luna
circle

2" (5cm)

MC
Stella Luna
circle

23 (24)" [58.5 (61)cm]

Seam   FRONT   Seam

¾" (2cm)

¾" (2cm)   28½ (30)" [72.5 (76)cm]   ¾" (2cm)

Size
One size

Knitted Measurements
- Shrug Length 15¼" (39cm), Neck circumference 19" (48.5cm), Lower edge circumference 106" (270cm)
- Cape Length 25" (63.5cm), Neck circumference 22¾" (58cm), Lower edge circumference 159" (404cm)

Materials
Shrug
- Cascade Yarns Magnum (100% wool), each approximately 123 yards (113m) and 1.75 oz (50g); 3 skeins of #8400 Charcoal (A)
- HPKY Venice (50% baby alpaca/22% nylon/21% polyester/7% merino), each approximately 300 yards (275m) and 3.5 oz (100g); 1 skein of Charcoal (B)
- Size U.S. 15 (10mm) straight needles or size needed to obtain gauge
- 3 Helping Hand buttons (Nicky Epstein #93362)

Cape
- The Bag Smith Big Stitch Yarn Bump (70% alpaca/15% wool/15% nylon), each approximately 40 oz (1.13kg); 2 bumps Gray (A)
- HPKY Venice (50% baby alpaca/22% nylon/21% polyester/7% merino), each approximately 300 yards (275m) and 3.5 oz (100g); 1 skein of Charcoal (B)
- Size U.S. 50 (25mm) circular needle (to accommodate large number of stitches) or size needed to obtain gauge
- 2 yards (1.8m) of 1½" (4cm) plaid ribbon
- 3 Heart clasps (Nicky Epstein #4045)
- Tapestry needle

Gauge
Shrug 5½ stitches and 11 rows = 4" (10cm) in Garter st using yarns A and B together
Cape 5 stitches and 10 rows = 6" (15cm) in Garter st using yarns A and B together
Take time to check gauge.

SHRUG/CAPE
With one strand each of A and B held together, cast on 21 stitches.

For shrug only Knit 6 rows. Work rows 1–14 of Rotate circle (see page 55) 20 times total. Knit 6 rows. Bind off.

For cape only Work rows 1–14 of Rotate circle 19 times total.
Bind off.

FINISHING
Block pieces lightly to measurements.

Shrug
Locate a space in the Garter st band on the right front, approximately 1¼" (3cm) from the top, and tease it open with the knitting needle into an opening large enough for the button. Make two more buttonholes approximately 3" (7.5cm) and 6" (15cm) from the first one. With B, outline the openings using Buttonhole stitch. Sew buttons to correspond on the left front.

With the shrug buttoned, align the "wedges" as follows (counting from the button band): 2–3 for the right front, 4 for the right sleeve, 6 for the back, 4 for the left sleeve, and 3 for the left front. Using B, sew a 3½" (9cm) chain stitch seam from the lower edge, at the point where the sleeves meet at front and back for an underarm/side seam. Repeat on the other side.

Cape
Thread the ribbon below the 3 stockinette stitches across the neck edge of the cape. Sew the first set of clasps at this same point, and the other two sets 4" (10cm) apart.

SHRUG

CAPE

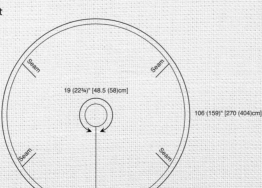

19 (22¾)" [48.5 (58)cm]

106 (159)" [270 (404)cm]

15¼ (25)" [39 (63.5)cm]

CRYSTAL LACE JACKET PAGE 12

Size
Small–Medium (Large–XL)

Knitted Measurements
• Bust 36–38(40–42)" [91–96.5(101.5–106.5)cm]
• Length 30(32)" [76(81)cm]
• Sleeve Length to underarm 16" (40cm), 18" (45.5cm) with optional fur

Materials
• Prism Symphony (80% merino wool/10% cashmere/10% nylon) 2 oz (57g) and 118 yards (108m); 11 (12) skeins of #103 (A)
• Prism Plume (100% nylon) 2.8 oz (79g) and 45 yards (41m); 4(5) skeins of Mink (B)
• Size U.S. 8(9) (5mm) 40" (101.5cm) and 60" (152.5cm) circular needles and 1 set of 5 double-pointed needles
• Stitch markers
• Tapestry needle

Gauge
18 stitches and 28 rows = 4" in St st on size 8 (5mm) needles
16 stitches and 24 rows = 4" in St st on size 9 (5.5mm) needles, or size needed to obtain gauge
Take time to check gauge.

PATTERN STITCH
Rnds 1–50 of Elegant Leaf Lace Circle (see page 105), then the following rnds 51–123 as directed.

Round 51 *[K1tbl, yo, k1, yo, ssk, k2, yo, ssk, k5, k2tog, yo, k2, k2tog, yo, k1, yo] 2 times; rep from * around. (44 stitches)

Round 52 and all even rounds Knit.

Round 53 *(K1tbl, yo, k3, yo, ssk, k2, yo, ssk, k3, k2tog, yo, k2, k2tog, yo, k3, yo) 2 times; rep from * around. (48 stitches)

Round 55 *[K1tbl, yo, k2tog, (yo) 2 times, ssk, k1, yo, ssk, k2, yo, ssk, k1, k2tog, yo, k2, k2tog, yo, k1, k2tog, (yo) 2 times, ssk, yo] 2 times; rep from * around. (52 stitches)

Round 57 *K1tbl, yo, k1tbl, yo, k2, k2tog, (yo) 2 times, (ssk) 2 times, k2, yo, s2kp, yo, k2, (k2tog) 2 times, (yo) 2 times, ssk, k2, yo, s2kp, yo, k2, k2tog, (yo) 2 times, (ssk) 2 times, k2, yo, s2kp, yo, k2, (k2tog) 2 times, (yo) 2 times, ssk, k2, yo, k1tbl, yo; rep from * around. (52 stitches)

Round 59 *(Yo, k1tbl, yo, k1) 2 times, k2tog, (yo) 2 times, ssk, k2tog, yo, ssk, k5, k2tog, yo, ssk, k2tog, (yo) 2 times, ssk, yo, s2kp, yo, k2tog, (yo) 2 times, ssk, k2tog, yo, ssk, k5, k2tog, yo, ssk, k2tog, (yo) 2 times, ssk, k1, yo, k1tbl, yo, k1; rep from * around. (54 stitches)

Round 61 *Yo, s2kp, yo, k2, yo, k1tbl, yo, k2, yo, ssk, k2tog, (yo) 2 times, (ssk) 2 times, k3, (k2tog) 2 times, (yo) 2 times, ssk, k2, yo, s2kp, yo, k2, k2tog, (yo) 2 times, (ssk) 2 times, k3, (k2tog) 2 times, (yo) 2 times, ssk, k2tog, yo, k2, yo, k1tbl, yo, k2; rep from * around. (54 stitches)

Round 63 *Yo, s2kp, yo, k3, yo, k1tbl, yo, k3, k2tog, (yo) 2 times, ssk, k2tog, yo, ssk, k1, k2tog, yo, ssk, k2tog, (yo) 2 times, ssk, yo, s2kp, yo, k2tog, (yo) 2 times, ssk, k2tog, yo, ssk, k1, k2tog, yo, ssk, k2tog, (yo) 2 times, ssk, k3, yo, k1tbl, yo, k3; rep from * around. (54 stitches)

Round 65 *Yo, s2kp, yo, k4, yo, k1tbl, yo, k4, ssk, k2tog, (yo) 2 times, ssk, yo, s2kp, yo, k2tog, (yo) 2 times, ssk, k2tog, yo, k3, yo, ssk, k2tog, (yo) 2 times, ssk, yo, s2kp, k2tog, (yo) 2 times, ssk, k2tog, yo, k4, yo, k1tbl, yo, k4; rep from * around. (57 stitches)

Round 67 *Yo, s2kp, yo, k5, yo, k1tbl, yo, k5, k2tog, (yo) 2 times, ssk, k2tog, yo, k3, (yo) 2 times, ssk, k1, k2tog, yo, k5, yo, ssk, k1, k2tog, (yo) 2 times, k2, (yo) 2 times, ssk, k2tog, (yo) 2 times, ssk, K5, yo, k1tbl, yo, k5; rep from * around. (64 stitches)

Round 69 *Yo, s2kp, yo, ssk, k3, yo, k1, yo, k1tbl, yo, k1, yo, k3, k2tog, yo, ssk, k2tog, (yo) 2 times, ssk, k2tog, (yo) 2 times, ssk, k2, k2tog, yo, k7, yo, ssk, k2, [k2tog, (yo) 2 times,

ssk] 2 times, k2tog, yo, ssk, k3, yo, k1, yo, k1tbl, yo, k1, yo, k3, k2tog; rep from * around. (68 stitches)

Round 71 *Yo, s2kp, yo, ssk, k3, yo, k2, yo, k1tbl, yo, k2, yo, k3, (k2tog) 2 times, (yo) 2 times, ssk, k2tog, (yo) 2 times, ssk, k2tog, (yo) 2 times, s2kp, yo, k9, yo, s2kp, (yo) 2 times, ssk, k2tog, (yo) 2 times, ssk, k2tog, (yo) 2 times, (ssk) 2 times, k3, yo, k2, yo, k1tbl, yo, k2, yo, k3, k2tog; rep from * around. (72 stitches)

Round 73 *S2kp, yo, ssk, (k3, yo) 2 times, k1tbl, (yo, k3) 2 times, k2tog, yo, ssk, [k2tog, (yo) 2 times, ssk] 2 times, k2tog, yo, k4, (yo, k1) 3 times, yo, k4, yo, ssk, [k2tog, (yo) 2 times, ssk] 2 times, k2tog, yo, ssk, (k3, yo) 2 times, k1tbl, (yo, k3) 2 times, k2tog, yo; rep from * around. (80 stitches)

Round 75 *K1tbl, yo, k1, yo, ssk, k3, yo, ssk, k5, k2tog, yo, k3, k2tog, [k2tog, (yo) 2 times, ssk] 2 times, k1, k2tog, yo, k5, (kfb) 7 times, k5, yo, ssk, k1, [k2tog, (yo) 2 times, ssk] 2 times, ssk, k3, yo, ssk, k5, k2tog, yo, k3, k2tog, yo, k1, yo; rep from * around. (87 stitches)

Round 77 *K1tbl, yo, (k3, yo, ssk) 2 times, (k3, k2tog, yo) 2 times, ssk, k2tog, (yo) 2 times, ssk, k3, k2tog, yo, k6, k1tbl, [(yo) 2 times, k2] 6 times, (yo) 2 times, k1tbl, k6, yo, ssk, k2, k2tog, (yo) 2 times, ssk, k2tog, (yo, ssk, k3) 2 times, (k2tog, yo, k3) 2 times, yo; rep from * around. (101 stitches)

Round 79 *Yo, k1tbl, yo, k2tog, (yo) 2 times, ssk, k1, yo, ssk, k3, yo, ssk, k1, k2tog, yo, k3, k2tog, ssk, (yo) twice, ssk, k2tog, (yo) twice, s2kp, yo, k5, k2tog, (1/1LC) 14 times, ssk, k5, yo, s2kp, (yo) twice, ssk, k2tog, (yo) twice, (ssk) twice, k3, yo, ssk, k1, k2tog, yo, k3, k2tog, yo, k1, k2tog, (yo) 2 times, ssk. (99 stitches)

Round 81 *K1, yo, k1tbl, yo, k1, yo, ssk, k2tog, (yo) 2 times, (ssk) 2 times, k3, yo, s2kp, yo, k3, k2tog, yo, ssk, k2tog, (yo) 2 times, ssk, k2tog, yo, k5, k2tog, k1, (1/1LC, k2) 6 times, 1/1LC, k1, ssk, k5, yo, ssk, k2tog, (yo) 2 times, ssk, k2tog, yo, ssk, k3, yo, s2kp, yo, k3, (k2tog) 2 times, (yo) 2 times, ssk, k2tog, yo; rep from * around. (95 stitches)

Round 83 *K2, yo, k1tbl, yo, k2, k2tog, (yo) 2 times, ssk, k2tog, yo, ssk, k7, (k2tog) 2 times, (yo) 2 times, ssk, k1, k2tog, yo, k5, k2tog, (1/1LC) 14 times, ssk, k5, yo, ssk, k1, k2tog, yo, k2, (yo) 2 times, (ssk) 2 times, k7, k2tog, yo, ssk, k2tog, (yo) 2 times, ssk; rep from * around. (91 stitches)

Round 85 *K3, yo, k1tbl, yo, k3, k2tog, ssk, (yo) 2 times, (ssk) 2 times, k5, k2tog, yo, ssk, k2, k2tog, yo, k5, k2tog, k1, (1/1LC, k2) 6 times, 1/1LC, k1, ssk, k5, yo, ssk, k2, k2tog, yo, ssk, k5, (k2tog) 2 times, (yo) 2 times, ssk, k2tog, yo; rep from * around. (87 stitches)

Round 87 *K4, yo, k1tbl, yo, k4, k2tog, (yo) 2 times, ssk, k2tog, yo, ssk, k3, (k2tog) 2 times, (yo) 2 times, s2kp, yo, k5, k2tog, (1/1LC) 14 times, ssk, k5, yo, s2kp, (yo) 2 times, (ssk) 2 times, k3, k2tog, yo, ssk, k2tog, (yo) 2 times, ssk; rep from * around. (83 stitches)

Round 89 *Ssk, k2, yo, k1, yo, k1tbl, yo, k1, yo, k2, k2tog, yo, ssk, k2tog, (yo) 2 times, (ssk) 2 times, k1, k2tog, yo, ssk, k1, k2tog, yo, k4, k2tog, k1, (1/1LC, k2) 6 times, 1/1LC, k1, ssk, k4, yo, ssk, k1, k2tog, ssk, k1, (k2tog) 2 times, (yo) 2 times, ssk, k2tog, yo; rep from * around. (78 stitches)

Round 91 *Ssk, (k2, yo) 2 times, k1tbl, (yo, k2) 2 times, (k2tog) 2 times, (yo) 2 times, ssk, k2tog, (yo) 2 times, s2kp, k2tog, (yo) 2 times, s2kp, yo, k3, k2tog, (1/1LC) 14 times, ssk, k3, yo, s2kp, (yo) 2 times, k1, s2kp, (yo) 2 times, ssk, k2tog, (yo) 2 times, ssk; rep from * around. (77 stitches)

Round 93 *Ssk, k2, yo, k3, yo, k1tbl, yo, k3, yo, k2, k2tog, yo, ssk, k2tog, (yo) 2 times, ssk, k2tog, (yo) 2 times, ssk, k1, k2tog, yo, k2, k2tog, k1, (1/1LC, k2) 6 times, 1/1LC, k1, ssk, k2, yo, ssk, k1, k2tog, (yo) 2 times, ssk, k2tog, (yo) 2 times, ssk, k2tog, yo; rep from * around. (77stitches)

Round 95 *SSk, k2, yo, ssk, k5, k2tog, yo, k2, (k2tog) 2 times, (yo) 2 times, ssk, k2tog, (yo) 2 times, ssk, k2tog, (yo) 2 times, s2kp, yo, k1, k2tog, (1/1LC) 14 times, ssk, k1, yo, s2kp, (yo) 2 times, ssk, k2tog, (yo) 2 times, ssk, k2tog, (yo) 2 times, ssk; rep from * around. (73 stitches)

Round 97 *Ssk, k2, yo, ssk, k3, k2tog, yo, k2, k2tog, yo, k2, k2tog, (yo) 2 times, ssk, k2tog, (yo) 2 times, ssk, k2tog, (yo) 2 times, k3tog, yo, k1, (1/1LC, k2) 6 times, 1/1LC, k1, yo, s2kp, (yo) 2 times, ssk, k2tog, (yo) 2 times, ssk, k2, yo; rep from * around. (73 stitches)

Round 99 *Ssk, k2, yo, ssk, k1, k2tog, yo, k2, k2tog, yo, k1, k2tog, (yo) 2 times, ssk, k2tog, (yo) 2 times, ssk, k2tog, (yo) 2 times, ssk, k1, k2tog, yo, (1/1LC) 14 times, yo, ssk, k1, k2tog, [(yo) 2 times, ssk, k2tog] 2 times, (yo) 2 times, ssk, k1, yo; rep from * around. (73 stitches)

Round 101 *Ssk, k2, yo, s2kp, yo, k2, k2tog, yo, [k2tog, (yo) 2 times, ssk] 3 times, k2tog, (yo) 2 times, s2kp, yo, k1, (1/1LC, k2) 6 times, 1/1LC, k1, yo, s2kp, (yo) 2 times, ssk, [k2tog, (yo) 2 times, ssk] 3 times, yo; rep from * around. (73 stitches)

Round 103 *Ssk, k5, k2tog, yo, k3, [k2tog, (yo) 2 times, ssk] 3 times, k1, k2tog, yo, (1/1LC) 14 times, yo, ssk, k1, [k2tog, (yo) 2 times, ssk] 3 times, k3, yo; rep from * around. (73 stitches)

Round 105 *Ssk, k3, k2tog, yo, k2, [k2tog, (yo) 2 times, ssk] 3 times, k2tog, (yo) 2 times, s2kp, yo, k1, (1/1LC, k2) 6 times, 1/1LC, k1, yo, s2kp, (yo) 2 times, ssk, [k2tog, (yo) 2 times, ssk] 3 times, k2, yo; rep from * around. (73 stitches)

Round 107 *Ssk, k1, k2tog, yo, k1, [k2tog, (yo) 2 times, ssk] 4 times, k1, k2tog, yo, (1/1LC) 14 times, yo, ssk, k1, [k2tog, (yo) 2 times, ssk] 4 times, k1, yo; rep from * around. (73 stitches)

Round 109 *S2kp, yo, [k2tog, (yo) 2 times, ssk] 4 times, k2tog, (yo) 2 times, s2kp, yo, k1, (1/1LC, k2) 6 times, 1/1LC, k1, yo, s2kp, (yo) 2 times, ssk, [k2tog, (yo) 2 times, ssk] 4 times, yo; rep from * around. (73 stitches)

Round 111 *K2tog, (yo) 2 times, ssk, [k2tog, (yo) 2 times, ssk] 4 times, k1, k2tog, yo, (1/1LC) 14 times, yo, ssk, k1, [k2tog, (yo) 2 times, ssk] 4 times, k2tog, (yo) 2 times, k1; rep from * around. (74 stitches)

Round 113 *Yo, ssk, [k2tog, (yo) 2 times, ssk] 4 times, k2tog, (yo) 2 times, s2kp, yo, k1, (1/1LC, k2) 6 times, 1/1LC, k1, yo, s2kp, (yo) 2 times, ssk, [k2tog, (yo) 2 times, ssk] 4 times, k2tog, yo; rep from * around. (74 stitches)

Round 115 *[K2tog, (yo) 2 times, ssk] 5 times, k2tog, (yo) 2 times, k1, ssk, k2tog, yo, (1/1LC) 10 times, yo, ssk, k2tog, k1, (yo) 2 times, ssk, [k2tog, (yo) 2 times, ssk] 5 times; rep from * around. (74 stitches)

Round 117 *Yo, ssk, [k2tog, (yo) 2 times, ssk] 5 times, k2tog, (yo) 2 times, s2kp, yo, k1, (1/1LC, k2) 4 times, 1/1LC, k1, yo, s2kp, (yo) 2 times, ssk, [k2tog, (yo) 2 times, ssk] 5 times, k2tog, yo; rep from * around. (74 stitches)

Round 119 *[K2tog, (yo) 2 times, ssk] 6 times, k2tog, (yo) 2 times, k1, ssk, k2tog, yo, (1/1LC) 6 times, yo, ssk, k2tog, k1, (yo) 2 times, ssk, [k2tog, (yo) 2 times, ssk] 6 times; rep from * around. (74 stitches)

Round 121 *Yo, ssk, [k2tog, (yo) 2 times, ssk] 6 times, k2tog, (yo) 2 times, s2kp, yo, k1, (1/1LC, k2) 2 times, 1/1LC, k1, yo, s2kp, (yo) 2 times, ssk, [k2tog, (yo) 2 times, ssk] 6 times, k2tog, yo; rep from * around. (74 stitches)

Round 123 *[K2tog, (yo) 2 times, ssk] 8 times, k2tog, yo, k1, (1/1LC) 2 times, k1, yo, ssk, [k2tog, (yo) 2 times, ssk] 8 times; rep from * around. (74 stitches)

Notes When working in rounds, knit all even-numbered rounds, knitting into the front and back of (yo) 2 times of previous round.

When working in rows, purl all even-numbered rows, purling into front and back of (yo) 2 times of previous row.

JACKET

Start with dpn, work rnds 1–50 of Elegant Leaf Lace Circle (see page 105), then work rnds 51–59 as given above, changing to progressively longer circular needles when there are too many stitches to fit on the needle being used. Rnd 59 is worked on 60" (152.5cm) circular needle.

Right Sleeve

With RS of circle facing, sl first 14 stitches of section 1 to 16" (40.5cm) circular needle, turn. Pfb, p13. With WS of circle facing purl 10 stitches of section 8, then pfb in eleventh stitch. (Leave remaining stitches on 60" [152.5cm]

circular needle.) Sleeve is worked in rows (see second note above).

Row 61 K1 (edge stitch), pm, m1, k2tog, (yo) 2 times, ssk, k2tog, yo, k2, yo, k1tbl, yo, k2, yo, s2kp, yo, k2, yo, k1tbl, yo, k2, yo, ssk, k2tog, (yo) 2 times, ssk, m1, pm, k1 (edge stitch). (31 stitches plus 2 edge stitches)

Row 62 and all even rows Purl.

Row 63 K1, sm, m1, k1, yo, ssk, k2tog, (yo) 2 times, ssk, k3, yo, k1tbl, yo, k3, yo, s2kp, yo, k3, yo, k1tbl, yo, k3, k2tog, (yo) 2 times, k2tog, yo, k1, m1, slm, k1. (37 stitches plus 2 edge stitches)

Row 65 K1, sm, m1, yo, ssk, k2tog, (yo) 2 times, ssk, k2tog, yo, k4, yo, k1tbl, yo, k4, yo, s2kp, yo, k4, yo, k1tbl, yo, k4, yo, ssk, k2tog, (yo) 2 times, ssk, k2tog, yo, m1, sm, k1. (43 stitches plus 2 edge stitches)

Row 67 K1, sm, m1, k1, [k2tog, (yo) 2 times, ssk] 2 times, k5, yo, k1tbl, yo, k5, yo, s2kp, yo, k5, yo, k1tbl, yo, k5, [k2tog, (yo) 2 times, ssk] 2 times, k1, m1, slm, k1. (49 stitches plus 2 edge stitches)

Row 69 K1, sm, m1, [k2tog, (yo) 2 times, ssk] 2 times, k2tog, yo, ssk, k3, yo, k1, yo, k1tbl, yo, k1, yo, k3, k2tog, yo, s2kp, yo, ssk, k3, yo, k1, yo, k1tbl, yo, k1, yo, k3, k2tog, yo, ssk, [k2tog, (yo) 2 times, ssk] 2 times, m1, sm, k1. (55 stitches plus 2 edge stitches)

Row 71 K1, sm, m1, k1, yo, ssk, [k2tog, (yo) 2 times, ssk] 2 times, ssk, k3, yo, k2, yo, k1tbl, yo, k2, yo, k3, k2tog, yo, s2kp, yo, ssk, k3, yo, k2, yo, k1tbl, yo, k2, yo, k3, k2tog, [k2tog, (yo) 2 times, ssk] 2 times, k2tog, yo, k1, m1, sm, k1. (61 stitches plus 2 edge stitches)

Row 73 K1, sm, m1, yo, ssk, [k2tog, (yo) 2 times, ssk] 2 times, k2tog, yo, ssk, (k3, yo) 2 times, k1tbl, (yo, k3) 2 times, k2tog, yo, s2kp, yo, ssk, (k3, yo) 2 times, k1tbl, (yo, k3) 2 times, k2tog, yo, ssk, [k2tog, (yo) 2 times, ssk] 2 times, k2tog, yo, m1, sm, k1. (67 stitches plus 2 edge stitches)

Row 75 K1, sm, m1, k1, [k2tog, (yo) 2 times, ssk] 3 times, ssk, k3, yo, ssk, k5, k2tog, yo, k3, k2tog, yo, k1, yo, k1tbl, yo, k1, yo, ssk, k3, yo, ssk, k5, k2tog, yo, k3, k2tog, [k2tog, (yo) 2 times, ssk] 3 times, k1, m1, sm, k1. (69 stitches plus 2 edge stitches)

Row 77 K1, sm m1, [k2tog, (yo) 2 times, ssk] 3 times, k2tog, yo, ssk, k3, yo, ssk, k3, (k2tog, yo, k3) 2 times, yo, k1tbl, yo, k3, (yo, ssk, k3) 2 times, k2tog, yo, k3, k2tog, yo, ssk, [k2tog, (yo) ssk] 3 times, m1, sm, k1. (71 stitches plus 2 edge stitches)

Row 79 K1, sm, m1, k1, yo, ssk, [k2tog, (yo) 2 times, ssk] 3 times, ssk, k3, yo, ssk, k1, k2tog, yo, k3, k2tog, yo, k1, k2tog, (yo) 2 times, yo, ssk, k1, yo, k1tbl, yo, k2tog, (yo) 2 times, ssk, k1, yo, ssk, k3, yo, ssk, k1, k2tog, yo, k3, k2tog, [k2tog, (yo) 2 times, ssk] 3 times, k2tog, yo, k1, m1, sm, k1. (73 stitches plus 2 edge stitches)

Row 81 K1, sm, m1, yo, ssk, [k2tog, (yo) 2 times, ssk] 3 times, k2tog, yo, ssk, k3, yo, s2kp, yo, k3, k2tog, k2tog, (yo) 2 times, ssk, k2tog, yo, k1, yo, k1tbl, yo, k1, yo, ssk, k2tog, (yo) 2 times, ssk, ssk, k3, yo, s2kp, yo, k3, k2tog, yo, ssk, [k2tog, (yo) 2 times, ssk] 3 times, k2tog, yo, m1, sm, k1. (73 stitches plus 2 edge stitches)

Place a removable marker in each edge stitch after row 82 is completed to mark underarm.

Row 83 K1, sm, k1, [k2tog, (yo) 2 times, ssk] 4 times, ssk, k7, k2tog, yo, ssk, k2tog, (yo) 2 times, ssk, k2, yo, k1tbl, yo, k2, k2tog, (yo) 2 times, ssk, k2tog, yo, ssk, k7, k2tog, [k2tog, (yo) 2 times, ssk] 4 times, k1, sm, k1. (71 stitches plus 2 edge stitches)

Row 85 K1, sm, k1, yo, ssk, [k2tog, (yo) 2 times, ssk] 3 times, k2tog, yo, ssk, k5, k2tog, k2tog, (yo) 2 times, ssk, k2tog, yo, k3, yo, k1tbl, yo, k3, yo, k2tog, ssk, (yo) 2 times, (ssk) 2 times, k5, k2tog, yo, ssk, [k2tog, (yo) 2 times, ssk] 3 times, k2tog, yo, k1, sm, k1. (69 stitches plus 2 edge stitches)

Row 87 K1, sm, k1, [k2tog, (yo) 2 times, ssk] 4 times, ssk, k3, k2tog, yo, ssk, k2tog, (yo) 2 times, ssk, k4, yo, k1tbl, yo, k4, k2tog, (yo) 2 times, ssk, k2tog, yo, ssk, k3, k2tog, [k2tog, (yo) 2 times, ssk] 4 times, k1, sm, k1. (67 stitches plus 2 edge stitches)

Row 89 K1, sm, k1, yo, ssk, [k2tog, (yo) 2 times, ssk] 3 times, k2tog, yo, ssk, k1, k2tog, k2tog, (yo) 2 times, ssk, k2tog, yo, ssk, k2, yo, k1, yo, k1tbl, yo, k1, yo, k2, k2tog, yo, ssk, k2tog, (yo) 2 times, ssk, ssk, k1, k2tog, yo, ssk, [k2tog, (yo) 2 times, ssk] 3 times, k2tog, yo, k1, sm, k1. (65 stitches plus 2 edge stitches)

Row 91 K1, sm, k1, [k2tog, (yo) 2 times, ssk] 4 times, s2kp, (yo) 2 times, ssk, k2tog, (yo) 2 times, ssk, ssk, (k2, yo) 2 times, k1tbl, (yo, k2) 2 times, k2tog, (yo) 2 times, ssk, k2tog, (yo) 2 times, s2kp, [k2tog, (yo) 2 times, ssk] 4 times, k1, sm, k1. (65 stitches plus 2 edge stitches)

Row 93 k1, sm, k1, yo, ssk, [k2tog, (yo) 2 times, ssk] 5 times, k2tog, yo, ssk, k2, yo, k3, yo, k1tbl, yo, k3, yo, k2, k2tog, yo, ssk, [k2tog, (yo) 2 times, ssk] 5 times, k2tog, yo, k1, sm, k1. (67 stitches plus 2 edge stitches)

Row 95 K1, sm, k1, [k2tog, (yo) 2 times, ssk] 6 times, ssk, k2, yo, ssk, k5, k2tog, yo, k2, k2tog, [k2tog, (yo) 2 times, ssk] 6 times, k1, sm, k1. (65 stitches plus 2 edge stitches)

Row 97 K1, sm, k1, yo, ssk, [k2tog, (yo) 2 times, ssk] 5 times, k2tog, yo, ssk, k2, yo, ssk, k3, k2tog, yo, k2, k2tog, yo, ssk, [k2tog, (yo) 2 times, ssk] 5 times, k2tog, yo, k1, sm, k1. (63 stitches plus 2 edge stitches)

Row 99 K1, sm, k1, yo, ssk, [k2tog, (yo) 2 times, ssk] 6 times, ssk, k2, yo, ssk, k1, k2tog, yo, k2, k2tog, [k2tog, (yo) 2 times, ssk] 6

times, k1, sm, k1. (61 stitches plus 2 edge stitches)

Row 101 K1, sm, k1, yo, ssk, [k2tog, (yo) 2 times, ssk] 5 times, k2tog, yo, ssk, k2, yo, s2kp, yo, k2, k2tog, yo, ssk, [k2tog, (yo) 2 times, ssk] 5 times, k2tog, yo, k1, sm, k1. (59 stitches plus 2 edge stitches)

Row 103 K1, sm, k1, [k2tog, (yo) 2 times, ssk] 6 times, ssk, k5, k2tog, [k2tog, (yo) 2 times, ssk] 6 times, k1, sm, k1. (57 stitches plus 2 edge stitches)

Row 105 K1, sm, k1, yo, ssk, [k2tog, (yo) 2 times, ssk] 5 times, k2tog, yo, ssk, k3, k2tog, yo, ssk, [k2tog, (yo) 2 times, ssk] 5 times, k2tog, yo, k1, sm, k1. (55 stitches plus 2 edge stitches)

Row 107 K1, sm, k1, [k2tog, (yo) 2 times, ssk] 6 times, ssk, k1, k2tog, [k2tog, (yo) 2 times, ssk] 6 times, k1, sm, k1. (53 stitches plus 2 edge stitches)

Row 109 K1, sm, k1, yo, ssk, [k2tog, (yo) 2 times, ssk] 5 times, k2tog, yo, s2kp, yo ssk, [k2tog, (yo) 2 times, ssk] 5 times, k2tog, yo, k1, sm, k1. (51 stitches plus 2 edge stitches)

Row 111 K1, sm, yo, k1, [k2tog, (yo) 2 times, ssk] 6 times, k3tog, (yo) 2 times, ssk, [k2tog, (yo) 2 times, ssk] 5 times, k1, yo, sm k1. (52 stitches plus 2 edge stitches)

Row 113 K1, sm, [k2tog, (yo) 2 times, ssk] 13 times, sm, k1. (52 stitches plus 2 edge stitches)

Row 115 K1, sm, yo, ssk, [k2tog, (yo) 2 times, ssk] 12 times, k2tog, yo, sm, k1. (52 stitches plus 2 edge stitches)

Rep rows 113–116 until 16" (40.5cm) from underarm marked row or 2" (5cm) less than desired length to wrist. End having worked a WS row. Break yarn and place stitches on stitch holder.

Return to stitches left on circular needle and join yarn to first unworked stitch of section 1. Using 40" (101.5cm) circular needles continue with Rnd 60, knitting across remaining stitches of section 1, all stitches of sections 2 and 3, then 43 stitches of section 4.

Left Sleeve

Slip last 11 stitches of section 4 and first 14 stitches of section 5 to a 16" circular needle (25 stitches). Leave rem stitches on hold. Turn work so that WS is facing, and join yarn to first stitch. Pfb in first stitch, purl to last stitch, and pfb in last stitch. Starting with row 61, work same as right sleeve.

Back Sleeve Gussets

RS facing, starting at right side underarm marker of left sleeve, join yarn, pu and knit 14 stitches to top of sleeve cap onto right end of the 60" (152.5cm) circular needle. Break yarn and rejoin to last st on this needle. Pu and knit

14 stitches down left side of right sleeve cap to underarm marker.

Row 60 Sl 1, purl to end.

Row 61 Sl 1, work pattern row 61 to last 2 stitches, turn.

Row 62 Sl 1. Purl to last 2 stitches, turn.

Row 63 Sl 1, work pattern row 63 to last 4 stitches, turn.

Row 64 Sl 1, purl to last 4 stitches, turn.

Row 65 Sl 1, work pattern row 65 to last 6 stitches, turn.

Row 66 Sl 1, purl to last 6 stitches, turn.

Row 67 Sl 1, work pattern row 67 to last 8 stitches, turn.

Row 68 Sl 1, purl to last 8 stitches, turn.

Row 69 Sl 1, work pattern row 69 to last 10 stitches, turn.

Row 70 Sl 1, purl to last 10 stitches, turn.

Row 71 Sl 1, work pattern row 71 to last 12 stitches, turn.

Row 72 Sl 1, purl to last 12 stitches, turn.

Row 73 Sl 1, work pattern row 73 to last 14 stitches, turn.

Row 74 Sl 1, purl to last 14 stitches, turn.

Row 75 Pm, work pattern row 75 to last 14 stitches, pm, k14.

Short Row Shaping for Right Front

Row 1 Continue at end of row 75, pu and knit 14 stitches up right-hand edge of right sleeve cap, then on stitches left on 40"circular needle, k2tog, (yo) 2 times, ssk, k1, turn.

Row 2 Sl 1, purl 9, turn.

Row 3 Sl 1, yo, ssk, [k2tog, (yo) 2 times, ssk] 2 times, k1, turn.

Row 4 Sl 1, p13, turn.

Row 5 Sl 1, yo, ssk, [k2tog, (yo) 2 times, ssk] 3 times, k2tog, k1, turn.

Row 6 Sl 1, p17, turn.

Row 7 Sl 1, yo, ssk, [k2tog, (yo) 2 times, ssk] 4 times, k1, turn.

Row 8 Sl 1, p21, turn.

Row 9 Sl 1, yo, ssk, [k2og, (yo) 2 times, ssk] 5 times, k1, turn.

Row 10 Sl 1, p25, turn.

Row 12 Sl 1, p29, turn.

Row 13 Sl 1, yo, ssk, [k2tog, (yo) 2 times, ssk] 7 times, k1, turn. Continue in this manner until there are 12 repeats of [k2, (yo) 2 times, ssk] on row 23.

Row 24 Sl 1, purl all stitches to end of needle, pu and purl 14 stitches up left edge of left sleeve cap, then p5 from left end of 40" (101.5cm) circular needle, turn.

Short Row Shaping for Left Front

Row 1 Sl 1, yo, ssk, k2tog, (yo) 2 times, ssk, k1, turn.

Row 2 Sl 1, p9, turn.

Row 3 Sl 1, yo, ssk, [k2tog, (yo) 2 times, ssk] 2 times, k1, turn.

Row 4 Sl 1, p13, turn.

Row 5 Sl 1, yo, ssk, [k2tog, (yo) 2 times, ssk] 3 times, k1, turn.

Row 6 Sl 1, p17, turn.

Row 7 Sl 1, yo, ssk, [k2tog, (yo) 2 times, ssk] 4 times, k1, turn.

Row 8 Sl 1, p21, turn.

Row 9 Sl 1, yo, ssk, [k2tog, (yo) 2 times, ssk] 5 times, k1, turn.

Row 10 Sl 1, p25, turn.

Row 11 Sl 1, yo, ssk, [k2tog, (yo) 2 times, ssk] 6 times, k1, turn.

Row 12 Sl 1, p29, turn.

Row 13 Sl 1, yo, ssk, [k2tog, (yo) 2 times, ssk] 7 times, k1, turn. Continue in this manner until row 24 is completed.

Row 25 Sl, yo, ssk, [k2tog, (yo) 2 times, ssk] 13 times, k1, pm, work from chart row 77, start at C work to B, then rep from A to B twice, then from A to D, pm, k1, [k2tog, (yo) 2 times, ssk] 13 times, k1, turn.

Body

Row 78 and all even rows through 100 Sl 1, purl all sts on 60" (152.5cm) needle, purl 2 from 40" (101.5cm) needle, turn.

Row 79 Sl 1, yo, ssk, [k2tog, (yo) 2 times, ssk] 14 times, k1, sm, work from chart row 79 starting at C working to B, then rep from A to B twice, then from A to D, sm, k1, [k2tog, (yo) 2 times, ssk] 14 times, k1.

Rows 80–101 Work as established in rows 78 and 79, having one more rep of [k2tog, (yo) 2 times, ssk] on each front (25 reps on row 101) and working chart rows between markers.

Back Short Rows Shaping

Row 102 Sl 1, purl to E on chart, pm and turn.

Row 103 Work chart row 103 from E to B, A to B twice, then A to F, pm and turn. Work as established in rows 102 and 103 until row 123 is completed, moving markers at end of each row. Next row, turn, purl to end of needle, purl all stitches remaining on 40" (101.5cm) needle onto 60" (152.5cm) needle, purl remaining stitches on 60" (152.5cm) needle. (480 sts) Turn and bind off all stitches knitwise.

Finishing

With yarn B and 60" (152.5cm) needle, * k2, k2tog; rep from * around body. (360 stitches) Knit around for 2" (5cm). Bind off. Slip 54 sleeve stitches to needle and join B, (k3, k2tog) 5 times, k4 (k2tog, k3) 5 times.

Work in St st for 2" (5cm). Bind off. Repeat for second sleeve. Sew sleeve seams.

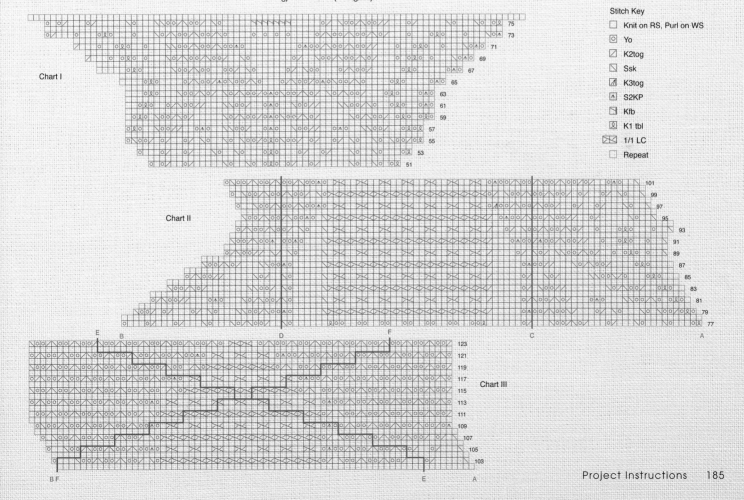

SPRING LEAVES JACKET PAGE 13

Size
Medium

Knitted Measurements
• Bust 40" (101.5cm)
• Length 26" (66cm)
• Sleeve Length to underarm 18" (45.5cm)

Materials
• Manos del Uruguay Rittenhouse Merino 5-ply Space-Dyed (100% wool), each approximately 241 yards (220m) and 3.5 oz (100g); 6 skeins of #596 Succulent (MC)
• Manos del Uruguay Silk Blend (70% wool/30% silk), each approximately 150 yards (135m) and 1.75 oz (50g); 1 skein of #3207 Willow (CC)
• U.S. 7 (4.5mm) needles as follows: 1 set of 5 double-pointed needles, 1 pair of straight needles, 16" (40cm), 40" (101.5cm) and 2 each 24" (61cm) circular needles or size needed to obtain gauge
• Stitch markers
• Stitch holders
• Tapestry needle

Gauge
20 stitches and 28 rows = 4" (10cm) in Box pattern
Take time to check gauge.

M2P (make 2 purlwise) Insert the left-hand needle from front to back under the horizontal strand between the last stitch and the next stitch, purl in the front and back loop of this strand.

PATTERN STITCH
Box Pattern (multiple of 4 stitches + 2)
Row 1 (RS) K2, *p2, k2; repeat from * to the end.
Rows 2 and 3 P2, *k2, p2; repeat from * to the end.
Row 4 Repeat row 1.
Repeat rows 1–4 for pattern, working new stitches into the established pattern.

CIRCLE
With CC, make a Ringed Leaves Circle (see page 82), working rnds 1–33.
Rnds 34–37 Purl.
Place 15 stitches of Section 1 on a stitch holder, 60 stitches of Sections 2–5 on a second 24" (61cm) circular needle,

and 15 stitches of Section 6 on a stitch holder. Leave remaining 60 stitches of Sections 7–10 on the needle. Cut yarn, leaving a 6" (15cm) tail. Set circle aside.

BACK
With straight needles and MC, cast on 50 stitches.
Rows 1 and 4 K2, *p2, k2; repeat from * to end.
Rows 2 and 3 P2, *k2, p2; repeat from * to end.
Rows 5–10 Repeat rows 1–4 once, then work rows 1 and 2.
Cast on 15 stitches at end of row 10 (65 stitches).
Row 11 P1, *k2, p2; repeat from * to end, cast on 15 stitches (80 stitches).
Row 12 K1, *p2, k2; repeat from * to the last stitch, k1.
Rows 13 and 16 K1, *p2, k2; repeat from * to the last stitch, k1.
Rows 14 and 15 P1,* k2, p2; repeat from * to the last stitch, p1.
Rows 17–20 Repeat rows 13–16.
Cast on 15 stitches at end of row 20 (95 stitches).
Row 21 P2, *k2, p2; repeat from * to the last stitch, k1, cast on 15 stitches (110 stitches).
Rows 22 and 23 K2, *p2, k2; repeat from * to end.
Row 24 P2, *k2, p2; repeat from * to end.
Rows 25 and 28 P2, *k2, p2; repeat from * to end.
Rows 26 and 27 K2, *p2, k2; repeat from * to end.
Rows 29–43 Repeat rows 25–28 three times, then work rows 25–27.
Row 44 (decrease row) P2tog, k2, *p2, k2; repeat from * to the last 2 stitches, p2togtbl.
Continuing in pattern, decrease 1 stitch each end every 6th row 7 more times (94 stitches).
Work 5 rows even in pattern.
Next row (RS) P2, [k2, p2] 11 times, k1, m1, k1, [p2, k2] 11 times, p2 (95 stitches).
Next row (join circle) [P2, k2] 10 times; with RS together, use 3-needle bind-off (see page 213) to join Section 1 of the circle to the center 15 stitches of Back, [K2, p2] 10 times (40 stitches each side).
Place 40 stitches of Left Back onto a holder.

Right Back
Row 1 (RS) (P1, k1) in the first stitch, k1, [p2, k2] 8 times, p2, k3tog, SK2P (using 1 Back stitch and 2 Circle stitches), turn.
Row 2 P2, [p2, k2] 9 times, p1 (39 stitches in work).
Row 3 K1, [p2, k2] 8 times, p2, k3tog, SK2P.
Row 4 P2, [p2, k2] 8 times, p2, k1 (37 stitches in work).
Row 5 P1, [k2, p2] 8 times, k3tog, SK2P.
Row 6 P2, [p2, k2] 8 times, p1 (35 stitches in work).

Row 7 K1, [p2, k2] 7 times, p2, k3tog, SK2P.
Row 8 P2, [p2, k2] 7 times, p2, k1 (33 stitches in work).
Row 9 P1, [k2, p2] 7 times, k3tog, SK2P.
Row 10 P2, [p2, k2] 7 times, p1 (31 stitches in work).
Row 11 K1, [p2, k2] 6 times, p2, k3tog, SK2P.
Row 12 P2, [p2, k2] 6 times, p2, k1 (29 stitches in work).
Row 13 P1, [k2, p2] 6 times, k3tog, SK2P.
Row 14 P2, [p2, k2] 6 times, p1 (27 stitches in work).
Row 15 K1, [p2, k2] 5 times, p2, k3tog, SK2P.
Row 16 P2, [p2, k2] 5 times, p2, k1 (25 stitches in work).
Row 17 P1, [k2, p2] 5 times, k3tog, SK2P.
Row 18 P2, [p2, k2] 5 times, p1 (23 stitches in work).
Row 19 K1, [p2, k2] 4 times, p2, k3tog, SK2P.
Row 20 P2, [p2, k2] 4 times, p2, k1 (21 stitches in work).
Row 21 Pfb, [k2, p2] 4 times, k3tog, SK2P.
Row 22 P2, [p2, k2] 4 times, p2 (20 stitches in work).
Row 23 [K2, p2] 4 times, k3tog, SK2P.
Row 24 P2, [p2, k2] 4 times (18 stitches in work).
Row 25 [P2, k2] 3 times, p2, k3tog, SK2P.
Row 26 P2, [p2, k2] 3 times, p2 (16 stitches in work).

Row 27 [K2, p2] 3 times, k3tog, SK2P.

Row 28 P2, [p2, k2] 3 times (14 stitches in work).

Row 29 [P2, k2] 3 times, sl 1, SK2P.

Row 30 P2, [k2, p2] 3 times (14 stitches in work).

Row 31 [K2, p2] 3 times, sl 1, SK2P.

Row 32 P2, [p2, k2] 3 times (14 stitches in work).

Row 33 [P2, k2] 3 times, M2P, sl 1, SK2P.

Row 34 P2, [p2, k2] 3 times, p2 (16 stitches in work).

Row 35 [K2, p2] 3 times, k2, M2P, sl 1, SK2P.

Row 36 P2, [p2, k2] 4 times (18 stitches in work).

Row 37 [P2, k2] 4 times, M2P, sl 1, SK2P.

Row 38 P2, [P2, k2] 4 times, p2 (20 stitches in work).

Row 39 [K2, p2] 4 times, k2, M2P, sl 1, SK2P.

Row 40 P2, [p2, k2] 5 times (22 stitches in work).

Row 41 (K1, p1) in the first stitch, p1, [k2, p2] 4 times, k2, M2P, sl 1, SK2P.

Row 42 P2, [p2, k2] 5 times, p2, k1 (25 stitches in work).

Row 43 P1, [k2, p2] 5 times k2, M2P, sl 1, SK2P.

Row 44 P2, [p2, k2] 6 times, p1 (27 stitches in work).

Row 45 K1, [p2, k2] 6 times, M2P, sl 1, SK2P.

Row 46 P2, [p2, k2] 6 times, p2, k1 (29 stitches in work).

Row 47 P1, [k2, p2] 6 times, k2, M2P, sl 1, SK2P.

Row 48 P2, [p2, k2] 7 times, p1 (31 stitches in work).

Row 49 K1, [p2, k2] 7 times, M2P, sl 1, SK2P.

Row 50 P2, [p2, k2] 7 times, p2, k1 (33 stitches in work).

Row 51 P1, [k2, p2] 7 times, k2, M2P, sl 1, SK2P.

Row 52 P2, [p2, k2] 8 times, p1 (35 stitches in work).

Row 53 K1, [p2, k2] 8 times, M2P, sl 1, SK2P.

Row 54 P2, [p2, k2] 8 times, p2, k1 (37 stitches in work).

Row 55 P1, [k2, p2] 8 times, k2, M2P, sl 1, SK2P.

Row 56 P2, [p2, k2] 9 times, p1 (39 stitches in work).

Row 57 K1, [p2, k2] 9 times, M2P, sl 1, SK2P.

Row 58 P2, [P2, k2] 9 times, p2, k1 (41 stitches in work).

Row 59 P1, [k2, p2] 9 times, k2, M2P, sl 1, SK2P.

Row 60 P2, [p2, k2] 10 times, p1 (43 stitches).

Place stitches on a holder. DO NOT BREAK YARN.

Left Back

Place the Left Back stitches onto a needle ready to work a RS row. Join MC. Slip the first 2 stitches from the circular needle onto the beginning of the same needle.

Row 1 (joining row, RS) K3tog (using 1 Back stitch and 2 Circle stitches), SK2P, [p2, k2] 8 times, p2, k1, (k1, p1) in the last stitch.

Row 2 P1, [k2, p2] 9 times, p2, slip the next 2 stitches from the circle onto the working needle.

Rows 3–28 Keeping in the established pattern, continue to join 2 stitches from the circle to the back and decrease

2 stitches on right side rows until 28 of the Circle stitches have been joined. AT THE SAME TIME increase 1 stitch at the end of row 21.

Row 29 K3tog, sl 1, [k2, p2] 3 times.

Row 30 [P2, k2] 3 times, p2, slip 2 stitches from the Circle.

Row 31 K3tog, sl 1, [k2, p2] 3 times.

Row 32 [K2, p2] 3 times, p2, slip 2 stitches from the Circle.

Row 33 K3tog, sl 1, M2P, [k2, p2] 3 times.

Row 34 [P2, k2] 3 times, p2, p2, sl 2 stitches from the Circle.

Row 35 K3tog, sl 1, M2P, [k2, p2] 3 times, k2.

Row 36 [K2, p2] 4 times, p2, slip 2 stitches from the Circle.

Rows 37–59 Keeping in the established pattern, continue to join 2 stitches from the Circle to the back and sl 1, M2P on RS rows until all the Circle stitches on the circular needle have been joined to the left back. AT THE SAME

TIME, increase 1 stitch at the end of row 41.

Row 60 P1, [k2, p2] 10 times, p2. Break the yarn, leaving a 4" (10cm) tail. Slip the remaining 15 stitches from the Circle that are on a holder to the needle, then slip the 43 Right Back stitches to the needle (101 stitches).

Row 61 (RS) Working across the Right Back, k1, [p2, k2] 10 times, p2; working across the top of the Circle, k2, p2, k2, p3, k2, p2, k2; working across the Left Back, p2, [k2, p2] 10 times, k1.

Row 62 K1, [p2, k2] 12 times, p2tog, p1, [k2, p2] 12 times, k1 (100 stitches).

Row 63 Bind off 2 stitches, work in pattern to the last 2 stitches, bind off 2 stitches (96 stitches).

Place stitches onto a holder.

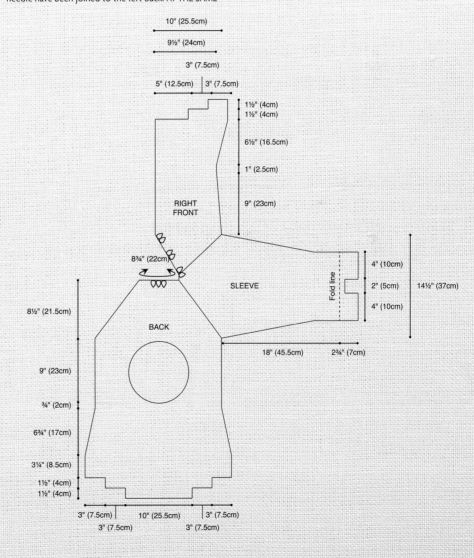

FRONT

Left Front

With MC cast on 15 stitches.

Row 1 (WS) K1, [p2, k2] 3 times, p2.

Row 2 K2, [p2, k2] 3 times, p1.

Row 3 P1, [k2, p2] 3 times, k2.

Row 4 P2, [k2, p2] 3 times, k1.

Rows 5–10 Repeat rows 1–4 once, then work rows 1 and 2. Cast on 15 stitches at the end of row 10 (30 stitches).

Rows 11 and 14 [K2, p2] 7 times, k2.

Rows 12 and 13 [P2, k2] 7 times, p2.

Rows 15–20 Repeat rows 11–14 once, then work rows 11 and 12. Cast on 25 stitches at the end of row 20 (55 stitches).

Row 21 K1, [p2, k2] 13 times, p2.

Row 22 K2, [p2, k2] 13 times p1.

Row 23 P1, [k2, p2] 13 times, k2.

Row 24 (decrease row) P2tog, [k2, p2] 13 times, k1 (54 stitches).

Row 25 K1, [p2, k2] 13 times, p1.

Keeping in the established pattern, decrease 1 stitch at the beginning of every 6th row 7 more times (47 stitches).

Work 7 rows even in pattern.

Next row (increase row, RS) (P1, k1) in the first stitch, k1, [p2, k2] 11 times, p1 (48 stitches).

Keeping in the established pattern, increase 1 stitch every 20th row twice more (50 stitches).

Work 21 rows even in pattern.

Last row (RS) Bind off 2 stitches, work in pattern to the last 2 stitches, k2tog. Mark this stitch for the start of neck shaping (47 stitches).

Place remaining 47 stitches onto a holder.

Right Front

With MC, cast on 15 stitches.

Row 1 (WS) P2, [k2, p2] 3 times, k1.

Row 2 P1, [k2, p2] 3 times, k2.

Row 3 K2, [p2, k2] 3 times, p1.

Row 4 K1, [p2, k2] 3 times, p2.

Rows 5–10 Repeat rows 1–4 once, then work rows 1 and 2.

Row 11 K2, [p2, k2] 3 times, p1, cast on 15 stitches (30 stitches).

Rows 12 and 13 [P2, k2] 7 times, p2.

Rows 14 and 15 [K2, p2] 7 times, k2.

Rows 16–21 Repeat rows 12–15 once, then work rows 12 and 13. Cast on 25 stitches at the end of row 21 (55 stitches).

Row 22 P1, [k2, p2] 13 times, k2.

Row 23 K2, [p2, k2] 13 times, p1.

Row 24 K1, [p2, k2] 13 times, p2tog, p1 (54 stitches).

Row 25 P1, [k2, p2] 13 times, k1.

Keeping in the established pattern, decrease 1 stitch at the end of every 6th row 7 more times (47 stitches).

Work 7 rows even in pattern.

Next row (RS) K1, [p2, k2] 11 times, p1 (p1, k1) in the last stitch (48 stitches).

Keeping in the established pattern, increase 1 stitch at the end of every 20th row twice more (50 stitches).

Work 21 rows even in pattern.

Last Row (RS) Ssk (mark this stitch for the start of neck shaping), work in pattern to the last 2 stitches, bind off 2 stitches (47 stitches).

Place remaining stitches onto a holder.

SLEEVES (MAKE 2)

Cuff

Section 1

With MC, cast on 20 stitches.

Row 1 (WS) [P2, k2] 5 times.

Rows 2 and 3 [K2, p2] 5 times.

Row 4 [P2, k2] 5 times.

Rows 5–10 Repeat rows 1–4 once, then work rows 1 and 2. Set aside.

Section 2

With a separate ball of MC, cast on 20 stitches.

Row 1 (WS) [K2, p2] 5 times.

Rows 2 and 3 [P2, k2] 5 times.

Row 4 [K2, p2] 5 times.

Rows 5–10 Repeat rows 1–4 once, then work rows 1 and 2. Set aside.

Joining row (WS) [K2, p2] 5 times across Section 1, cable cast on 10 stitches, [p2, k2] 5 times across section 2 (50 stitches).

Row 12 [P2, k2] 12 times, p2.

Row 13 [P2, k2] 12 times, p2.

Rows 14 and 15 [K2, p2] 12 times, k2.

Row 16 [P2, k2] 12 times, p2.

Rows 17–20 Repeat rows 13–16.

Row 21 (turning ridge) Knit.

SLEEVE

Rows 1–27 Repeat rows 13–16 of cuff 6 times, then work rows 13–15.

Row 28 (increase, RS) (K1, p1) in the first stitch, p1, [k2, p2] 11 times, k2, p1, (p1, k1) in the last stitch (52 stitches).

Working new stitches into the established pattern, increase 1 stitch each end every 6th row twice more, every 8th row 3 times, then every 10th row 5 times (72 stitches). Work 11 rows in pattern or to desired length, ending with a WS row (sleeve measures 18" [45.5cm] from turning ridge).

Next row Bind off 2 stitches, work in pattern to the last 2 stitches, bind off 2 stitches (68 stitches).

Place stitches onto a holder.

RAGLAN YOKE AND V-NECK SHAPING

With RS facing, transfer body and sleeve stitches to a 40" (101.5cm) circular needle as follows: 47 right front stitches, pm, 68 sleeve stitches, pm, 96 back stitches, pm, 68 sleeve stitches, pm, and 47 left front stitches (326 sts).

Joining Row (WS) *Work in the established pattern to 2 stitches before the next marker, p2, sm, p2; repeat from * 3 more times, work in pattern to end.

Row 1 (neck and raglan decrease, RS) Ssk, *work in pattern to 3 stitches before the next marker, k2tog, k1, sm, k1, ssk; repeat from * 3 more times, work in pattern to the last 2 stitches, k2tog (316 stitches).

Row 2 (raglan decrease, WS) *Work in pattern to 3 stitches before the next marker, p2togtbl, p1, sm, p1, p2tog; repeat from * 3 more times, work in pattern to end (308 stitches).

Row 3 Repeat row 1 (298 stitches).

Row 4 *Work in pattern to 2 stitches before the next marker, p2, sm, p2; repeat from * 3 more times, work in pattern to end.

Rows 5–8 Repeat rows 1–4 (270 stitches).

Row 9 Repeat row 1 (260 stitches).

Row 10 Repeat row 4.

Row 11 *Work in pattern to 3 stitches before the next marker, k2tog, k1, sm, k1, ssk; repeat from * 3 more times, work in pattern to end (252 stitches).

Row 12 Repeat row 4.

Rows 13–52 Repeat rows 9–12 ten times (72 stitches).

Rows 53–56 Repeat rows 11 and 12 twice (56 stitches).

Row 57 Ssk, *sm, k1, ssk, work in pattern to 3 stitches before the next marker, k2tog, k1; repeat from * twice more, sm, k2tog (48 stitches).

Row 58 P1, remove marker, *p2, work in pattern to 2 stitches before the next marker, p2, sm; repeat from * twice more, remove marker, p1.

Row 59 Ssk twice, *work in pattern to 3 stitches before the next marker, k2tog, k1, sm, k1, ssk; repeat from * once, work in pattern to the last 4 stitches, k2tog twice (40 stitches).

Row 60 P2, work 2 stitches in pattern, p2, remove marker, p2, work 28 stitches in pattern, p2 remove marker, p2, work 2 stitches in pattern, p2.

Bind off.

FINISHING

Sew side, underarm, and sleeve seams.

BRAIDED CORD (MAKE 3)

With MC and dpns, cast on 5 stitches.

*Do not turn. Slide stitches onto the other end of the needle, k5; repeat from * until cord measures approximately 60" (152.5cm).

Tack the 3 ends of the cords together and make a braid. Starting at the lower right front, sew cord along fronts and back neck. Adjust for length, bind off, and tack ends in place.

LEAF (MAKE 17)

With CC, cast on 5 stitches.

Row 1 (RS) K2, yo, k1, yo, k2 (7 stitches).

Row 2 and all even-numbered rows Purl.

Row 3 K3, yo, k1, yo, k3 (9 stitches).

Row 5 K4, yo, k1, yo, k4 (11 stitches).

Row 7 Ssk, k7, k2tog (9 stitches).

Row 9 Ssk, k5, k2tog (7 stitches).

Row 11 Ssk, k3, k2tog (5 stitches).

Row 13 Ssk, k1, k2tog (3 stitches).

Row 15 SK2P (1 stitch).

Fasten off.

Sew 3 leaves to the center back neck; 3 pairs evenly spaced on each side from the back raglan seam to the start of the V-neck shaping; fold the cuffs and sew 1 leaf to each front cuff.

ESTHER'S PINWHEEL CAP & SLOUCHY HAT PAGE 14

Size

One size

Knitted Measurements

- Fitted version Circle measures 6" (15cm) diameter, 19" (48.5cm) circumference
- Slouch version Circle measures 8" (20cm) diameter, 21" (53.5cm) circumference

Materials

- Fitted version Misti Alpaca Worsted (100% baby alpaca) 109 yards (99m) and 1.75 oz (50g); 1 skein each #NT100 Natural White (MC) and #4270 Cornflower Blue (CC)
- U.S. 4 (3.5mm) needles
- Slouch version Alisha Goes Around Stable of Horses (100% merino wool) 200 yards (183m) and 3.5 oz (100g); 1 skein each Pavement (MC) and Charred (CC)
- U.S. 6 (4.25mm) needles (Note: For larger sizes, use needles one size larger.)
- Tapestry needle

Gauge

Fitted version 32 stitches and 34 rows = 4" (10cm) in pattern stitch

Slouch version 24 sts and 25 rows = 4" (10cm) in pattern stitch

Take time to check gauge.

Pattern stitch (multiple of 2 stitches)

Row 1 (RS) Knit.

Row 2 *K1, p1; repeat from * to end.

Repeat rows 1 and 2 for pattern.

SIDE CIRCLES (MAKE 2)

Follow instructions for Orbit (Bi-Color) (see page 134).

CENTER

With MC, cast on 20 stitches.

Rows 1–5 Work in Pattern st.

Row 6 K1, m1, k to the last stitch, m1, k1.

Rows 7–30 Repeat rows 1–6, incorporating the new stitches into the pattern as established (30 stitches after row 30).

Rows 31–110 Work in Pattern st.

Rows 111–114 Knit.

Bind off knitwise.

FINISHING

Fitted version Starting with the cast-on end of the center section (back neck) and a MC section of a side circle, sew the pieces together, matching rows and leaving 2½ sections free. Repeat for the other side.

PINWHEEL CAP

SLOUCHY HAT

Slouch version Sew one section of the circles together in the back, leaving 2 sections free for the edge of the hat. Make a pleat at the back end of the center section and sew into the *V* formed above the back seam. Sew edges of the center section to the circles.

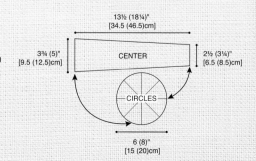

13½ (18¼)"
[34.5 (46.5)cm]

3¾ (5)"
[9.5 (12.5)cm]

CENTER

2½ (3¼)"
[6.5 (8.5)cm]

CIRCLES

6 (8)"
[15 (20)cm]

Size
One size

Knitted Measurements
• Brunhilda 26" (66cm) diameter
• Capella 25" (63.5cm) diameter

Materials
Brunhilda
• Malabrigo Rasta (100% merino wool), each approximately 90 yards (82m) and 5.25 oz (150g); 5 skeins of #856 Azules
• Size U.S. 15 (10mm) circular needle and double-pointed needles or size needed to obtain gauge
• Stitch markers

Capella
• Plymouth Baby Alpaca Grande (100% baby alpaca), each approximately 110 yards (99m) and 3.5 oz (100g); 5 skeins of #208 Brown
• Size U.S. 10 (6mm) circular needle and double-pointed needles or size needed to obtain gauge
• Stitch markers
• Tapestry needle

Gauges
• Brunhilda 8 stitches and 10 rnds = 4" (10cm) in St st
• Capella 14 stitches and 20 rnds = 4" (10cm) in St st
Take time to check gauge.

CIRCLES
Make 2 Brunhilda's Whirl (see page 83) or Capella circles (see page 89).

CAPELLA CIRCLE ONLY
Rnds 44, 46, 48, 50, and 52 Purl.
Rnd 45 *K19, m1; repeat from * around (20/160 stitches).
Rnd 47 *K20, m1; repeat from * around (21/168 stitches).
Rnd 49 *K21, m1; repeat from * around (22/176 stitches).
Rnd 51 *K22, m1; repeat from * around (23/184 stitches).
Rnd 53 *K23, m1; repeat from * around (24/192 stitches).
Rnd 54 Knit.
Rnd 55 *[K2, p2] 6 times, m1, sm, [p2, k2] 6 times, m1P; repeat from * around (25/200) stitches).
Rnd 56 *[K2, p2] 6 times, k1, sm, [p2, k2] 6 times, p1; repeat

CAPELLA

from * around.
Rnd 57 *[K2, p2] 6 times, k1, m1, sm, [p2, k2] 6 times, p1, m1P; repeat from * around (26/208 stitches).
Rnds 58–60 *K2, p2; repeat from * around.
Bind off in pattern using a needle one size larger.

FINISHING
Block lightly to measurements.
Place one circle over the other with WS together.

BRUNHILDA
Leaving one shell open for the neck opening, sew 6" (15cm) shoulder seams.

CAPELLA
Leaving one section open for the neck opening, sew 5" (12.5cm) shoulder seams.

BRUNHILDA

COLLAR (OPTIONAL)
Cast on 92 stitches. Work in K2, P2 Rib for 5" (12.5cm). Bind off loosely in pattern.
Cut 7 strands of yarn, 12" (30.5cm) in length, and sew to one corner of the collar.
Wrap the collar around the neck and use a brooch to fasten it in place.

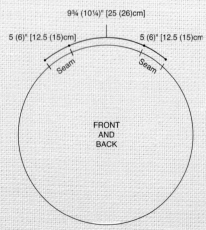

9¾ (10¼)" [25 (26)cm]
5 (6)" [12.5 (15)cm]   5 (6)" [12.5 (15)cm
Seam   Seam
FRONT
AND
BACK

Size
One size

Knitted Measurements
• Length 8" (20cm) without fringe
• Lower edge circumference 100" (254cm)

Materials
• Aslan Trends Del Sur (100% wool) 1.4 oz (40g) and 87 yards (80m); 3 skeins of #0037 Ecru (A)
• Namaste Farms Charmed (mohair blend) 1.4 oz (40g) and 40 yards (36m); 1 skein Ecru Skulls (B)
• Namaste Farms Mohair Fringe (100% mohair) 2.4 oz (68g) and 20 yards (18m); 1 skein each of Ecru (C) and 1 skein in your choice of color (D)
• Size U.S. 11 (8mm) straight needles or size needed to obtain gauge
• 2 yards (1.8m) ½" (13mm) silk ribbon in turquoise
• 2 yards (1.8m) ½" (13mm) silk ribbon in a contrasting color
• Size H (5mm) crochet hook
• 18" (45.5cm) cardboard for fringe
• Stitch markers

Gauge
16 stitches and 20 rows = 4" (10cm) in St st
Take time to check gauge.

CIRCLES (MAKE 2)
With A, make 2 Illuminator circles (see page 117). Do not sew to complete the circles.

FINISHING
With RS facing, sew the bound-off edge of one circle to the cast-on edge of the second circle.

Front Bands
With RS facing, pick up and k15 stitches along the center front edge. Knit 4 rows. Bind off. Repeat on the other side.

Front Ties
Cut the turquoise ribbon into 6 even lengths. Attach 3 to each front band above the sawtooth edge as for fringe.

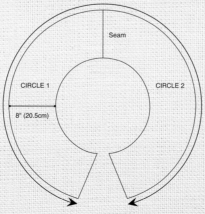

Seam

CIRCLE 1   CIRCLE 2

8" (20.5cm)

100" (254cm)

Fringe
Working with one strand each of B, C, and D, wrap around cardboard 56 times to make 168 36" (91.5cm) strands. Using 2 strands per fringe, attach to the WS through the eyelets running just above the sawtooth edge in 7 groups of 12, as pictured, or as desired.

Thread the contrasting color ribbon through the eyelets running above the fringe and sew in place at each end.

Note This is also cute without the fringe.

ENTRELAC CAPELET PAGE 17

Sizes

Small (Medium/Large)

Knitted Measurements

Each circle measures approximately 13½ (15½)" [34.5 (39.5)cm] in diameter, including cord edging

Materials

• Crystal Palace Mochi Plus (80% Superwash merino/20% nylon) 1.75 oz (50g) and 95 yards (85m); 5 (6) skeins of #551 Intense Rainbow
• Size Small U.S. 7 (4.5mm) circular and double-pointed needles
• Size Medium/Large U.S. 9 (5.5mm) circular and double-pointed needles or size needed to obtain gauge
• Stitch marker

Gauge

20 (16) stitches and 28 (24) rows = 4" (10cm) in St st
Take time to check gauge.

CIRCLES

Make 3 Entrelac circles (see page 84).

CORD EDGING

Using double-pointed needles, cast on 5 stitches. *Do not turn. Slide stitches onto the other end of the needle, k5; repeat from * to desired length. Make 3 cords, approximately 46 (52)" [117 (132)cm] for the right circle, 40 (46)" [102 (117)cm] for the center circle, and 43 (49)" [109 (124.5) cm] for the left circle.

Note Do not graft the ends until the cords are attached and the length is determined to be correct.

FINISHING

Right Circle

Fold the cord at its center and make an overhand knot using both strands of the folded loop. Sew the cord around the edge of the circle, adjust for length, and graft the ends together.

Left Circle

Fold the cord at its center to make a loop large enough to fit the knot on the right circle, and tack in place. Sew the cord around the edge of the circle, adjust for length, and graft the ends together.

Center Circle

Sew cord around the edge of the circle, adjust for length, and graft the ends together.

Block circles lightly to measurement.

ASSEMBLY

Place circles in an open *V*, with the loop and knot pointing straight up. Leaving the top 8 (9)" [20 (23)cm] of the center circle open and 8 (9)" [20 (23)cm] between the seam and the loop/knot, sew a 5" (12.5cm) seam between each circle.

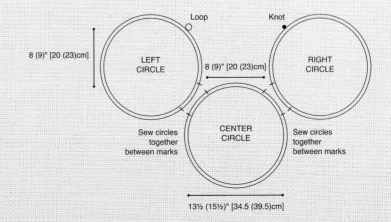

CIRCULATE CAPE PAGE 18

Sizes
Small/Medium (Large/X-Large)

Knitted Measurements
Each circle measures 16 (17¾)" [40.5 (45)cm] in diameter

Materials
- Cascade Baby Alpaca Chunky (100% baby alpaca), each approximately 108 yards (98m) and 3.5 oz (100g); 4 (5) skeins of #565 Ecru (MC)
- Namaste Farms Mohair Fringe (100% mohair), each approximately 20 yards (18m) and 2.4 oz (68g); 1 skein in your choice of color (CC)
- Size U.S. 10 (10 ½) [6 (6.5mm)] double-pointed and circular needles or size needed to obtain gauge
- Stitch markers
- Tapestry needle

Gauge
14 (12) stitches and 20 (18) rnds = 4" (10cm) in St st using smaller (larger) needles and MC
Take time to check gauge.

CIRCLES
Make 4 Lacy Swirl circles with MC (see page 116), working rnds 1–34.

Rnd 35 *[Yo, k1] twice, yo, k13, k2tog; repeat from * around (19/152 stitches).

Rnd 36 *K17, k2tog; repeat from * around (18/144 stitches).

Rnds 37–39 Purl.

Bind off knitwise using a needle one size larger.

Block lightly to measurements.

FINISHING
Place circles in a diamond pattern, as in the diagram. Leaving 5½" (14cm) of each circle open at the neck edge, sew 8" (20cm) seams from the neck edge down.

Neckband
With MC, pick up and knit 75 stitches evenly around the neck opening. Place marker.

Rnds 1, 3, 5, and 7 Purl.

Rnds 2, 4, and 6 Knit.

Bind off knitwise.

Thread a strand of CC through the yo swirls.

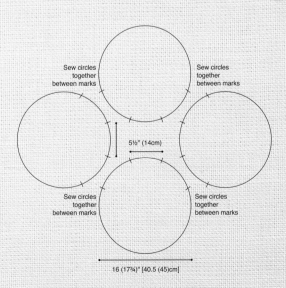

Sew circles together between marks

Sew circles together between marks

5½" (14cm)

Sew circles together between marks

Sew circles together between marks

16 (17¾)" [40.5 (45)cm]

DAISY MAE PULLOVER PAGE 19

Sizes
Small (Medium)

Knitted Measurements
Each circle measures 16 (18)" [40.5 (45.5cm)] in diameter
- Bust 32 (36)" [81.5 (91.5cm)]
- Length 18 (19)" [45.5 (48.5)cm]

Materials
- Madelinetosh Tosh Chunky (100% Superwash merino wool), each approximately 165 yards (151m) and 3.5 oz (100g); 5 (6) skeins of Betty Draper's Blue
- Size U.S. 8 (5mm) circular and double-pointed needles or size needed to obtain gauge
- Size U.S. 7 (4.5mm) 16" (40cm) circular needle
- Stitch markers
- Tapestry needle

Gauge
14 stitches and 20 rnds = 4" (10cm) in St st using larger needles
Take time to check gauge.

CIRCLES
Make 4 Daisy Mae Circles (see page 80), rnds 1–36.

For Size Small
Work Garter St Edging.

For Size Medium
Rnd 37 Purl.
Rnd 38 *P13, m1P, p13; repeat from * around (27/162 stitches).
Rnds 39–41 Purl.
Work Garter St Edging.
Bind off.

FINISHING
Make 4 bobbles (see page 80) and sew 1 to the center of each circle.
Block lightly to measurements.

Place circles in a diamond pattern as in the diagram, positioning 2 petal points of each circle as pictured. Leaving the space between petal points open at the top of each circle for the neck opening, sew "raglan" seams from the neck point down to the next point. Then sew 3½ (4)" [9 (10)cm] side seams and 4 (4½)" [10 (11.5)cm] sleeve seams.

Neck Band
With RS facing and smaller needle, pick up and knit 84 (88) stitches evenly around the neck opening. Place marker. Work in K2, P2 Rib for 1½" (4cm). Bind off in pattern.

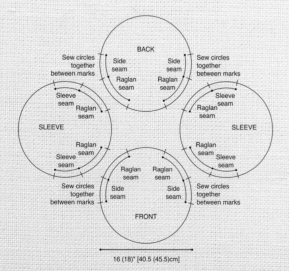

16 (18)" [40.5 (45.5cm)]

BIG BLOOMS CAPELET PAGE 20

Size
Small/Medium

Knitted Measurements
Each circle measures approximately 14½" (37cm) in
  diameter

Materials
• Cascade Magnum (100% wool) 8.8 oz (250g) and 123
  yards (110m); 4 skeins of #9479 Periwinkle
• Size U.S. 15 (10mm) circular and double-pointed
  needles or size needed to obtain gauge
• Matching yarn in a finer gauge for sewing
• 1 yard (91.5cm) of 1½" (4cm) ribbon in matching color
• Tapestry needle

Gauge
6 stitches and 10 rows = 4" (10cm) in St st
Take time to check gauge.

CIRCLES
Make 3 Bold Petal circles (see page 170).

FINISHING
Place circles in an open *V*. Leaving the top 12" (30.5cm) of
the center circle open, sew an 8" (20cm) seam between
each circle. Cut the ribbon in half and sew an end to each
side circle approximately 8" (20cm) from the seam.

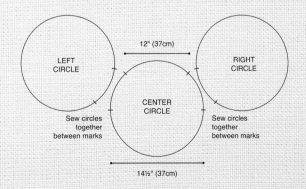

LEFT CIRCLE

12" (37cm)

RIGHT CIRCLE

CENTER CIRCLE

Sew circles
together
between marks

Sew circles
together
between marks

14½" (37cm)

STARSTRUCK TUNIC PAGE 21

Size
Small/Medium

Knitted Measurements
- Each oval measures approximately 15" x 21" (38cm x 53.5cm), including single crochet border
- Top edge measures approximately 27" (68.5cm) to fit above bustline

Materials
- ArtYarns Beaded Mohair (80% silk with glass beads/20% mohair), each approximately 114 yards (104m) and 1.75 oz (50g); 4 skeins of Burgundy with silver beads
- Size U.S. 8 (5mm) straight needles or size needed to obtain gauge
- Size U.S. 6 (4.00mm) double-pointed needles
- Size F-5 (3.75mm) crochet hook
- 1 yard (91.5cm) of 1" (2.5cm) pleated velvet ribbon in matching color
- Sewing needle and matching thread
- 1 yard (91.5cm) of ¼" (6mm) elastic
- 1 medium-size sew-on snap
- Tapestry needle
- Ribbon for flower (optional)

Gauge
18 stitches and 22 rows = 4" (10cm) in St st using larger needles
Take time to check gauge.

OVAL (MAKE 4)
Using larger needles, cast on 31 stitches.
Knit 1 row, purl 1 row.
Inc row (RS) K1, m1, k to the last stitch, m1, k1.

Repeat Inc row every RS row until there are 55 stitches, every 4th row until there are 63 stitches, then every 6th row until there are 67 stitches.
Work even in St st for 1" (2.5cm), ending with a WS row.
Dec row (RS) Ssk, k to the last 2 stitches, k2tog.
Repeat Dec row every 6th row until there are 63 stitches, every 4th row until there are 55 stitches, then every RS row until there are 31 stitches.
Bind off, placing the last stitch onto the crochet hook.

EDGING
Work 1 round of single crochet evenly around the 2 sides and the cast-on edge. Fasten off.

FINISHING
Position Ovals as in the diagram, with side panels overlapping the front and back panels approximately 4" (10cm) down from the top edge. Sew in place with 4" (10cm) seams. Connect the sides of the front and back panels 14" (35.5cm) from the top edge, with a 1" (2.5cm) seam.

Cord Straps and Trim
With dpns, cast on 5 stitches.
*Do not turn. Slide stitches onto the other end of the needle, k5; repeat from * to desired length.
Make 4 cords approximately 16" (40.5cm) or to desired length for shoulder straps. Make 1 cord approximately 27" (68.5cm) for trim.

Cut the elastic 2–3" (5–7.5cm) shorter than the desired fit measured around the top of the bust. Weave the elastic through the crochet trim across the WS of the top edge. Tack down the ends. Cut the ribbon 2" (5cm) longer than the top edge of the tunic and sew in place with a 1" (2.5cm) hem at each end.

Sew cord trim across the RS of top edge to cover the elastic. Sew the ends of the cord straps to the top edge as indicated on the diagram.

Ribbon Corsage (optional)
Wrap ribbon around 4 spread fingers approximately 20 times so you create uniform loops. Remove and fold in half. Cut a V on the corners of the fold, being careful not to cut all the way through the center. Unfold and tie another piece of ribbon around the V's to secure the bow. Separate the loops one by one to the right and left, from the inside out, working one side at a time, until you achieve the look you want.

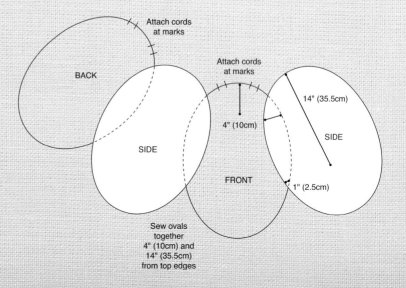

RAMBLING REVERSIBLE CABLE SCARF PAGE 22

Size
One size

Knitted Measurements
Approximately 8" x 58" (20.5cm x 147.5cm)

Materials
- Mountain Colors Monarch (100% merino wool)
  3.5 oz (100g) and 200 yards (182m); 4 skeins of
  Ruby River
- Size U.S. 8 (5mm) straight needles or size needed to
  obtain gauge
- Stitch markers
- Tapestry needle

Gauge
18 stitches and 22 rows = 4" (10cm) in St st
Take time to check gauge.

CIRCLES
Make 8 Bold Reversible Cable circles (see page 88).
Place circles side by side and sew a 4" (10cm) seam
between each circle.
Block lightly to measurements.

8" (20.5cm)

58" (147.5cm)

Size

One size

Knitted Measurements

Approximately 40" x 50" (101.5cm x 127cm)

Materials

- Aslan Trends Royal Alpaca (100% alpaca), each approximately 220 yards (200m) and 3.5 oz (100g); 7 skeins of #402 Andean Coal (A), 4 skeins of #18 Gray (B), 3 skeins each of #19 Black (C) and #6314 Crimson (D), and 2 skeins of #37 Bone (E)
- Size U.S. 6 (4mm) straight, double-pointed, and circular needles or size needed to obtain gauge
- Stitch markers
- Tapestry needle
- Polyfill
- Optional 32 Silver pearl beads (8mm) for Honeycomb Cable circle

Gauge

20 stitches and 26 rows = 4" (10cm) in St st
Take time to check gauge.

CIRCLES

Notes Make 20 large circles as follows, without edgings. Letters indicate colors—first MC and second CC. Additional letters correspond with the number of colors in the charts. Circles will not be uniform in size.

Sailing (2) using B/A and B/C (see page 140)

Stallion (2) using B/C (see page 141)

Modern Fair Isle (2) using A/E and B/D (see page 138)

Fair Isle Image (2) using B/C/D and B/A/E (see page 139)

Tree Circle (1) using E (see page 90)

Honeycomb Circle (1) using B (see page 64)

Meridian (2) using A and E (see page 78)

Rosey (1) using A/D (see page 145)

Morning Bloom (2) using B and D (see page 115)

Bobbled Burst (1) using E (see page 87)

Daisy Mae (1) using D (see page 66)

Rotate (1) using B (see page 55)

Cathedral Window (2) using B (see page 62)

EDGING

With A, work a 4-row Garter St Edging using stitch counts as indicated in each respective pattern.

FILLER CIRCLES (MAKE 12)

With A, cast on 70 stitches. Pm and join.

Rnd 1 *K2tog, k5; repeat from * around (60 stitches).

Rnds 2, 4, 6, 8, and 10 Knit.

Rnd 3 *K2tog, k4; repeat from * around (50 stitches).

Rnd 5 *K2tog, k3; repeat from * around (40 stitches).

Rnd 7 *K2tog, k2; repeat from * around (30 stitches).

Rnd 9 *K2tog, k1; repeat from * around (20 stitches).

Rnd 11 *K2tog; repeat from * around (10 stitches).

Break off yarn, leaving a 4" (10cm) tail. Thread the tail through the remaining stitches, pull tight, and secure.

TASSELS (MAKE 6)

With A, cast on 30 stitches, leaving a 6" (15cm) tail.

Rows 1 and 3 (WS) K2, *p2, k2; repeat from * to end.

Row 2 P2, *k2, p2; repeat from * to end.

Row 4 P2, *k2tog and leave stitches on the needle, knit the first stitch again, slip both stitches off the needle, p2; repeat from * to end.

Rows 5–12 Repeat rows 1–4.

Rows 13–15 Repeat rows 1–3.

Row 16 P2, *k2tog, p2; repeat from * to end (23 stitches). Change to B.

Rows 17 and 18 Purl.

Rows 19–28 Work in Reverse St st.

Row 29 (WS) K1, *k2tog; repeat from * to end (12 stitches).

Row 30 *P2tog; repeat from * to end (6 stitches). Break the yarn, leaving a 6" (15cm) tail. Thread the tail through the remaining stitches, pull tight, and secure.

Stuff the cap with polyfill and sew the seam of the cap. With the cast-on tail, sew the seam of the skirt. Use the ends at the color change to tighten the neck of the tassel. With a crochet hook and 2 strands of A, chain 8. Fasten off. Attach one end to the top of the tassel.

FINISHING

Block all circles.

Position circles as pictured or as desired. Position filler circles, overlapping to accommodate the uneven spacing. Using A, sew circles in place. Sew 3 tassels to each end of the afghan, as pictured.

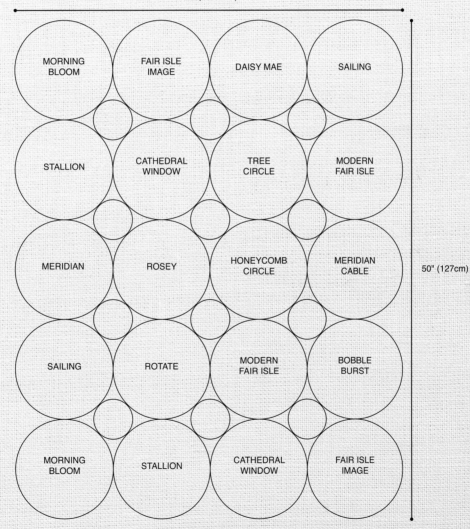

Smaller circles are filler circles

Size
One size

Knitted Measurements
Approximately 48" x 58" (122cm x 147cm)

Materials
• Cascade Yarns Pacific (60% acrylic/40% Superwash merino wool), each approximately 213 yards (191m) and 3.5 oz (100g); 7 skeins of #48 Black (A), 2 skeins of #21 Aqua (B), 2 skeins of #16 Light Green (C), 2 skeins #26 Lavender (D)
• Size U.S. 7 (4.5mm) circular needles in 24" (61cm) and 16" (40cm) lengths or size needed to obtain gauge
• Size U.S. 7 (4.5mm) double-pointed needles
• Stitch markers
• Tapestry needle
• Cardboard 6" x 6" (15cm x 15cm) for tassels

Gauge
18 stitches and 20 rnds = 4" (10cm) in stranded 2-color St st
Take time to check gauge.

LOOP EDGING (INSTRUCTIONS FOR SMALL CIRCLE IN PARENTHESES)
With CC, cast on 200 (136) stitches.
Row 1 Bind off 3 stitches, *k1, bind off the next 3 stitches; repeat from * to end (50 [34] stitches).
Row 2 *K1, cast on 2 stitches; repeat from * to end (150 [102] stitches). Pm and join.

LARGE CIRCLES
All circles begin after having worked the Loop Edging (150 stitches).

Make 6 Kismet circles (see page 141) as follows, with the first letter indicating the Loop Edging color, the second letter MC, and the third letter CC:
1 each A/B/A, A/A/D, C/C/A, C/A/C, D/D/A, and B/B/A

Make 11 Spheroid circles (see page 140) as follows:
2 each A/D/A, A/B/A, and B/A/B
1 each A/C/A, A/A/C, A/A/B, D/A/D, and C/C/A

Make 8 Karma circles (see page 136) as follows:
2 each A/C/A
1 each A/A/B, A/D/A, D/A/D, D/D/A, C/C/A, and B/B/A

SMALL CIRCLES
All circles begin after you have worked the Loop Edging (102 stitches).

Work Rnds 9–24 of the specified chart.
Rnd 25 *S2KP; repeat from * around (6 stitches).
Break the yarn. Thread the tail through the remaining 6 stitches, pull tight, and secure.

Make 2 Spheroid circles as follows:
1 each A/A/B and A/A/D

Make 2 Kismet circles as follows:
1 each A/C/A and D/A/D

Make 2 Karma circles as follows:
1 each A/C/A and B/B/A

TASSELS (MAKE 14)

Make 5 each in B and C, and 4 in D, wrapping 50 times for each tassel (see page 198).

Tassel Tie

With A, cast on 8 stitches. Knit 2 rows. Bind off. Wrap Tie around tassel, 1" (2.5cm) from the top, and sew in place.

FINISHING

Position circles following the diagram or as desired. Sew in place. Sew 7 tassels evenly across each end of the afghan.

48" (122cm)

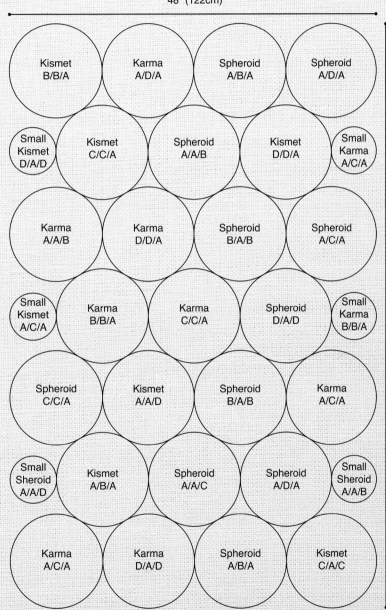

58" (147.5cm)

HOOPLA BAG PAGE 25

Knitted Measurements

Approximately 12" x 15" (30cm x 38cm)

Each circle measures approximately 6 (6½, 7, 8)" [15 (16.5, 18, 20.5cm) in diameter]. Final dimensions of the bag will depend on assembly.

Materials

- Berroco Blackstone Tweed Metallic (63% wool/24% mohair/10% angora/3% other) 1.75 oz (50g) and 127 yards (116m); 2 skeins of #4647 Nor'easter (A), 1 skein each of #4646 Salt Water (B), #4601 Clover Honey (C), #4651 Forest Floor (D), #4642 Rhubarb (E), #4650 Sugar Pumpkin (F), and #4603 Ancient Mariner (G)
- Size U.S. 7 (4.5mm) double-pointed and circular needles or size needed to obtain gauge
- Stitch markers
- Tapestry needle
- 8 decorative buttons (optional)
- Aslan Trends Luxury Handbag Handles (#20711)
- 1 yard (91.5cm) fabric for lining
- 5" x 7" (12.5cm x 18cm) cardboard for base
- Fabric glue
- Sewing needle and matching thread

Gauge

18 stitches and 25 rows = 4" (10cm) in St st

Take time to check gauge.

CIRCLES

Notes The first letter indicates MC and second CC.

Make 12 Hoops circles (see page 134) as follows, then change to A and purl 1 rnd, knit 1 rnd, purl 1 rnd, and bind off.

Make four 3-ridge (3R) working rnds 1–21, as follows: 1 each in A/B, A/C, A/D, and A/E

Make five 4-ridge (4R) working rnds 1–27, as follows: 1 each in A/E, A/B, A/D, A/G, and A/F

Make two 5-ridge (5R) working rnds 1–33, as follows: 2 in A/F

Make one 6-ridge (6R) in A/A, working rnds 1–39 for the base.

FINISHING

Position circles as follows, overlapping as needed to create a solid fabric.

Lower row (left to right) 3R A/B, 4R A/E, 4R A/G, 3R A/E, 4R A/B, 4R A/D.

Sew in place.

Upper row 5R A/F, 3R A/D, 5R A/F, 3R A/C.

Sew in place.

Center 3R A/D of upper row above 4R A/E and 4R A/G of lower row, overlapping to close gaps. Sew in place and sew side seam. Sew the 6R base to the lower row, overlapping the lower row all around. Sew 4R A/F flap above 3R A/D of upper row, overlapping by approximately 2" (5cm). Sew buttons to the centers of the circles as desired. Sew straps to the front and back of the bag.

LINING

Cut the cardboard into an oval and glue it to the inside base of the bag.

Cut 2 circles from the fabric, 14" (35.5cm) in diameter. With the RS together, sew around using a ½" (13mm) seam, leaving an 8" (20cm) opening at the top.

Cut a 6" (15cm) circle from the fabric. Turn under ½" (13mm) and sew it to the flap.

Insert the lining into the body of the bag so the WS of the lining is against the WS of the bag. Turn under ½" (13mm) along the top edge and sew in place, overlapping the flap lining.

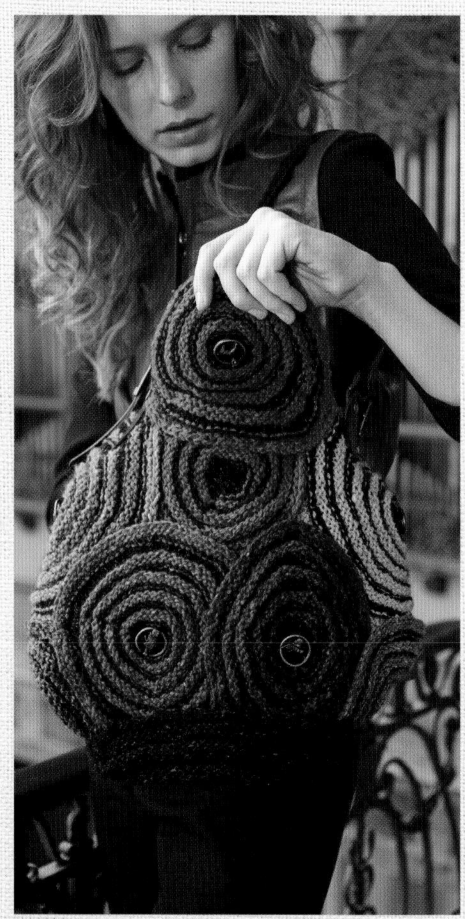

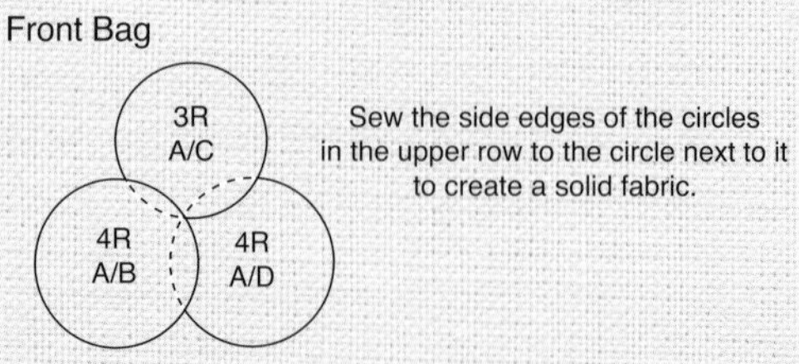
Front Bag
3R A/C
4R A/B
4R A/D
Sew the side edges of the circles in the upper row to the circle next to it to create a solid fabric.

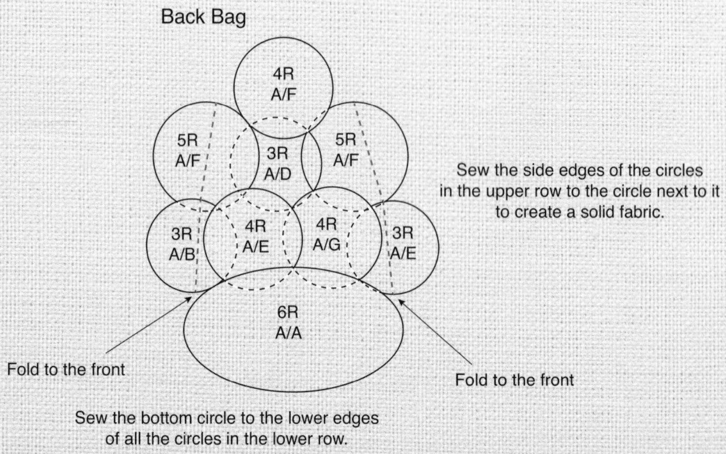
Back Bag
4R A/F
5R A/F
3R A/D
5R A/F
3R A/B
4R A/E
4R A/G
3R A/E
6R A/A
Fold to the front
Fold to the front
Sew the side edges of the circles in the upper row to the circle next to it to create a solid fabric.
Sew the bottom circle to the lower edges of all the circles in the lower row.

CELESTIAL SHAWL PAGE 26

Size
One size

Knitted Measurements
40" x 32" (101.5cm x 81.5cm)
Each circle measures approximately 10" (25.5cm) in
  diameter

Materials
- Tilly Tomas Disco Lights (100% silk with sequins), each
  approximately 225 yards (206m) and 3.5 oz (100g);
  4 skeins of Dusty Purple
- Size U.S. 8 (5mm) straight needles or size needed to
  obtain gauge
- Tapestry needle

Gauge
16 stitches and 32 rows = 4" (10cm) in Garter st
Take time to check gauge.

CIRCLES
Make 10 Celestial Bloom circles (see page 112).
Position circles in a triangle following the diagram. Sew
in place.
Block lightly to measurements.

ETERNITY DRESS PAGE 27

Sizes
Small/Medium (Large)

Knitted Measurements
- Bust Approximately 34 (40)" [86.5 (101.5)cm]
- Length Approximately 39½ (43½)" [100.5 (110.5)cm]

Note Adjustments can be made to width and length when positioning circles during assembly.

Materials
- ArtYarns Rhapsody Light Silver Glitter (50% silk/50% kid mohair w/Lurex), each approximately 400 yards (366m) and 3.8 oz (80g); 4 (5) skeins of #137 Cappucino with Silver
- Small/Medium Size U.S. 4 (3.5mm) double-pointed and circular needles or size needed to obtain gauge
- Large Size U.S. 5 (3.75) double-pointed and circular needles or size needed to obtain gauge
- Stitch markers
- Tapestry needle
- 21 Swarovski crystal beads (8mm Aurora Borealis)
- Sewing needle and matching thread
- Purchased or handmade slip lining
- Dress form (optional, but recommended)

Gauges
- Small/Medium 24 stitches and 30 rows = 4" (10cm) in St st using smaller needles
- Large 22 stitches and 28 rows = 4" (10cm) in St st using larger needles

Take time to check gauge.

CIRCLES (MAKE 33)

Make 11 small circles (approximately 5") working rnds 1–22 of Lacy Swirl circle (see page 116).

Make 16 medium circles (approximately 7½") working rnds 1–28.

Make 6 large circles (approximately 9") working rnds 1–34.

For all circles, work edging as follows:
Rnds 1 and 3 Purl.
Rnd 2 Knit.
Bind off using a needle one size larger.

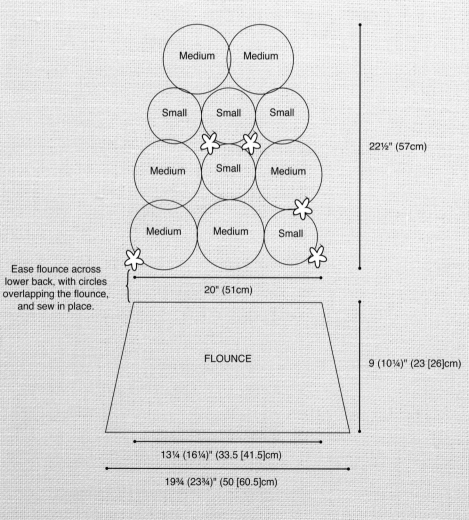

BACK

22½" (57cm)

Ease flounce across lower back, with circles overlapping the flounce, and sew in place.

20" (51cm)

FLOUNCE

9 (10¼)" (23 [26]cm)

13¼ (16¼)" (33.5 [41.5]cm)

19¾ (23¾)" (50 [60.5]cm)

BACK FLOUNCE

With the needle for your size, cast on 80 (90) stitches.

Inc row (RS) K1, m1, k to the last stitch, m1, k1.

Continuing in St st, repeat Inc row every RS row 18 (20) more times [118 (130) stitches]. Work even in St st until flounce measures 14 (16)" [35.5 (40.5)cm] or desired length, ending with a WS row.

Dec row (RS) K10, *k2tog, k10; repeat from * to the end of the row [109 (120) stitches].

Next row Purl.

Bind off.

Flounce Edging

With RS facing, pick up and knit [approximately 290 (310)] stitches evenly around side and cast-on edges of the flounce.

Knit 3 rows.

Bind off loosely.

FINISHING

Note Use a dress form for easier fitting and sewing. Position circles following the diagram, starting at the top and working down, overlapping circles as needed. Sew pieces in place. Ease the flounce across the lower back, with circles overlapping the flounce, and sew the top and side edges of the flounce in place.

FLOWER (MAKE 13)

Cast on 6 stitches.

Row 1 (RS) K3, yo, k3 (7 stitches).

Row 2 and all WS rows Knit.

Row 3 K3, yo, k4 (8 stitches).

Row 5 K3, yo, k5 (9 stitches).

Row 7 K3, yo, k6 (10 stitches).

Row 9 K3, yo, k7 (11 stitches).

Row 11 K3, yo, k8 (12 stitches).

Row 12 Bind off 6 stitches, knit to end (6 stitches).

Repeat [rows 1–12] 4 more times.

Bind off remaining 6 stitches and cut yarn, leaving an 8" (20.5cm) tail.

Sew bound-off edge to cast-on edge, then weave tail through the eyelets, pull tight to gather, and secure.

Sew 3 beads to the centers of 4 flowers, and 1 bead to the center of 9 flowers.

Sew flowers to the dress, as pictured.

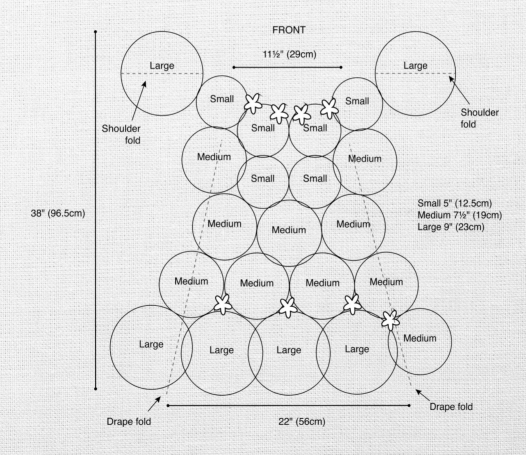

FRONT

11½" (29cm)

Large — Shoulder fold

Large — Shoulder fold

Small

Small

Small

Small

Medium

Medium

Small

Small

Small 5" (12.5cm)
Medium 7½" (19cm)
Large 9" (23cm)

Medium

Medium

Medium

Medium

Medium

Medium

Medium

Medium

Large

Large

Large

Large

Medium

38" (96.5cm)

Drape fold

Drape fold

22" (56cm)

LE CIRQUE BABY AFGHAN

Size
One size

Knitted Measurements
Approximately 58" x 58" (147.5cm x 147.5cm)

Materials
• Lion Brand Yarn Baby Wool (100% easy care wool) 1.75 oz (50g) and 98 yards (90m); 3 skeins of #108 Blue Bonnet (A), 2 skeins each of #172 Pear (B), #132 Papaya (C), #144 Lavender (D), #157 Sunflower (E), #106 Blue Bell (F), 1 skein each of #102 Peony (G), #174 Sprout (H), and #143 Orchid (I)
• Size U.S. 8 (5mm) straight and circular needles or size needed to obtain gauge
• Size U.S. 6 (4mm) double-pointed needles
• Size H-8 (5mm) crochet hook
• Stitch markers
• Tapestry needle

Gauge
16 stitches and 32 rows = 4" (10cm) in Garter st using larger needles
Take time to check gauge.

CIRCLES
Make 9 Orbit circles (see page 134) as follows:
4 small circles, working each section to 18 stitches.
1 each in C/E, B/H, A/F, and D/I.
5 large circles, working each section to 24 stitches.
1 each in A/D, C/A/F, E/A/H, B/A/D, and G/A/I.

Note For 3-color circles, the first letter indicates the color in every other section; the 2nd and 3rd letters indicate the alternating colored sections.

CIRCUS FACE CIRCLE
With larger needles, cast on 12 stitches.
Rows 1 and 2 Knit.
Row 3 (RS) Kfb, k to the last stitch, kfb. (14 stitches)
Row 4 Knit.
Rows 5–16 Repeat rows 3 and 4 (26 stitches after row 16).
Rows 17–26 Knit.
Row 27 (RS) Ssk, k to the last 2 stitches, k2tog (24 stitches).
Row 28 Knit.

Rows 29 to 40 Repeat rows 27 and 28 (12 stitches after row 39).
Rows 41 and 42 Knit.
Bind off.

CORKSCREW FRINGE
With larger needles, loosely cast on 12 stitches.
Row 1 *Kfb; repeat from * to end (24 stitches).

Bind off purlwise. Use your fingers to twist into a corkscrew.

CLOWN BOY
Face
With B, make 1 Circus Face Circle.
With 2 strands of A, embroider eyes using Cross stitches; with G, embroider mouth using Stem stitch and Crossed Straight stitch.

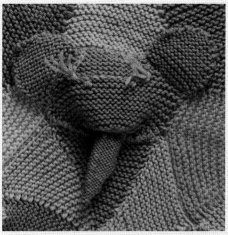

Hair

With H, make 6 Corkscrew Fringes. Sew 3 fringes to each side of the Face.

Nose

With larger needles and I, cast on 7 stitches.

Row 1 *Kfb; repeat from * to end (14 stitches).

Rows 2–8 Work in St st.

Row 9 *K2tog; repeat from * to end (7 stitches); pass the 2nd through the 7th stitches over the first stitch. Fasten off. Thread the cast-on tail through the cast-on stitches, pull tight, and secure. Stuff the nose with polyfill and sew the side seam. Sew to the center of the Face.

Bow

With larger needles and F, cast on 9 stitches. Work in K1, P1 Rib for 3½" (9cm). Bind off.

Tie

Cast on 6 stitches. Knit 1 row. Bind off.

Wrap the Tie around the center of the Bow and sew in place. Sew to the Neck of the Clown.

Hat

With larger needles and H, cast on 15 stitches. Knit 6 rows.

Dec row (RS) Ssk, k to the last 2 stitches, k2tog.

Continuing in Garter st, repeat Dec row every RS row once more (11 stitches).

Knit 4 rows.

Bind off. Sew to the top of the Face. With C, embroider the flower using Lazy Daisy stitch; with B, embroider stem using Stem stitch and flower center with a French knot.

CLOWN GIRL

Face

With G, make 1 Circus Face Circle.

With 2 strands of A, embroider eyes using Cross stitch; with D, embroider mouth the same as for the Clown Boy.

Hair

With E, make 6 Corkscrew Fringes.

Sew 3 fringes to each side of the top of the Face.

Nose

With larger needles and F, make the same nose as the Clown Boy's.

Sew the Nose to the center of the Face.

Bow and Tie

With larger needles and H, make the same Bow and Tie as the Clown Boy's.

Sew the Bow to top of the Face.

Ruffle

With larger needles and D, cast on 15 stitches.

Row 1 (RS) K1, *p1, k1; repeat from * to end.

Row 2 P1, *k1, p1; repeat from * to end.

Row 3 K1, *p1, m1P, k1; repeat from * to end (22 stitches).

Row 4 P1, *k2, p1; repeat from * to end.

Row 5 K1, *p2, m1P, k1; repeat from * to end (29 stitches).

Row 6 P1, *k3, p1; repeat from * to end.

Row 7 K1, *p3, m1P, k1; repeat from * to end (36 stitches).

Row 8 *P2, k3; repeat from * to the last stitch, p1.

Row 9 K1, *p4, m1P, k1; repeat from * to end (43 stitches).

Row 10 *P2, k4; repeat from * to the last stitch, p1.

Row 11 K1, *p5, m1P, k1; repeat from * to the end (50 stitches).

Bind off knitwise. Sew to the Neck of the Clown.

LION HEAD

Face

With C, work rows 1 to 41 of the Circus Face Circle.

Row 42 *K2tog; repeat from * to end (6 stitches).

Bind off. With 2 strands of F, embroider eyes using Straight stitch; with H, embroider Nose and Mouth using Satin and Stem stitches, respectively.

Ears (make 2)

With larger needles and C, cast on 16 stitches.

Rows 1–12 Knit.

Row 13 Ssk, k3, ssk, k2, k2tog, k3, k2tog (12 stitches).

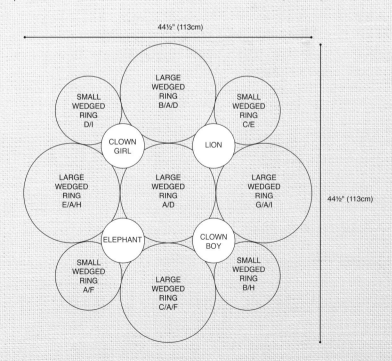

LE CIRQUE BABY AFGHAN CONTINUED FROM PREVIOUS PAGE

Rows 14 and 16 Knit.

Row 15 Ssk, k1, ssk, k2, k2tog, k1, k2tog (8 stitches).

Row 17 [Ssk] twice, [k2tog] twice (4 stitches).
Bind off. Fold over with rows 1–12 facing outwards, as pictured, and sew to the Lion Head.

Outer Mane

With E, cast on 66 stitches.

Row 1 (WS) K1, *insert the right-hand needle into the next stitch knitwise, wind yarn over the right-hand needle and the first and second fingers of your left hand 3 times, then over the right-hand needle point once more, draw all 4 loops through the stitch and slip them onto the left-hand needle, insert the right-hand needle through the back of these 4 loops and the original stitch and knit them together tbl, k1; repeat from * to the last stitch, k1.
Bind off. Sew around the edge of the circle.

Inner Mane

With E, cast on 12 stitches. Work the same as for the Outer Mane. Sew between the Ears at the top of the Face.

ELEPHANT HEAD

Face

With A, work rows 1–32 of Circus Face Circle (20 stitches).

Row 33 *K4, k2tog; repeat from * to the last 2 stitches, k2 (17 stitches).

Rows 34, 36, and 38 Knit.

Row 35 *K3, k2tog; repeat from * to the last 2 stitches, k2 (14 stitches).

Row 37 *K2, k2tog; repeat from * to the last 2 stitches, k2 (11 stitches).

Row 39 *K1, k2tog; repeat from * to the last 2 stitches, k2 (8 stitches).
Cast on 2 stitches, pm for end of the rnd, cast on 2 stitches and join. Divide these 12 stitches evenly onto 3 dpns.
Work even in Reverse St st (purl every rnd) for 1" (2.5cm).
*Dec rnd P1, p2tog, p to the last 3 stitches, p2tog, p1 (10 stitches).
Work even in Reverse St st for ½" (13mm).
Repeat from * 3 more times (6 stitches). Bind off.

With C, embroider headdress using Chain stitch; with G, embroider eyes and mouth using French knots and Stem stitch, respectively; with H, make a 2-strand fringe at each corner of the headdress.

Ears (make 2)

With A, cast on 13 stitches.

Rows 1–14 Knit.

Row 15 Ssk, k to the last 2 stitches, k2tog (11 stitches).

Row 16 Knit.

Rows 17–24 Repeat rows 15 and 16 (3 stitches after row 24).
Bind off. Sew the Ears to the Elephant Head, as pictured.

FINISHING

Position circles following the diagram and sew in place.

Edging

With A and crochet hook, work 1 round of single crochet and 1 round of slip stitch evenly around the entire edge of the afghan.

CIRCLES INTO HATS

How to Turn a Circle into a Hat

Many of the circles in this book can be made into hats (berets, slouches, and cloche hats can easily be made) simply by adding an edging.

For an adult head, your circle should be at least 10" (25.5cm) in circumference. The larger the circle, the more overlap you will have.

Adult Head Measurements Are as Follows:

Extra Small	20" (51cm)
Small	21" (53.5cm)
Medium	22" (56cm)
Large	23" (58.5cm)
X-large	24" (61cm)

Adding the edging depends on the direction in which the circle is knitted. Once you've decided on an edging, adjust the technique and stitch counts to correspond with your circle and the size of your head. (See sample beret.)

Knit from the outer edge to the center. Cast on and work the edging before you begin and continue with the circle pattern you have chosen.

Knit from the center to the outer edge. Adjust stitches for the edging and continue with the edging until you reach the desired length.

Knit flat or sideways. Calculate the stitch amounts. Pick up the stitches around the circle and then work the edging for your desired length.

A sewn-on edging can be used on most of the circles. Use a running stitch around the edge of the circle, gather the stitch until the circle fits the head, and secure. Make the edging you chose. Fit it around the circle's gathered edge and sew on. You can also pick up stitches at the gathered edge of the circle and work the edging of your choice.

TIP:

Ribbed edgings work well because of their elasticity

"OH NO . . . DON'T RIP!"

If your hat doesn't fit, here are a few of my favorite fixes.

Too Big:

- Make a pleat at the back or side and you can also add a cool button.
- Run thin elastic through the edging band.
- Make an I-cord, weave it in and out of the band stitches. Pull and tie to fit your head. Ribbon can also be used.

Too Small:

- Give it to a child.

Or:

- OK . . . go ahead and rip!

AUTUMN LEAF BERET

Size
Average adult

Knitted Measurements
Headband approximately 19" (48.5cm) unstretched

Materials
- Cascade Yarns Cascade 220 (100% Peruvian highland wool), approximately 220 yards (198m) and 3.5 oz (100g); 1 skein of #4010 Straw (A), small amounts of #2453 Pumpkin Spice (B), and #9322 Silver Spruce Heather (C)
- Size U.S. 5 (3.75mm) straight and double-pointed needles
- Size U.S. 6 (4.25mm) straight needles or size needed to obtain gauge
- Stitch markers
- Tapestry needle

Gauge
20 stitches and 26 rows = 4" (10cm) in St st using larger needles
Take time to check gauge.

Note Hat is worked back and forth from the ribbed band to the center top.

With smaller needles and A, cast on 102 stitches, leaving a 16" (40.5cm) tail for sewing seam.
Work in K1, P1 Rib for 1¼" (3cm).
Change to larger needles.
Row 1 (RS) K1, *kfb, k9; repeat from * to the last stitch, k1 (112 stitches).
Row 2 and all WS rows Purl.
Row 3 K1, *kfb, k10; repeat from * to the last stitch, k1 (122 stitches).
Row 5 K1, *kfb, k11; repeat from * to the last stitch, k1 (132 stitches).
Row 7 K1, *kfb, k12; repeat from * to the last stitch, k1 (142 stitches).
Row 9 K1, *kfb, k13; repeat from * to the last stitch, k1 (152 stitches).
Row 11 K1, *kfb, k14; repeat from * to the last stitch, k1 (162 stitches).
Beginning with a WS row, work 5 rows in St st.

CROWN DECREASES
Work rows 1–29 of 10-Spiral Decrease (2-needle with seam) circle (see page 46).
Row 30 *P2tog; repeat from * to end (6 stitches).
Do not cut yarn.
Note You may use any of the circles worked from outer edge to center in this pattern; however, an increase or decrease may be necessary to achieve the 162 stitches needed to begin the crown decreases.

LOOP
Slip stitches onto a dpn, ready to work a RS row. Continuing with A, k2tog, k4 (5 stitches).
*Do not turn. Slide stitches onto the other end of the needle, k5; repeat from * for 3" (7.5cm).
Do not cut yarn.

LEAF
Note Make color changes with B and C, as pictured, using the Intarsia technique.
Row 1 (RS) K2, yo, k1, yo, k2 (7 stitches).
Row 2 and all even-numbered rows Purl.
Row 3 K3, yo, k1, yo, k3 (9 stitches).
Row 5 K4, yo, k1, yo, k4 (11 stitches).
Row 7 Ssk, k7, k2tog (9 stitches).

Row 9 Ssk, k5, k2tog (7 stitches).
Row 11 Ssk, k3, k2tog (5 stitches).
Row 13 Ssk, k1, k2tog (3 stitches).
Row 15 SK2P (1 stitch).
Fasten off.

FINISHING
Weave in ends. Using the cast-on tail, sew back seam. Fold loop in half and tack the base of the leaf to the base of the loop. Tack down the leaf as needed. Block hat over an 11" (28cm) plate.

5 EASY PIECES TO MAKE

EASY PROJECTS YOU CAN MAKE WITH JUST ONE OR TWO CIRCLES

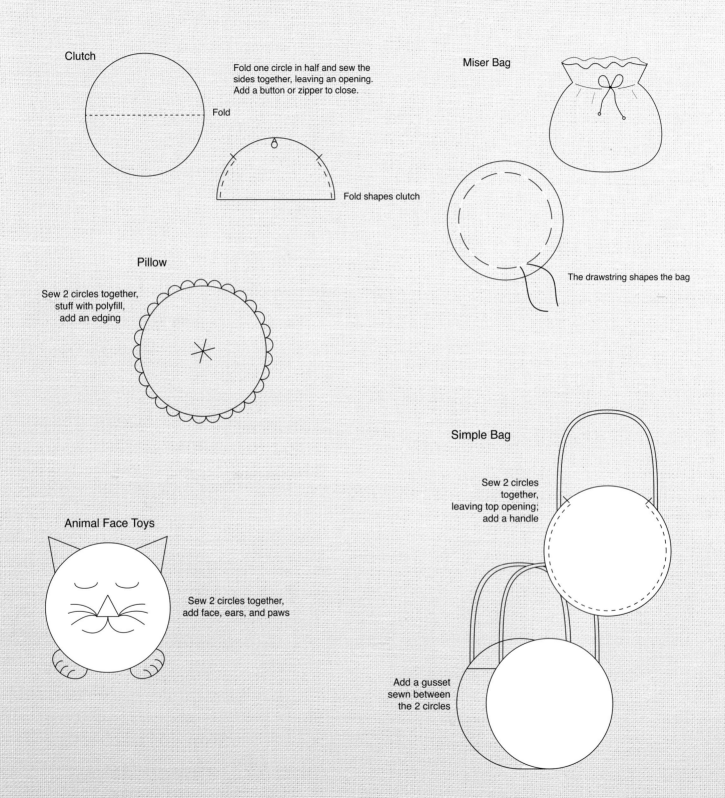

Clutch

Fold one circle in half and sew the sides together, leaving an opening. Add a button or zipper to close.

Fold

Fold shapes clutch

Miser Bag

The drawstring shapes the bag

Pillow

Sew 2 circles together, stuff with polyfill, add an edging

Simple Bag

Sew 2 circles together, leaving top opening; add a handle

Animal Face Toys

Sew 2 circles together, add face, ears, and paws

Add a gusset sewn between the 2 circles

HOW TO SHAPE CIRCLES

CIRCLES WORKED FLAT FROM BOTTOM UP
Cast on desired number of stitches on straight or circular needles, and increase to half the circle. This establishes the width of the circle. Continue working evenly for 1–2" to establish length of half the circle. Then decreases are worked to mirror the first half of circle. Bind off.

CIRCLES WORKED FROM CENTER TO OUTER EDGE
Using one of the methods given (see pages 45 or 48), these circles begin at the center and are worked in the round (page 213) using symmetrical increases that are incorporated into the pattern being used.

CIRCLES WORKED FROM OUTER EDGE TO CENTER
CIRCULARLY WITH NO SEAM
Circular needles are used to cast on the number of stitches to make the outer circumference, which establishes the circle size. Circle is then decreased in segments incorporated in pattern stitch being used. At midpoint it becomes necessary to switch to a shorter circular needle or a set of double-pointed needles in order to finish the circle.

To close the center hole:

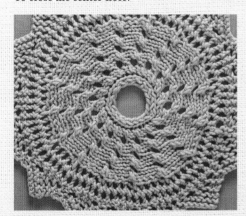

Often when casting on for a circle, the hole remains open.

Run a tapestry needle threaded with yarn through the cast-on stitches to close the loop.

Pull each end of the yarn tightly to the back of the circle and knot to secure.

CIRCLES WORKED FROM OUTER EDGE WITH SEAM
These circles are worked by using straight needles. The circumference size is cast on plus a selvedge stitch at each end. Then decreases are worked in pattern to center. This shapes the circle. The remaining few stitches are pulled together for the circle core, and the seam is sewn using the selvedge stitches, which makes the seam invisible.

CIRCLES WORKED IN SHORT ROWS SIDEWAYS
Made with straight needles, the stitches are cast on and worked back and forth. Each row is worked to a given number of stitches and turned before the end of the row, and then repeated. The technique of shortening the rows creates a fan shape; when continued, this forms the circle.

CIRCLES WORKED IN QUADRANTS AND JOINED
The domino, entrelac, and bulbiform brioche are examples of this technique. Stitches are picked up, increased, decreased, and turned, making intricate shapes to form the circles. They can be worked from the center out or circumference to center on straight or circular needles, depending on the technique being used.

CIRCLES MADE BY TWIRLING OR SPIRALING

These circles are made by using long strips of cord or a narrow pattern stitch, then turning them to shape a circle. Circumference size depends on the length of the strip. They are then sewn together around each spiral.

Shaping a strip into a circle:

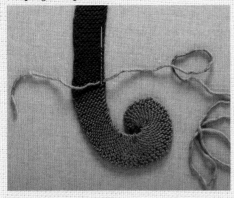

Make the strip per instructions. Thread a needle with yarn and run it through the first 2–3 inches at the inner edge. Pull to form a small spiral. Secure the spiral.

Continue to thread the inner edge, pulling and sewing the strip to shape the circle.

TIP: You may use the same yarn the strip is knitted with, or 2 strands of matching sewing thread to keep the stitches invisible.

TO WORK WEDGES FROM THE CENTER TO THE OUTER EDGE

As each stitch is picked up, the row count is increased, forming the 18-stitch section.
Note: To make the section larger or smaller, cast on more or fewer stitches.

This photo shows 6 sections completed.

Pin first and last sections together. With threaded tapestry needle, pick up 1 garter stitch from each section and weave the seam closed.

With the seam closed, all live section stitches are on the outer circumference together. Ready to bind off.

All stitches are bound off.

KNITTING TECHNIQUES

3-NEEDLE BIND-OFF

Step 1: With the right side of the two pieces facing each other, and the needles parallel, insert a third needle knitwise into the first stitch of each needle, wrap the yarn around the needle as if to knit, as shown. Knit these two stitches together and slip them off the needles.

Step 2: Knit the next two stitches together in the same way as in Step 1.

Step 3: Slip the first stitch on the third needle over the second stitch and off the needle. Repeat steps 2 and 3 across the row until all the stitches are bound off.

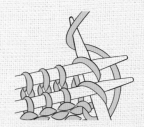

CIRCULAR KNITTING ON DOUBLE-POINTED NEEDLES

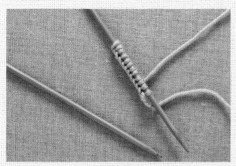

Cast on the required number of stitches on the first needle, plus one extra. Slip the extra stitch to the next needle, as shown. Continue in this way, casting on the required number of stitches on the needles (or cast on all stitches onto one needle, then divide them evenly among the other needles).

Arrange the needles with the cast-on edge facing center of triangle or square, making sure not to twist the stitches.

Place a stitch marker to indicate the start of the round. With the free needle, knit the first cast-on stitch, pulling the yarn tightly. Continue knitting rounds, slipping the marker before beginning each round.

COLOR STRANDING/FAIR ISLE

Stranding one-handed:

On the knit side, drop the working yarn. Bring the new color (now the working yarn) over the top of the dropped yarn and work to the next color change.

Drop the working yarn. Bring the new color under the dropped yarn and work to the next color change. Repeat these two steps.

On the purl side, drop the working yarn. Bring the new color (now the working yarn) over the top of the dropped yarn and work to the next color change.

Drop the working yarn. Bring the new color under the dropped yarn and work to the next color change. Repeat these two steps.

I-CORD

Using two double-pointed needles, cast on three to five stitches.

*Knit one row on RS. Without turning the work, slip the stitches to the right end of needle to work the next row on the RS. Repeat from * until desired length. Bind off.

INTARSIA

On the knit side, drop the old color. Pick up the new color from under the old color and knit to the next color change.

On the purl side, drop the old color. Pick up the new color from under the old color and purl to the next color change.

Repeat these two steps.

MAKE A DAISY

Make an I-cord to desired length. Shape like an accordion, as shown, and run a needle threaded with yarn through the bottom loops.

Pull each end of the yarn thread to shape the flower.

Pull tightly and knot to secure. Attach to the background as desired.

MAGIC LOOP

On a long circular needle, cast on the required number of stitches. Divide the stitches so that half are on one needle and half are on the other. The working yarn should be hanging off the back needle, with the needle cable looped on the left side of your stitches. Make sure the stitches are not twisted.

Slide the stitches on the back needle onto the cable. You will use the back needle tip to knit the front stitches. You now have a loop of cable on either side of your work.

When you have worked all stitches on the front needle, half of a round has been completed. Turn the work around and return the stitches to the position shown in the first illustration. The stitches you're about to knit are in front, and the working yarn is on the right side of the needle in the back. Knit the second half of the round.

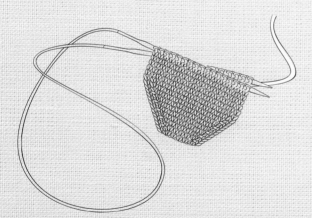
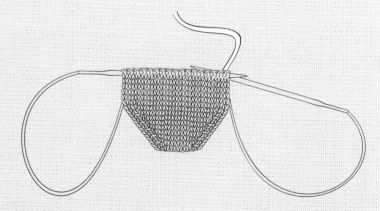

PROVISIONAL CAST-ON

Leaving tails about 4" (10cm) long, tie a length of waste yarn together with the main yarn in a knot. With a knitting needle in your right hand, hold the knot on top of the needle close to the tip, then place your thumb and index finger between the two yarns and hold the long ends with your other fingers. Hold your hand with your palm facing upwards and spread your thumb and index finger apart so that the yarn

forms a V with the main yarn over your index finger and the scrap yarn over your thumb. Bring the needle up through the scrap yarn loop on your thumb. Place the needle over the main yarn on your index finger and then back through the loop on your thumb. Drop the loop off your thumb and, placing your thumb back in the V configuration, tighten up the stitch on the needle. Repeat for the desired number of

stitches. The main yarn will form the stitches on the needle and the scrap yarn will make the horizontal ridge at the base of the cast-on row.

When picking up the stitches along the cast-on edge, carefully cut and pull out the scrap yarn as you place the exposed loops on the needle. Take care to pick up the loops so that they are in the proper direction before you begin knitting.

JOINING

Don't like to sew? Get over it!

If you can knit these lovely circles with two needles, you can certainly sew with one. You're gonna love it! . . . This is a fun sewing circle!

Sewing the circles together will be the final step in creating your circle masterpieces. You will find it intensely gratifying and you'll develop a whole new appreciation for the process. You may even find it to be fun!

Sewing the circles together is really easy, and I believe you'll change your knitter's attitude toward sewing and actually look forward to it. So get out that sewing needle and start putting those beautiful circles together, and you'll never say "I hate sewing" again!

Here are some diagrams showing easy ways of sewing pieces together.

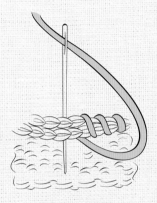

Whipstitch

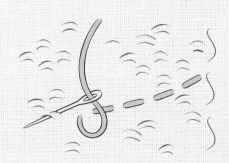

Running Stitch

ATTACHING AN EDGING

Choose and make an edging for your circle. Pin it in place and, using a tapestry needle and yarn, whipstitch the edging onto the wrong side of your circle. You may use corresponding yarn or 2 strands of matching sewing thread to attach.

MAKING A LINK FRAME

Work circle. Make a long I-cord (page 213), leaving live stitches on a holder so the cord can be easily lengthened or shortened.

Loop cord as shown and pin in place.

Gently weave another cord length in and out of the loops.

Turn to shape into a circle.

Sew onto the circumference of the knitted circle, making sure both the loops and straight cord are sewn together. **TIP**: I use an ironing board when pinning and shaping the cord. Use your iron to steam the cord lightly to help hold the link shape.

EMBROIDERY

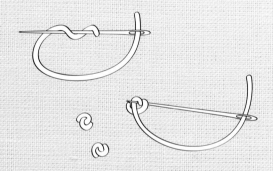

French Knot

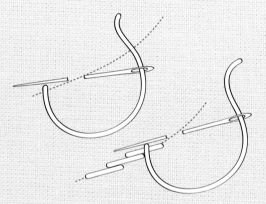

Stem Stitch

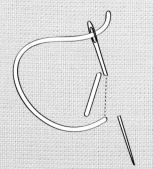

Long Stitch

Duplicate Stitch

Copy and cut out these circles, and then place them into the assembly diagrams to design your own creations!

MIX-AND-MATCH CIRCLES

GENERAL ABBREVIATIONS

beg	begin(ning)(s)	**MB**	make bobble	**SK2P**	sl 1 st as if to k, k2tog, pass slipped st over k2tog
CC	contrasting color	**MC**	main color	**skp**	sl 1 knitwise, k1, pass slipped st over k1
cn	cable needle	**p**	purl	**sl**	slip
cont	continue	**p2tog**	purl 2 together	**sm**	slip marker
dec	decrease	**patt**	pattern	**ssk**	sl next 2 sts knitwise, one at a time, to RH needle, insert tip of LH needle into fronts of these sts, from left to right. Knit them tog—2 sts decreased.
dpn(s)	double-pointed needles	**pwise**	purlwise		
est	establish(ed)	**pfb**	p in front and back of st		
foll	follow(ing)(s)	**pm**	place marker		
inc	increase	**psso**	pass slipped stitch over	**St st**	Stockinette stitch
k	knit	**RC**	right cable	**st(s)**	stitch(es)
kwise	knitwise	**rem**	remain(ing)	**tbl**	through back loop
k2tog	knit 2 together	**rep**	repeat	**tog**	together
kfb	knit in front and back of st	**RH**	right-hand	**W&T**	wrap and turn
LC	left cable	**rnd(s)**	round(s)	**WS**	wrong side
LH	left-hand	**RPC**	right purl cable	**wyib**	with yarn in back
LPC	left purl cable	**RS**	right side	**wyif**	with yarn in front
m1	make 1 — insert LH needle into horizontal strand between last st and next st on needle, k through back loop of this strand.	**S2KP**	sl 2 sts as if to k2tog, k1, pass slipped st over k1	**yo**	yarn over

RESOURCES

ArtYarns
39 Westmoreland Ave.
White Plains, NY 10606
(914) 428-0333
www.artyarns.com

AslanTrends
8 Maple Street
Port Washington, NY 11050
(800) 314-8202
www.aslantrends.com

The Bagsmith
20600 Chagrin Blvd., Suite 101
Shaker Heights, OH 44122
www.bagsmith.com

Berroco, Inc.
14 Elmdale Road
P.O. Box 367
Uxbridge, MA 01569
(508) 278-2527
www.berroco.com

Cascade Yarns
1224 Andover Park East
Tukwila, WA 98188
www.cascadeyarns.com

Crystal Palace Yarns
www.straw.com

HPKY
www.hpkylic.com

Jade Sapphire Exotic Fibres
(866) 857-3897
www.jadesapphire.com

JHB Buttons
1955 South Quince Street
Denver, CO 80231
(800) 525-9007
www.buttons.com

Leisure Arts
www.leisurearts.com

Lion Brand Yarn
34 West 15th Street
New York, NY 10011
www.lionbrand.com

Madelinetosh
7515 Benbrook Parkway
Benbrook, TX 76126
(817) 249-3066
www.madelinetosh.com

Malabrigo Yarn
(786) 866-6187
www.malabrigoyarn.com

Manos de Uruguay
Eduardo Víctor Haedo 2187
11200 Montevideo, Uruguay
(+5982) 400 48 39
www.manos.com.uy/en/

Mountain Colors
P.O. Box 156
Corvallis, MT 59828
(406) 961-1900
www.mountaincolors.com

Plymouth Yarn Company, Inc.
500 Lafayette Street
Bristol, PA 19007
(215) 788-0459
www.plymouthyarn.com

Prism Yarns
www.prismyarn.com

Tilli Tomas
(617) 524-3330
www.tillitomas.com

Yarn Market for Namaste Farms
www.yarnmarket.com

ACKNOWLEDGMENTS

Many, many thanks go out to my circle of friends and associates who went round and round with me in creating a beautiful book all about knitting circles!

The Potter Craft/Random House team, headed up by my always efficient and supportive editor Betty Wong, superb art director Jess Morphew, my "go-to" gal and book designer Chi Ling Moy, assistants Caitlin Harpin and La Tricia Watford, publicity director Kim Small, the talented stylist Meg Goldman, and hair and makeup stylist Ingeborg—and the rest of the gang.

The breathtaking fashion photography of the great Rose Callahan, whose energy, enthusiasm, and talent are evident in every frame.

The lovely photography of Heather Weston, who made each and every one of my circles radiate with details.

The intrepid knitters of my private knitting circle: Jo Bradon, Nancy Henderson, Dianne Weitzul, Kristy Lucas, Eve Wilkin, Dana Vessa, Steven Hicks, Miriam Tegels, Victoria Russell, Holly Neiding, Stephanie Alchinger, Randi Sherman, Shirley Spencer, and my old standby Eileen Curry.

My hardworking, reliable instruction writers and technical editors: Eve Ng, Nancy Henderson, and Charlotte Quiggle, and Therese Chynoweth for the schematics and illustrations.

A great big thank-you to the very popular yarn company Cascade Yarns, whose team has always championed my work, and who generously contributed their beautiful 220 Superwash yarn from which all the circles were made and several of the design pieces—Jean, Bob, Shannon, Rob, and David Dunbabin, you are Seattle's finest.

And to: ArtYarns, AslanTrends Yarns, Prism Yarns, Manos De Uruguay, Lion Brand, Berroco, Mountain Colors, Crystal Palace, Malabrigo, Plymouth, Bagsmith, Madelinetosh, Tilli Tomas, HPKY, and Yarn Market for Namaste Farms for their generosity and gorgeous yarns.

Thanks to that great bunch at JHB Buttons: Jay and Barbara Barr, Lynita Haber, Eloise Wagner, and Lisa Lambright—you are really buttoned up!

And thanks, as always, to my closest circle of personal supporters, Emily Brenner, Jo Brandon, Chris Farrow, Leigh Merrifield, Steven Berg, Angie DeFazio, and my greatest supporter and helper—Howard.

INDEX

ABOUT THE AUTHOR

Nicky Epstein is the beloved knitwear designer and bestselling author of numerous books, including *Knitting Block by Block*, the Knitting on the Edge series, *Knitting on Top of the World*, and *Nicky Epstein's Knitted Flowers*. Her award-winning knitting and crochet books range from highly original resource books to knitting/travel books to collections for Barbie, and are must-haves in the libraries of designers and knitters alike. She is a three-time winner of the National Independent Book Publisher's Award for Best Craft Book of the Year.

Her innovative and fashion-forward designs have appeared in every major knitwear magazine, in museum exhibits, and on television. She loves to share her expertise and enthusiasm for knitting with countless fans around the world and has traveled and taught throughout the United States and in England, Australia, New Zealand, Italy, Canada, Argentina, Uruguay, and France, gaining a loyal following. She hosts popular knitting tours and recently launched the Nicky Epstein Knitting Club. Her line of designer buttons, clasps, scarves, note cards, and artwork can be found on her website: www.nickyepstein.com.

Nicky lives in New York City but is constantly on the go, sharing her love of knitting with a fun-loving army of fans.